MW00575351

ETs ON EARTH

VOLUME 1

THE EXPLORER RACE SERIES

The Explorer Race Series

mlin's official voice confir
-FOOT ALIENS
ALKABOUT IN
City in terror

channeled through **Robert Shapiro**

Other Books by Robert Shapiro

EXPLORER RACE SERIES

THE EXPLORER
RACE SERIES

ETs ON
EARTH

VOLUME 1

through **Robert Shapiro**

LIGHT
Technology
PUBLISHING

* * *

ISBN-13: 978-1891824-91-3
ISBN-10: 1-891824-91-0

Light Technology Publishing, LLC
Phone: 800-450-0985
Fax: 928-714-1132
PO Box 3540
Flagstaff, AZ 86003
www.lighttechnology.com

CONTENTS

CHAPTER 23:
YOUR SHIFT IN FOCUS IS CAUSING DREAMS
AND VISIONS

ET Visitor • July 17, 2010

INTRODUCTION

Greetings. This is Zoosh.

In the beginning of the Explorer Race adventure—that means you, all humans on Earth—way back, ETs on Earth were a normal thing. In fact, you were ETs who came from many different planets those thousands of years ago, and you felt that Earth was a wonderful place where you could thrive.

I want you to keep that in mind when you read about these ETs that happen to be still visiting the Earth. In this book, as well as in other books that have material like this, if you can keep that in mind, it will not be too surprising or shocking. In fact, for most of you, you will be ETs again in another life, and your youngsters just might be ETs from Earth visiting other planets in the future.

This should be a fun read and a gentle reminder that ETs are just friends from some place—you might say from another neighborhood.

Good life.

ET BEINGS USE GREEN LIGHT TO SUPPORT EARTH BEINGS

ET Traveler

September 6, 2007

Greetings! I am a traveler from a galaxy far from here. You have lightbeings here as well, but you do not usually observe them. You yourselves are lightbeings who are passing through these physical forms in order to learn something, but you are not physical in your natural state. You are like me. I happened to be nearby when Robert began speaking of having seen the green light in the sea. That green light was emanated because there was a vehicle under the sea. Sometimes the beings in the vehicle are working with sea creatures—in this case, they were working to support whales and turtles—and it is only when they are doing that that they will emanate that green light, because that light has a way of improving the quality of energy in the sea.

The sea on your planet is a living being, not unlike the way your own bodily fluids are alive and support your life. If it were not for the fluids in your body, you could not occupy the body. The fluids create a connection between your light and the physical form of the body. That is why your light can be temporarily expressed through these physical bodies. Without the fluid, you could never do that. And the saline fluid is particularly helpful, because your light is incompatible with blood—totally incompatible. If it were not for the saline systems of your body, along with other liquids, you could not function in the body—you would instantly move out of the body.

So why do we have blood, then?

Your blood has to do with Earth. Through the woman, Earth produces the body it can produce. Earth is composed of iron to a great degree, you understand, and iron makes up a large part of your blood. That is what your light is incompatible with. So if it were not for the saline systems of your body, you could not be in your body.

The Light Associated with Your Planet Is Red

Why are you here?

I am just passing through. In the past, I have been associated in my form— as I am now, not in body—with those beings on the ship who like to support whales and turtles and sometimes dolphins on your planet.

Are they from Sirius?

No. They do not wish it to be known where they are from. But where they are from is closer than that—they are in your galaxy.

Our galaxy. Okay. Why did your own light show as red or orange? Is there a significance to that?

That is because of the iron on your planet.

You reflect the iron just by being here?

I don't reflect it. My light shows up, but the light associated with your planet—with the structures, the stone, of your planet—is red. That is the light that it exudes, and that is the light that it consumes. Visiting your planet, you as a being made of your planet would see me that way. Robert saw me that way, but the color that would be seen beyond this planet would be a different one. It is a pale yellow with some portion that is white. The color when you are beyond here, regardless of how you appear on Earth, is similar.

I hate to make the channel talk so much when his voice is going. Would you like to talk to us another time and tell us about yourself?

No, I am just passing through. Now or never!

All right. Are you on your way somewhere, or are you just observing the planet?

I am just passing through; this space is part of my route. Perhaps I was attracted because of the ship's activities in this area.

These Beings Who Emit Green Light Feel Like Long-Lost Friends

The ship is still here, and while it is not exuding that light in the water, it is exuding that light in the air. One does not see it, though, because it is presently exuding the light in a forest where green light would be less noticeable. The trees breathe it in, and they breathe it out. Trees are often compatible with other life, including sea life.

I didn't know that. Do these beings in that craft come frequently to help the sea life?

They have been coming more frequently. They are able to come and go on your planet when they choose, for their energy causes no harm to any form of life here, of course. And their energy, as it comes to your planet, appears to be something natural when noted.

Ah! So nobody from the various military forces is going to shoot at them.

No one is going to be offended at their presence or feel frightened by them. If you met the individuals on the ship, regardless of who you are on the planet, you would feel as if you had met a long-lost friend. You would relate to them that way, and they would relate to you that way. You might even have some shared recollections, even though you would know as you were speaking of the recollections that this was not something that you did with this being or others in this life, because you would be speaking about matters that are not associated with Earth life. But in those moments, you would be able to recall them.

They would be experiences that we had on other planets, in other places?

Yes, but you would be able to recall them as well as you could recall what you did yesterday.

Would these beings speak to us through Robert?

I do not know. I do not speak for them. You would have to ask another time.

I will. All right, I am going to let you go, because he can't channel as long as he used to anymore, but thank you so much. Thank you.

Have a most benevolent life and passage to the beyond.

Thank you. Bless you.

HUMANS ARE GOING THROUGH RAPID CHANGES ON EARTH

ET Traveler Focused on Rapid Change

August 7, 2009

Greetings. I am a visitor to your planet.

Welcome, welcome to our planet. What would you like to talk about?

I travel more to the outer planets these days, especially yours, because there is so much happening here. My culture is very focused on rapid change, and from our perspective, your planetary peoples are going through a rapid change that is not typical of that which is found elsewhere. My peoples are not embodied physically the way yours are, so we traverse space through what you call portals, or windows. I believe, as I've noticed, that there is a great deal of such traversing on this planet now. Some travel seems to have to do with previous humans who have lived here and are getting a last look at what was, because you are apparently just about at the point where you will transfer over to being on a future-connected course of travel and life rather than a past one. So as near as I can tell, those particularly affectionate toward the past and who have been human on this focus of Earth are coming to Earth, as much as they get permission, to look about and see what is and to witness the change.

I feel also that there is quite a bit of particle visiting. By "particle," I mean material, mass, not bodies or souls—personalities, you would say. Some of the greatest interest comes from materials. Well, your race, the human race, is an adaptive one, and you are particularly good at adapting to whatever is available to form it toward your needs. From my point of view, materials would fall under the heading as anything that human beings use to form to their needs, though I rule out nonhuman beings who people your planet in that case, even though

5

you use them also. I rule them out because, from my point of view, they are just like you, only you do not know that—meaning most of your peoples do not know that these are simply other life forms from other planets who are exactly the same as you but look different, as one would find in traveling beyond Earth.

So the materials I'm talking about might be what you would call minerals. I've seen a lot of visitation from a mineral world to your planet, because when you get on this new path and are locked on to it, everything will change. The change will come gradually, yes, but some things will change more rapidly— not necessarily the human soul and personality, but the other beings on the planet, including the materials themselves. There will be very rapid change in, say, buildings that are made of minerals. The material, the composition of the material, will change quite a bit. You will not notice it because everything will change relative to everything else, but if you were able to stand back and look at it, everything will be bigger.

So molecular structures will transform to being about one-third larger than they were before this change. This has less to do with the so-called dimension than the fact that in order to live through such a transformation, it is necessary to have more room to be able to flex, you would say, and thus materials need to do that as well. I have looked ahead to see what this would look like, and it's quite different. Imagine, if you could, that your buildings will be one-third larger, though you will not notice that and it might not even be observable to your contemporary science. However, I do feel the science you are developing will, in about eighteen to twenty years, be able to detect that on the basis of . . . well, you'll be able to look into the past a little bit then scientifically in terms of sequenced past as compared to momentary past, which you can do now an-thropologically and scientifically, to a degree.

This is something that interests me: the expansion of materials. But then there's the other factor too. When you get on that future-anchored track of travel and motion, something else happens, and that's that the other life forms besides the human soul will rapidly transform into their more natural state. This does not mean that they will necessarily be one-third larger [chuckles]— because everything will be that, relative to everything else—but it means that they will have less interest in being on the planet. So other than those life forms you consciously welcome as human beings, you might find that many of the life forms you are dependent on for your very lives will simply depart.

Some of them are departing now, such as honeybees—but these are not really natural bees. You will have to either learn to accommodate natural bees, which are a little more aggressive—meaning learn how to get along with them, which simply means you have to give them their distance—or you will have to welcome honeybees. They do not feel welcome. They have often been confused with the more natural bees and eliminated. You cannot do that to a species as gentle as honeybees; they will just leave, and they are doing that now.

Other species wish to leave because of feeling mistreated. Cows and a lot of beings you consume or who are vital to your existence, such as honeybees, are leaving. So if you want them to stay, you will have to consciously welcome them and treat them as well as possible, meaning better than you do now. It might be good to gather less honey from honeybees and to recognize that [chuckles] the honey is meant for the young bees—it is their food. If you want honeybees to stick around and multiply, you're going to have to find a way to welcome them.

My Peoples Are in the First Loop of This Galaxy

My peoples have been in and around, not the very center of this galaxy, but perhaps if you were to look at the galaxy from a different perspective—science has speculated on this and it's pretty accurate—our planetary system is within the first loop, coming out from the center of solidified mass. However, when our culture, which is not only associated with a planet, has in the past been in what is now in the second loop, we simply moved to the first loop, because we find it more comfortable to be as close to the light of emergence. We like this better than being in some of the more outer loops.

The centers of galaxies like this contain the emergence of substance coming directly from creation outward. It is an immortal thing; it will always be. But it is very much light and not substance. Substance happens afterward. The closest thing I can come to here, scientifically, would be to describe it as a precipitate. But to put it in more conventional terms, it would not be unlike a very light steam vapor condensing into a droplet of water, which you could feel but you might not feel. So just translate that into light. When it comes far enough away from the point of emergence, it gradually condenses into mass, which eventually becomes planets and suns and so on.

There are many peoples associated with my culture—"personalities" might be a better statement, but our personalities are revolving. This means that we are not focused only as one personality, as you would identify each other on this planet, but rather at any given moment, a hundred or so personalities would pass through us. Therefore in order to communicate, it is necessary to tap into that portion of ourselves that might be more capable of such communication, as is going on now. But even during this now time, fully 90 to 95 percent of my being is doing other things—some of them here, some elsewhere.

You Are Moving Much Faster Than You Realize

Your culture, the human race on this planet, is moving much faster than you realize. Of course, you are aware of the physical motion you make and you are at least dimly aware of the planet's motion—since you see night and day and the motion of the stars in the sky, and so on. But the actual traversing of different focuses of being is happening very rapidly within the context of such transformations. I have had the opportunity to observe another such transformation many, many, [chuckles] many structures ago, as we would say. This was in a Pleiadian galaxy—the third galaxy, as they call it—and the peoples there, also a human race, very rapidly transformed from one focus to another. So this process is not unknown, but the difference is that in the Pleiadian situation, there was not the polarity you have on Earth. So the transference happened very quickly but in a way in which people were conscious of it and could experience the change within themselves.

You are mostly having this transference happening on an individual basis at the deep levels of sleep. Otherwise, it would be so very distracting for so many of you that I think you would find it hard to cope. But this is only for the human being; all other materials and all other beings on the planet, including particles and so on, are doing this rapidly. You might reasonably ask that if particles are doing this rapidly, then what about the particles inside yourselves? They are also doing it rapidly. You catch up—meaning your total physical being, yes, but more your mind, your personality as you understand it—during the deep sleep when you are less resistant to change and transformation. I do understand why you are resistant to change and transformation, because as a physical being, as a human being, you have had to adapt from a very fast life in your lightbodies to what your lightbodies would perceive as an exceedingly slow life in the physical body. But you are here to learn about physicality, so you must adapt.

So you can see that, at the deep levels of sleep, when your lightbody and soul travels about, your physical body automatically makes the shift—and since your lightbody and personality is in its more natural focus, it easily makes the shift. That is why this takes place in the simplest way at those deep levels of sleep. This does not cause you any immediate sense of discomfort and, more to the tune of an attunement, so to speak, happens with relative ease.

You Are at 40 Percent Discomfort

Perhaps you have a question?

Yes. I didn't know that any other species had moved in this way while they were alive in their bodies, but you're saying that one did in the Pleiades?

Yes, and the reason I bring that up, you understand, is that they were human beings also, so I feel it has relevance.

Absolutely. I just thought we were the first ones to do it without dying and then coming back in a different vibrational body.

But the really big difference, you see, is that these beings from the Pleiades were not experiencing polarity—nothing discomforting, you understand—so this might be why you have this impression. If they mentioned this to you before, other beings may well have felt that it wasn't relevant. But the reason I feel it is relevant is that these were human beings. Granted, they were not identical in physical makeup, but they were so close that if you were standing next to one, somebody else, an observer would say, "Well, two human beings!" They wouldn't necessarily notice much difference. There might be a little noticeable difference, but short of a physical examination, it wouldn't be obvious.

They shifted to a different timeline? How did they transform?

Well, they didn't transform in the same way you are transforming. They shifted to a different focus, and from my perspective, that's what you're doing. I realize that others have told you it's a different timeline, but that is because it's easier for you to understand things within the context of time than it is for you to understand things in the context of space. Space seems very understandable to you—you walk across the room; you walk around the block—but I'm talking about vast reaches of space. You don't think about, "Oh, you walk over to the next galaxy." I might think that, though walking isn't involved. I mention this because the Pleiadian humans shifted focus from one focus of existence to another, allowing them to . . . oh, I can't say too much, but allowing them to migrate here and there with greater ease.

"Travel with greater ease"—what does that mean?

As I said, I can't say too much.

Are we moving to a different focus of the same planet, or are we moving in space to another focus somewhere else?

No, you are moving in focus to the same planet, but it will be a different focus of that planet. When you get to that point where you're fast-tracking, from your perspective—meaning everybody notices changes every day when they wake up from deep sleep—then you will have dropped a great deal of your polarity. The first thing you will notice, though you won't be measuring it, is that you will drop down to about 12 percent discomfort. The next big shift goes down to 8 percent, then 4 percent, then 2 percent, and it kind of stays at 2 percent for quite a while through the next focus. So that's the big change that you'll notice.

Right now there's a little pause, because everybody is now involved in waking up. Before there were some people doing it, and they were sort of pioneering, but the whole point of pioneering is to create a pathway for others and to try to create it in such a way that the others who are coming along will be able to traverse that pathway without the problems the first ones encountered. The job of the first few thousand or so that traverse any pathway is to discover what the problems are and come up with at least workable solutions—ideally, flexible solutions—which can then be adapted by the others as they come along and have that in place. So now that the rest of the people are coming along, you have to kind of slow down and wait up for them.

Will I be able to see 12 percent discomfort while I'm in this human body?

Oh, no. I wouldn't think so. It could happen "tomorrow," but . . .

It probably won't.

If you were, as a physical person ensouled with your personality, present to experience the change to about 12 percent, you would basically no longer identify your persona as the person you were. It would be a dim memory. So even if you were alive for that, you wouldn't be able to get excited and say, "Wow! Here we are at 12 percent! I can remember . . ." In short, you won't be able to remember. Your memory will change entirely.

Right. What is the percentage of discomfort right now?

Let's see if I can get that figure. [Pause.] You understand, this isn't a constant, but taking into account the entire human race, what everybody is experiencing all the time and then averaging it, oh, it's about 40 percent. It's a big difference all right, because it used to be 47 percent discomfort. The range has changed during the past twenty years or so; the past twenty years have seen that change.

But the way the memory process works, it just falls away; it's just not even available. It's just like, "Well, it's always been like this." Is that how we will feel?

That is how you'll feel, but there will be a dim sense of it being different. By "dim," I mean that there will be a feeling that it was different before, but you won't have images and you won't have thoughts. But the feeling of there being a change and that things were different in the past will be present at 12 percent. By the time you get to 8 percent, you won't have much of that feeling left. By the time you get to 4 percent, you won't have any of that feeling left. And by the time you get to 2 percent, you will be looking forward to the next focus, eh?

Fantastic.

You All Have Multiple Personalities

Tell me a little about yourself. Have you been physical in your past, or have you always been lightbeings?

No, our people have never been physical.

If I could see you and I looked at you, what would I see?

If you were able to see us, you might just see a varying shape of light.

You're not a particular color or anything?

I will say no more.

That's a secret too?

[Pause.] I have been instructed by certain beings that it is important not to get you too excited about who and what I am so that you don't get distracted from who and what you are.

All right. This hundred-personality thing—tell me about that. Is that unusual?

You think it's unusual, but it really isn't. When you are in your natural state, you will have available to you the essence—granted, in its completely nonpolarized fashion, completely benevolent—of all the personalities you have ever been focused in, in any given life, anywhere. So you think it's unusual, but it really isn't. It is something you are totally familiar with at the deep-sleep level when you are traversing around here and there in your soul self. It is also typical of lightbeings, but it is not necessarily spoken of. Perhaps you had an encounter through this method of communication where one day you spoke to a being who went by this or that name temporarily, and the next time you spoke to that being, you had a definite sense that his or her personality was different. That is an example of that situation.

They were speaking from a different part of themselves.

Yes, that's right. So this is something actually normal. It's true that in your world there is a sense of self-discipline and even a sense of demand among friends and family that you remain who you were. For anybody who has ever moved away from home and made new friends and gotten a new job, a new life, you become yourself, whoever your self is. But even with new friends and a new life, old friends and family expect you to be who you were. Over time, naturally, you change. But then you go back to see those friends or you go back to see family, and there is an expectation, almost a demand, that you be who you were.

You see, in your life, you actually have multiple personalities going on now for every physical person. You have your youthful personality, you have your young years, your middle years, your old years, and so on. You think your personality has not changed, but you find out. The quickest way to find out that your personality has changed—and this happens; you can totally identify with this—is when you are with your blood family, because they talk to you the way they remember you and the way they were. Everybody becomes their children again, and as dysfunctional [chuckles] as that might seem in moments, it is a clear-cut reminder of how you are more than one being.

Yes, I understand that completely. I am from a large family.

We Travel with Other Portions of Beings within Us

How does it work, then, as a lightbeing? Have you always been in this galaxy?

I've always been, yes.

So if you're immortal and you stay the same—a lightbeing—how do you get a hundred personalities? What lives are you drawing from?

No, no. You're assuming that what I say is true for you is true for us, but it is not so. We get a hundred personalities or so, or more—I just picked that number out of the air—because it has to do with the rest of our culture, the rest of the beings. We have hundreds and thousands of us in our culture, but we're not comfortable being one. We're not comfortable unless there are at least a hundred, several hundred, maybe a thousand. It is like this: If you are a human being, it might be exciting to go out and travel in space, but after a few days, you'd be missing other human beings. Do you understand? For us, we travel all over time and we also are like that. We would get lonely. So then we travel with other portions of other beings within us.

It doesn't mean that they are then stuck inside us and can't be themselves. Right now, I am inside other beings as well, you see? It is a matter of being: I would be lonely without them, and they would be lonely without me. It is not the same. I explained something to you about how you are, and you extrapolated that this is how all lightbeings are, but it isn't so. I just utilized that as an example so that you could understand it. I know you're trying to make classifications, but it isn't that way.

So all of your beings are one culture, and you can become one of them, or they can become one of you, or a hundred of you can be together and you can switch your focus among different ones of you, and you're still you?

Yes, but that is an extremely simple way to put it. It's much more complex than that. Imagine a simple molecule. That would be the individual. But then you think of a more complex molecule, and it would have many portions of itself, the atomic structure and so on. It's like that. We are complex beings. We have many portions, but they are not fixed. At any given moment, I might have hundreds of different personalities that are associated with different beings in my culture revolving through me. They don't travel in me as one might travel in a bus—it's not like that.

Okay, but you can experience . . . you can be one of those or one of these or anyone at any time?

Yes, that's a good, simple way to put it.

Okay, I don't know a more complex way. [Chuckles.] It sounds like fun!

Well, the reason I'm saying that's a simple way to put it is that I consider it to be an advantage. It's better to have it spoken simply in a cross-cultural frame of reference like this than to attempt to break it down into its formulaic complexity.

You come in through a portal, you said. Did you come from your own culture to get here?

Yes, you might say that. Yes.

How do you know where the portals are? Do you see them? Do you feel them?

It's not like that, but I understand that you're speaking about spatial reference again. In our world, I have an interest to go to some place and then I am in that place. I am slowing down how I get there for you to understand. I am saying to you, "I get here . . ."

Because you want to be here.

Yes, it's like that. It is like a navigational aspect not based on time and space but on temporal need. It just so happens that I'll pass through a portal to make it comfortable for me and not harmful for others, but I don't look for the portal. It's just part of the process. If you were able to see the portal—and some human beings on Earth can do that now—you might see that traversing of a being through the portal, or you might simply see a being or you might simply see a portal. I know that this channel sees such things all the time, but you know, there are others who see it too.

So you know an awful lot about us. Had you ever been here before?

No, but I know about you because I am here now. When I go and do other things, I will not know that. I'll only know it again if ever I come here again. So the knowledge I have is purely temporal.

Yes, I think we're trained to call it vertical wisdom: you know what you need to know when you need to know it.

Yes, that's a good description.

What other things interest you? You travel every place in this galaxy or beyond?

No, I'm just interested in rapid change. Our peoples are interested in rapid change, and when any rapid change happens anywhere, we're very interested in that and we tend to migrate there for a short time. This is why I am here, and I am not alone—there are a few others around in different parts of your planet. But we do not have difficulty. Say I need to go someplace. From your point of view, a surface measurement would be, say, 3,000 miles away. But instead of going through the surface, I just go through the planet.

Why would you need to go there? Do you know where you are now?

I am inside the planet.

Ah. Why would you need to go from one place to another, for example?

It may be because I was curious. I wanted to see what was going on.

That's a trait that I highly admire.

[Chuckles.] I can understand that.

You're not one of the beings we will run into when we start traveling, are you?

Well, you won't see us, so you might run into us and simply not know about it.

Right through you, yes. You mentioned the Pleiadians. What other species or life forms have gone through rapid change? What are some examples of that?

When I mentioned the Pleiadians, I had meant that they're . . .

That was because they are human, yes?

Yes, even though it hadn't been mentioned to you before, but there are others. But to put it in a simple way—I am sort of on the borderline of what I can talk about here—all the others, including the Pleiadians, went from one focus to another without polarity. I'm only really allowed to slightly mention the Pleiadians, because they were humans. The others were not.

It's probably because you got it in there before anybody knew you were going to say it [chuckles].

No, that's not true; they always know. The reason you are not being told many things is that you—the human being on Earth—are a species who is very easily distracted. It is very easy. Just take a look at your day or take a look at the people around you: They are very easily distracted. Since you're doing something very important for yourselves and ultimately perhaps for others, we are not encouraged to distract you. It is felt that you already have enough distraction.

You Have to Redefine Comfort

When we are down to 2 percent discomfort, can you talk to us and talk more?

Oh, we will be talking to you more when you are at 12 percent. But when you're at 12 percent, then you'll be locked in and moving, but you'll notice. You understand, when you pass through the main point of change, you won't . . . when you drop to, say, 30 percent and then slowly down, it won't be "clicking" from 30 to 20 or anything like that—they'll go through notch by notch. When you get to 30 percent overall discomfort on the planet as an average, then you'll start to release a lot of distraction and you'll notice that something good is happening, and people will be excited and want to participate.

The reason for all of this talk coming through this being for the purpose of these books and articles and ways of sharing is so that when that time comes, that hopefully people will know what they can do. You won't be able to speed up the process, and there's no point in doing that—why speed it up if you've got beings who have to come along? Everybody has to go, so what's the point of stringing the line out? You want to go as a group; otherwise it doesn't work. So the whole point, then, is that you'll need to be informed of what you can do to welcome the change. It's not about stopping being polarized; it's about welcoming being in comfort. You have to redefine comfort. Some people might consider excitement and wild, violent movies to be comfortable, but in fact, they're not a good influence.

I think of the Zetas and their calm and peace, and that might truly be very boring for some people. [Chuckles.]

It would be boring if you were raised on that kind of excitement. But, you see, when you are born as a baby, that kind of excitement frightens and upsets you. You are conditioned to like this or want it or need it. So it remains a distraction your whole life.

How can we uncondition ourselves?

You can't. You can only welcome comfort, ease, and love—"love" meaning a good feeling between all beings. I'm not speaking about physical love here.

Benevolence, we call it.

Yes, you can welcome that. Welcome it for yourself and welcome it for others—you might say for all beings.

Have you been anyplace else where there is discomfort in this galaxy?

No, there isn't any in the rest of the galaxy.

While you're here, you can see it and observe it, but it doesn't affect you, right?

Certainly not. If it affected me, I wouldn't be able to go back. I know of several beings from other planets who have become caught up in the discomfort, and alas, tragically, they had to stay.

Just for the life they're living?

Oh, I cannot say. You'd have to talk to them. It might be worth talking to them now.

That's a good point.

Your Passage Toward Benevolence Is a Natural Motion

If you were a human on the planet and you wanted to somehow contribute toward everyone moving comfortably through this transformation, what would you do?

Well, for starters, I would do that living prayer process. Live as well as possible, in the most benevolent way. Be the example for your own sake. If others comment on the way you live, you can say why, but don't tell them that what they're doing is bad. Just say:

Living Prayer

"What I'm doing serves me and I feel good about it and my life flows in a better way for me."

But you will have to come up with examples, because people are going to want proof. In some cases, you would be simplifying your life; in other cases, your life may be more complex. It depends on the individual.

I came here today because I wanted to let you know that you are not alone in your passage. The passage that you make toward a more benevolent world is a worthy goal, but in a larger sense, it is a natural motion. For many of you who are very young—two years old, maybe—you might very well live to have a natural life of, say, 120 or so as the lifetime potential grows longer. And you might very well live to at least the point of an overall average of 30 percent discomfort—which will seem, overall on average, like a big change. But it's also possible that some of you will live to see 12 percent. So enjoy your life now, pay attention to the moment, live as well as possible in the most benevolent way, and help others when you can. Good night.

Happy traveling. Thank you.

UPDATE ON ETS AND UFOS

Zoosh

October 26, 2009

Greetings. This is Zoosh.

Welcome.

Now, I'm going to give a little update about ET and UFO activity and what isn't. Starting in the past few years and really picking up steam now in the latter part of 2009 (and this will pick up considerably more velocity over the next few years), is a combination of greed and only slightly—one might think it was more than that—disinformation. What's going on is not only a nervousness in some rarified circles that the spiritual transformation on Earth will lead to their downfall, which is not true, but also that their way of life is threatened. To a degree, that's true if you factor in only money and wealth, but if one considers that friends are also a form of wealth—and I mean friends who seem more like family: old friends, people you feel completely at ease with and who feel at ease with you, and such comforts are not always known in those rarified circles. Then, to a degree, it is merely a transformation: a redistribution of what is seen, when that time comes to not be so important, into what is oh so important, along with a realization about how much it's been missed. So there's that message to those circles.

But there's more. You'll find that there will be television programs, movies, and other forms of "entertainment" that function as a conditioning, in a way. Such versions of entertainment will not be entirely prompted by those who would condition you or remind you of the conditioning you've had for most of your life that ETs are something to be "afraid" of and that spirituality is only

17

safe in church or temple or in the mosque or other such places of comfort, brotherliness, and sisterliness.

You Maintain Your Right to Choose

Spirituality is your nature. It is your true source. It is who and what you are. You can choose, over the next few years, what you would create if you could, for those of you who might think that way. For those of you who might be more actively involved, you can choose what you would create—period. Choose: It's the time of your choosing.

There are opportunities and there will be continuing opportunities to experience benevolent ETs, benevolent ships, and benevolent spirits, but don't get caught up or attached to the idea of UFOs and big ships filled with happy ETs landing. That's not likely to happen, because it would almost be interference. It would take choice out of your hands. Ultimately, spirituality is about choice: who you would be if you could, yes? Or is it who you really are and have forgotten? Oh yes, that is it.

So you will find yourself almost surrounded with books and things on the Internet that try to frighten you, sometimes rationalizing that, "Oh, it's just entertainment! Just for fun." But you have to keep in mind that many religious books have made predictions—sometimes benevolent for a benevolent future, other times, including popular religions of the day, for a future that is frightening and represents a challenge, a hurdle, and yes, a test of the true believers. "What will you go through to prove to Creator that you are worthy?" Like that. But in reality, there is no need to prove anything. You are Spirit. And such creations that may interfere with that idea are purely temporary, for those who would keep you from knowing this will get past these minutes very soon.

Everyone needs reassurance, from the most frightened child—because the room is dark and the child doesn't feel safe—to that frightened child as an adult, who may have many very reasonable reasons to be frightened and others that he or she doesn't remember. So sometimes it's just greed: "The people are frightened. How can we make money off of this? Let's make it entertainment! We'll say it's that, anyway." And other times, it will be: "Well, the people are frightened. What can we do to reassure them?" Perhaps an entertainment will help, but ultimately it is to remind them of their own natural, native, normal personalities, which are portions of Creator.

If you understand that, then you'll recognize that the next few years leading to the time around 2012—including the latter part of 2011, 2012 itself, the early part of 2013, and to a lesser degree of intensity, the years beyond that—will offer you a great deal of choice. You can choose to believe in a fear —and you may very well have perfectly rational reasons to be frightened, and I'm not trying to take that away from you—but I am saying that you have more capability now to create than you've ever had on the planet as the human race on Earth.

So a recommendation: Picture what you would like—not what you're afraid of, but what you would like in a world. Don't think about revenge or harm: Think of a beautiful world, heaven on Earth, if you'd like. Picture it to the best of your ability. Then over time you can elaborate on that picture, that's all right too, but what I would recommend is to feel it. Put yourself in it, see the picture, and try to feel being in the picture. Imagine stepping in and feeling the ground or the water, if it's that—or the air, if it's that—under your feet. Make it as physical as possible. Touch it; be touched by it.

This is the easiest way to create something benevolent. You don't have to include everybody on the planet, but you might notice pleasant faces coming and going of this or that person or this or that animal or this or that plant or tree, perhaps. How about it? Let that be as long as it feels good. That's what I'm recommending, not only in regard to ETs and UFOs, but mostly in regard to the creationism that is available to you in and around 2012 especially, but also even now. That's your homework, if you'd like: very important.

Also, be nice to each other, if you would. Try to be friendly. Recognize that other people are feeling just as nervous and upset as you are. Sometimes, they may not speak about it, even loved ones. Sometimes, they'll keep it a secret for this or that reason: Possibly they don't wish to sound like they're complaining. Possibly they believe they must be strong at all costs and many other explanations. But if they act agitated, give them space. And when you see people on the street, if they smile a little bit and it feels safe, smile back and say, "Good life" or "have a good day" or "I wish you well" or whatever you say like that.

Look for Signs from Spirit in Crop Circles

Now know that many things that you see these days—lights, shapes, certain things that appear briefly and then, almost before you notice, are gone—are Spirit touching in with you. If there is a benevolent energy or you feel good immediately afterward—not as you think about it and maybe get frightened because of your conditioning, but right after or perhaps even during it (more likely right after)—that's Spirit paying a visit. It's possibly one of your guides, possibly an angel, possibly even Creator just reassuring you that you will go on no matter what, maybe not in the body you are in—no, of course not—but you are immortal in your personality, in your spirit, and things will get better. Maybe not today, maybe not tomorrow, but they will get better in time.

Many of the things called crop circles that you see are real. They are identified with UFOs and ETs, but in fact, about 50 percent of them are simply gifts from Creator. That is why if you are near them afterward, the energy is so wonderful. Sometimes it feels almost electrical, tingly. Other times it feels soft and gentle, more feminine and comforting and loving. If you have the opportunity, be near them. But if the opportunity does not present itself, know that it will, and that energy will not be denied you. It will come in other ways, in the form of those lights or dots of lights, as I have mentioned.

If you see a picture of a crop circle, take the picture and turn it slowly. The best picture would be taken from directly above, looking directly down, but of course that's not always available. Make the turn on the picture to the left, since that is the way the Earth moves when it is creating, and Earth is always creating. Turn it very slowly to the left—in a rotating way, you understand—and stop only when the picture feels just right to you. It will feel different in the "just right" position to different people. The picture is a universal language that goes beyond words—symbols, of course, pictures, yes? This is the most easily transcribed universal language, and crops are often welcoming of such gifts that come from Spirit.

Very, very few of these crop circles will be fake—very few. And they'll be easily told because of the damage done to the crops—because the crops did not feel the welcome from the visitation of such beautiful energies and did not lie down and relax without breaking a stem, because the energies were from Creator or from a visitor sent by Creator—often an angelic being. Sometimes the angelics will appear as spots or balls of light. Other times, and most of the time, they will not be seen.

Occasionally in the beginning, crop circles were associated with ETs and UFOs, but very rarely are they connected that way now, unless the ETs and UFOs, meaning those in the UFOs, were asked by Creator or one of Creator's messengers—and you can say angels, for that is an appropriate word also—to leave a mark on the ground to herald the coming of these messages, and so that was done. But now the message is come through angelics, and you'll always be able to tell the difference, because the crops lie down in a relaxed fashion and sometimes interweave with other stems because it feels good to be close to them. And the weaving will not break a stem—not one. Then you'll know it's from Creator through the angelic beings.

The pictures or patterns in crop circles that are produced are for each and every one of you. That's why I recommend that you turn the pictures. Turn them, because each and every one of you is unique and different. Granted, some of you are from families of consciousness. That is why sometimes people look similar, even though they're not related by blood—at least, not family. There might be some distant relationship in the past or possibly even in the future. The images in the crop circles will then help you, usually, to know, to feel, and to remember who you really are. These reminders and many others will come from the picture, the energy, the moment—or slightly after the moment, slightly after you saw the picture, slightly after you saw the light, slightly after you had the inspiration. It's all about the moment now: the moment of the feeling.

You Will All Move to a More Benevolent Time

You have the opportunity now to create, almost like an apprentice to Creator. Creator will teach you through angels, guides, and Spirit. All of these beings love you just the way you are. They don't always love everything you do, but they love you just the way you are in your personality, which is immortal, in your soul, which is immortal, and in your light, which is immortal. And these words and many others all mean the same thing: that portion of Creator that you are.

Don't be alarmed if there are reports of people being afraid of something they saw in the sky. There are things now that—because of a mistake in perception—are being seen in the sky by those who would demonstrate them in ways that might momentarily frighten but then be gone. Most of the things you see in the sky that prompt you to feel good—the lights, the UFOs—will be visitors from friendly places. Sometimes one or more of the crop circles will be a picture of one of these vehicles. Most of the time, though, they will be the universal language—not only to remind you of who you are in spirit, but also to demonstrate this universal language of form and function.

Form seems to follow function. Other times, function seems to follow form. And yet they are all a portion of personality—immortality, spirit. Trees, birds, animals—the biggest, the smallest—microbes, yes, atoms, particles, and of course human beings are always form and function. You can't be a unique portion of Creator without being form and function. Know this, and you will always feel at least partially enlightened.

In the times that come, don't get caught up in the fear. Try to be balanced and centered, as it is said, in who you really are. If you don't see crop circles, if you don't have such pictures, that's all right. Put your hand on the center of your chest or, if it feels better, just slightly below your chest. That is where Creator often resides. The heart is said to be where Creator resides, and yet it is really closer to the center of your chest where Creator resides. The heart, being a loving organ, is drawn to that center. Your stomach, being a portion of your feeling self, is also drawn to that center. Remember to place your hands on your chest: one hand over your heart, the other over your stomach—that part of your chest really pretty much just on the other side; your stomach, just on the other side of your chest from your heart. Know that these parts of your body, as well as your lungs, not only help to maintain your brief time on the Earth, compared to your immortality of existence, but also they are a center of your being, that which supports, loves, and nourishes.

You will be all right. You are all immortal. Every one of you will move through these times to a more benevolent time—no exceptions. And along the way, you will shed things—not because you are told to, but because before you shed them, you will find yourself doing something else that feels so very much like you, so completely you, that you don't need the old, which you've used to protect the unseen, the unfelt you. That unseen, unfelt you—form and function—will reveal itself more and more, and the function will feel more and more benevolent. So the old mask, as it were—the war, the old warrior—will be able to relax, sit down, put down the sword, put down the spear, or put down the gun: You are now coming into the time of your true being. Don't let it frighten you. It will come with love— and only with love. Remember that always.

ETs Help You Remember Who You Are

You've been very, very vague. Can you say something about the beings in the rarified circles who are going to create these horror movies about ETs?

No, I wanted you to feel into it. You want details, eh? You want names; you want to know what's coming. But if I tell you that, how will you use your natural spirit, your abilities, your instinct? How will you use that if I give you all that what is? And your question also suggests that these beings you are judging are the sole creators of these movies, but they are not. Only very slightly, through financial services, are they involved. Others will create these movies, because money is there to be made.

So why should I tell you who these people are who are helping money to come—not so much giving money, but helping it to come—to such productions, when they are the ones who need to be reassured? If you were one of these beings, would you want to be punished, or would you want to be reassured so you could relax—lay down your sword, lay down your spear, lay down your gun? Or would you want to be punished and thus activate your armies before your suffering and "show them all"? What would you prefer—not only as one of them, but as one of the people as you are?

What about the ETs and the UFOs? Are they going to come in to the planet, and if so, what are they going to be doing?

Helping to remind you who you are. In your natural state, you are happy to see them. They are friends. They are welcome. Granted, some of them in the past were checking you over to see what is going on, what is meant to be. There was a short time of—how can we say?—compromise and coercion. You might find it hard to believe that ETs could be coerced, but for a short time, some ETs were coerced because there were loved ones who were being held hostage on this planet. That's the way they saw it, but the people who were holding them felt that they had this wonderful gift: "Beings from another world! How can we learn from them and study them?" But of course, as you might feel if you were a rabbit in a laboratory—or a cat or a dog in a laboratory—you would want to be someplace else. You would want to be with your own kind—with your family, with your loved ones. And they would want to be with you. What's the difference, eh?

That was probably fifty years ago. Or has that been recently?

In recent times, those ETs who had been coerced have been mostly relieved of their coercion. They have been shown what has happened to their loved ones, and now they have retired far away to grieve on their own. There are a few left who are still coerced but not many. I am speaking nowadays and in this time to you and the reader and also to those who know these things in detail to let them know that Spirit is not blaming them, nor is there any effort to punish them. It happened, and that's that. Question?

What were the relatives of those ETs being held coerced to do?

To check up on the human beings and to find out, through sampling on a genetic basis and utilizing the advanced genetic techniques of these ETs, whether there was any "danger" of this transformation happening any time soon. But you see, it's a funny thing: There is no danger—period. The transformation is not going to bring about a tribunal in which people will be held responsible. Everyone will transform into their natural, native spirit personalities. It's not about blaming. There will be no tribunal.

So there is no reason to single them out, because it would just have the most lethal effect. If you were told, right now, who did something, or if you were given someone to blame, do you not think that some people might just act on that blaming? "It's her fault! It's his fault! It's their fault!" What has happened as a result in the past when such names were given? All you have to do is pick up any history book to find out.

I am being, as you say, "vague" because I want you to use your spiritual abilities to feel, to know, to detect, and to create benevolently. Why would I want you to use your spiritual abilities to blame—to harm, to have retribution, to have revenge—when that only fosters more and more revenge? Study history: History is largely about revenge, and usually with the revenge happening to those who never did anything to receive that vengeance but were named. I will not perpetuate human blaming history.

ETs Are Giving You Space Now

We were told over the course of years that ETs were measuring us for our level of benevolence: the way we treated people—old people, babies, prisoners.

That's what they were really doing, but there is no difference between what I just said and what the others wanted. The ETs would report on the human beings' level of benevolence, but you see, from those who told them they had to do this or they wouldn't get their loved ones back, they didn't take it as your "level of benevolence." They took it as the level of change—the most feared thing, the transformation. See, it's not what it is; it's how it's seen.

From their perception.

Have you seen one of those masks that looks happy and smiling on the one side, and then you flip it over, and on the other side, it's miserable and weeping? It depends on how you look at it. You might think, if you're standing there, that it's wonderful: "Look how benevolent they're becoming." On the other side, you might look at it and say, "This is terrible. The change is coming more rapidly than we realized." It depends on who's looking at it and from what position.

All right. If we were looking at it, how are we doing?

Very well, or I wouldn't have opened with the comments that I did.

Ah. Good. How long, then? We have to go through what you're calling these "changes" before we can openly interact with ETs—before they can land on the planet?

If I told you that you had a choice to be your full, natural, spiritual beings—that which you are, that which you wish to be; you could go anywhere and do anything, benevolently—or you could have the ETs come and do that for you, what would you choose? Now some of you would say, "Well, since I don't know how to be my true, natural, spiritual being on the planet and I'm just doing the best I can, it would be wonderful if benevolent ETs came and did that for me or at least showed me how to do it. I'd be happy to participate if only I were shown how to do it!"

But, you see, the ETs now know how very close you are to remembering how to do it for yourself. That's the reason for all the training in recent years. Slowly, very slowly: "This is how you do it." Homework—slowly, very slowly: no rush to remember, to know. You don't know on the basis of what you think; you know on the basis of what you do, because you haven't been rushed. You've done it yourself, and you can feel the outcome. And then that's built upon—one thing after another—and slowly, you realize: You can create. Slowly, you realize that what seemed impossible in the past now seems much more possible, maybe even easy.

It is true, Melody, that when you become your true, natural, spiritual selves, ETs will come and go like they do everywhere else. But they'll give you a little distance because they don't want to interfere now with what you're doing, because what you are doing is so very important, and they have been told it will be important for them as well. So of course they don't want to interfere. If a mom tells her youngsters, "Now, you have to keep out of the kitchen, because I'm making something, and you're going to love it. But if you come in the kitchen, you might distract me, and then maybe you won't love it so much." [Chuckles.] And they'll be very curious; they'll be huddled outside the kitchen door. "What's going on? What can you hear? What's she doing?" Making this wonderful cake, eh? "What is that smell? Oh, it's wonderful! Oh!"

In short, yes. The answer to your question is yes. The ETs will come and go, but they will give you distance now. They are happy to see you being reminded in the universal language—not only of crop circles, but in the language of light and energy—for many of you (many, many now) will see the quick blinks of light or the quick motion, something that seemed to move: "What was that?" and it will be Spirit. For some of you, as I said, it will feel tingly, almost electrical—sometimes even with a sudden sense of something that really feels almost electrical. You will experience no harm afterward: You'll notice it, but you'll just say, "Wow, what was that?" Other times, it will be soft and gentle, nurturing, and you might even feel a warmth in your body.

ETs are giving you a little distance so you can remember who you are, but you will still see them sometimes in the skies—something moving, quickly—especially when all around you is quiet and you can be more sensitive in your abilities (your auric field, you might say), because it's a quiet time. Often—not everywhere, but often all over the world—such quiet times exist. That's when it's easier to feel, because your auric field—your energy body, you understand—

doesn't leave your body; it just expands and takes with it the abilities that you know as touch, albeit a gentle one, but still something you can perceive.

The question went in a different way than I meant. ETs can't come here right now because of our accelerated movement in time, right?

You see, you want it black and white: "can, must, only, can't." No, they could come, but why would they? If your mother is baking a wonderful cake in the kitchen and going in there would ruin the cake, waiting in the dining room (or in the playroom or in the bedroom or wherever) will mean that at some point, that cake will be served and you can have some, what would you do? Would you barge into the kitchen and destroy it for yourself and others? Some might, but ETs are not like that. So they will wait. That's why I used the analogy, because many of you can understand it. Some of you might say, "Well, some children would barge into the kitchen." And that may be true. Maybe they would get a piece of cake anyway. But in time, they would learn patience and why it's valuable.

You Can Create the Outcome You Desire

Are we going to change? How is our form going to change as we become more of our natural selves?

You'll feel physically lighter on your feet. There won't be any apparent biological differences. There might, in time, be some differences that happen in terms of, say, the birthing cycle. Babies won't, when they're ready to become children—babies outside the womb—they'll be just as big as ever, but there may be a way to give birth without pain. That's in the works. There will be other things. You'll probably eat differently, and as a result, you'll feel different.

There will be a different kind of technology, one that does not involve—how can we say?—machines so much. Or those things you might call machines would last a long time, because they are happy to be that way, however temporarily. The machines you have now are often tolerant of being machines, because they know it is temporary and that at some point, in some form, they will return to the earth, and there is the hope that they might be able to find their way back home—meaning to where they were mined out of the ground. As long as they are on Earth, there is that hope. But even then, since everything is alive, even being on the Moon or in space would still be a portion of home, so there's that.

You will find that disease does not exist anymore and becomes a dimmer and dimmer memory, things like that. You will find that it is much easier to make friends and that friends and family become sort of blended, and family becomes a good thing, feeling more like friends. In short, a universal friendship will take place. It will be a good thing.

All right. You were giving us a lot of reassurance earlier. Is there something that we need to be aware of that's going to be difficult, like climate changes or . . . ?

Climate changes are happening now. It's up to you to change them into something more benevolent. Next time you hear about some big storm coming—not just rain that feeds the ground and ultimately becomes the water you drink (so don't just prevent rain) but if some terrible storm is coming, one that has already killed and maimed and destroyed—then start picturing what you would prefer. Wouldn't it be so much nicer to have a gentle rain that could be easily soaked up by the land and then ask the Sun to warm the land? Like that. Picture what you want, and then, picturing it to the best of your ability—not just for a minute or two, but as long as you can—put yourself into it. Include in that picture your home and where you live, the land upon which your home may sit, and put yourself into that picture and feel the sunlight or the gentle rain. The more of you who do that, the more likely the storm will be benevolent and light. It is up to you, now, to change the storms, for the changes you refer to are happening now. Why wait?

Perhaps there are volcanoes. Perhaps there are earthquakes. Give Mother Earth permission to move, but ask her to move more gently or in smaller increments so that they aren't huge earthquakes but are very soft and gentle ones maybe that happen every day—as you say on your scale of measurement: a 2.0, a 3.0, something like that, maybe even a 4.0. If it happens every day, you'll say, "Oh, Mother Earth is moving," and there will be no problem. Why wait? Do something about it now.

There Are Spirits of Ships in the Sky

You said on your sort of advance-notice tape that you would talk about what is not ETs. Would that relate to some of the cloud formations that are being sent around on email, purporting to be crafts, or something else?

Some of that may be vehicles, but a lot of it isn't. A lot of it is the memory of vehicles, and some of it is the spirit of vehicles. Look at the clouds in the sky any day: Look at their edges (you might say, "edges," eh?), even their whole mass. You will see faces all the time. These are faces of spirits that are in the sky. They were in the sky before the clouds got there or they were in the sky and have left an imprint, because the vehicle, in the case of a ship, was alive. Many vehicles—you say ships—are alive. You must be able to accept the belief that something that appears to be inanimate is alive. A stone is alive and moving.

Your scientists tell you, "Look—the atoms, the structure—it is moving!" "It must be alive," some of them have the courage to say.

When you see the things in the sky that appear to be clouds and yet they look all the world like the way you might picture a ship, a vehicle, maybe it's the spirit of the vehicle, all right? Most of the time, it will be the vehicle's spirit, its being, just like the faces are defining a spirit that's there. Move past your belief that a UFO, a flying saucer, a ship, is a thing in which beings travel. The beings travel and are able to travel through such great spaces and distances because the thing they're traveling in is alive. It is spirit first, and spirit knows no boundaries. Your spirit—when you are at the deep levels of sleep—can leap across the universe, go from one side of the universe to another in less than a second to visit a teacher, an angel, a guide, a being, a loved one, any kind of benevolent source being. And you do it every night—or every day, when you sleep, whenever—at the deepest levels of your sleep. It is a spirit. The ships are all alive, and the vehicles—the ships themselves—often come to visit, but there may not be any beings inside the ships.

So recognize when you see those shapes in the clouds: Sometimes they are just the shape of the clouds. Other times they are the spirit of the ships, for the spirit exists before any ship that travels across distances—travels, as you say, in time, but it's also in space. The spirit exists before the ship exists, and you exist before your body exists. What does that suggest? The ships are spirit. They are immortal; they are someone. That is why the benevolent beings—the ETs— who can only be exposed to that which is benevolent, will travel in something that is benevolent, that is spirit, that is like them: that is immortal. That's what you're seeing in the skies. Never forget that.

For your homework, whether you are very young or very old: Look at the sky more often. You might see someone you recognize, a spirit. Sometimes one is there all the time—watching over you, doing what it can to help. Other times, it is a face of someone passing, and then that one moves on. Spirits are with you always, and why not? You are spirits as well.

This Is a Time for Choosing

All right. Well, anything I want to ask is really in a different flavor than what you want to talk about, so I'll just say . . .

Ask about anything you want. Let me remind you that you are speaking for the reader, but you are also speaking for yourself, your own curiosity. You are, how can we say, the spokesperson for the reader and ultimately, in time, for the listener. But it's all right to ask the questions. Do you know that I am answering your questions? Though they do not satisfy your mind, I am answering your questions from the position of your soul, your spirit—not to satisfy your mind, because your mind, like the minds of many readers, is associated with the mysteries: "Who is that? What was that? Why is that?" and so on. But I answer your spirit's questions, the being I know—your soul, your spirit, your immortal personality—and I guide your conscious mind, who is still trying to remember who she is, but it's getting closer, day by day. Go ahead. Ask your questions.

Well, it's my understanding from one of the Founders in the Time book that ETs can't come here now, because the rate at which we're moving toward the benevolent focus, using the accelerated time frequency, would cause them to die if they came here and got out of their spaceship.

Well, it's possible. For some, yes—no question about it. But what is death, really, but transformation? They would change, and if they have always been something, some immortal personalities, right?—how many personalities do you know—people, you understand, even maybe cats or dogs too, personalities, who would be at peace with a change into something completely unknown? Some might be frightened, though they might not recognize the fear. They might just have an uncomfortable feeling, not knowing that it's fear, but recognizing, on the basis of their instinct—which has to do with feeling—that no, they don't want to do that.

So while some could come and be just fine, they've been requested not to come. They've been requested to stay away while the sleeper wakes up. Have you had a time when you've awakened—slowly, gradually—to relax to your surroundings, perhaps even with good smells in the background: food cooking, coffee or tea brewing? Oh, that's nice. Compare that to waking with an alarm clock: "Get up! Now!" Quite a difference, eh? They're told to let the sleeper wake gradually, no forcing. And they say, "Yes, of course."

Well, we've been told that that's how we're waking up.

It is how you're waking up.

Like going from light sleep to the deep-sleep stage, and just letting everything that's not benevolent go, releasing it.

There's that, but you have to remember that you've been told things in piecemeal—you knowing that, perhaps, better than many. You're told things in piecemeal on the basis of what you can hear, safely, at any given time. Nothing you've been told in the past has been false, but remember it is not only that you're being told from those who are looking at this thing that is happening but they are looking at this thing that is happening from the basis of who they are, from their perspective.

Imagine, if you would, something vast: a mountain, a cliff, if you would, a butte, a mesa. On this side, it looks this way. On that side, it looks that way. And when you get close up to it, there are many other minute pictures in the stone. It depends on who you are, what you see, what you know, what you believe, but it's all true, not just opinion. It's all true, what you've been told. And yet the more awake you get—using that as the analogy: the sleepers wake up and remember who they are—the more you can be told. And what you are told becomes simpler, not more complicated, because what you are is very simple and uncomplicated, and what you've been and the pathway you've searched for that simple, real thing is filled with complications and contradictions and always with choices.

This is the time of the choosing. You can choose what feels good, or you can remain attached to and desiring what you have known: the complications, the contradictions, what is, what isn't, what might be, what could be. "Was it them? Was it her? What did they do? When? Why? What should we do about it?" or "It's all us." I have to speak in these riddles sometimes, because it's the time of the choosing, and so many of you are choosing to remember who you are, and you can know more. And I am revealing a great deal today, because as so many of you are waking up—slowly, gradually—more can be known. And the more must always, always be simpler, not more complicated. It makes the choosing so much easier.

If we're all going together and we're choosing, do those who choose the complicated delay the others who chose the simple?

The others who choose the simple—you, your immortal spirits, who you really are—do not get delayed at all. You become that, but because you love those who are taking longer, you wait for them to catch up. Why would you rush over the hill, even to something beautiful, if loved ones are behind you? You want your loved ones to catch up, because when you are that thing—your immortal personality, your spirit, your soul—there is no more harm, no more hate, and no more resentment. You aren't angry at them for whatever reason; you only feel love for them, and you wait for them to catch up. That is what is happening.

That is reassuring.

Now we must finish. Know that your time of awakening is really happening now. Remember to put yourself in the picture of something beautiful, something wonderful. Do the homework every day. It might just improve the quality of your day-to-day life as well. Good life.

Thank you, Zoosh. Good life.

BLUE SPIRAL LIGHT OVER NORWAY

ET Human a Spaceship in the Sky over Norway

December 9, 2009

Greetings.

Greetings!

We are associated with certain beings who have been in the skies above Norway, Finland, and Sweden for the past week and a half. I must say that the phenomenon currently being discussed and witnessed by many thousands in the Norway sky is not directly associated with us, but we were able to influence it in a benevolent way, in an intention to keep everything peaceful. We're going to put it like this: There are those who know we are in the sky, and while we cannot usually be detected—though occasionally we are confused for satellites, sometimes functioning satellites or sometimes just debris that catches the light—there are also those who feel that we might represent a threat when their detection systems come close to an analysis suggesting a foreign country's threat. This has less to do with the Nordic countries I mentioned and more to do with an influential country of global power near there—but I will not say the name and I would prefer you do not. This is not about conflict; it is about conflict resolution.

The energized emanation that was directed toward us—and I will not elaborate on what it was—was redirected, and its sky signature was accentuated. Some of it had to do, then, with that fear, but other aspects of it had to do with finding out more about who and what we are. I can assure you that while we are closer to your northern polar region, we are not from within the Earth nor are we associated in any way with the Earth population or any portion of the Earth population.

31

Human Beings Are All Over the Universe

We come from a star system—you would say "solar system"—from within this galaxy, and we are meant to be some of the first beings you are likely to come in contact with as a global community. This is why we have vehicles that are pre-pared to repel the fear-based energy emanations that might be directed toward us in ways that have the least detrimental effect on your surface populations. That's what was accentuated in the photographs and also other moving images that have been on your Internet today.

I want to reassure the peoples in that area that if you could see us now on our vehicle, you would say, "Wow! You look like Earth people!"—and we do. We are of the human race, but we are not based on your planet, nor have we ever had a base there. Using our motive system, we are easily able to move from our solar system to yours in a very brief amount of time. Our ships, as I say, are practically never viewable but on occasion might appear as I mentioned before. When they move like that—in a way that they can easily be mistaken for other objects placed in the sky, which are, as you say, human-made—it has to do with a means we use to slow down and enter your atmosphere. We will follow that pattern to have the least effect. We do not wish to cause alarm. But now since our time of meeting approaches (I cannot say when; it depends a lot on the means you choose to befriend each other—person to person, community to community, country to country), the greater amount of befriending that goes on that is genuine, we will be able to meet you sooner, not later.

We have been trained to be able to tolerate a certain amount of radiated discomfort energy from individuals but not a tremendous amount of fear-based energy. We realize that you've had sixty or seventy years to build up a fear base. I want to reassure you that for at least another 700 or 800 of your years, you will never meet any beings who either come to visit your planet or your space travelers go to visit who do not look essentially humanoid. The first beings you will meet will most likely be human beings like us. They might be from differ-ent places. You will find it reassuring to know that human beings, the human race, is all over the universe.

There are other beings, of course, just like on your own planet. Many of these you call animals, which is ironic, since although they look a little differ-ent on their planets than they do on Earth, they wouldn't consider themselves to be a secondary class of beings, you might say. But this oversimplification has developed on your planet over many years during the time when you have not had, at large, contact with extraterrestrials. You have had individual contact, and some communities have kept up a contact longer than others. There has been a well-known contact in the Nordic countries with a man named Meyer, a totally genuine experience for which there has been much misinformation and misunderstanding. That situation will be understood much better in the coming years.

For now, I just wanted to say that we needed to transform that energy emanation from the Earth into something that was more beautiful and less—how can we say?—of conflict. That was our intention and, we believe, the outcome. We cannot exactly apologize to those who sent that energy emanation, since the intention was actually conflicted [chuckles] between, "Who and what is that?" and "Just in case, here's the big bang." We understand that you are still shy about these contacts, and we understand that the reason the energy emanation was aggressive was that there was a misunderstanding about who we are. So we just want to reassure those who sent the emanation that we recognize the misunderstanding.

The Energy Emanations Were Redirected

How long have you been out there?

As I said, about a week and a half.

Ah, I missed that. Do you come and go, or is this the first time you were here?

As peoples, we have not been near your planet too much. We have been contacted by humanoids who were originally going to be the first ones you would come into contact with, but it was felt that it might be more comfortable for you—and they felt this too—to meet beings who looked identical to human beings on the Earth. So when you do meet us, you will find us to be representative of the appearances of human beings on the Earth. We will not all look like the same type of human being, if I make myself clear.

You will be different shapes and colors and sizes?

We will generally have the same shape, but there would be what you call "racial" differences. We just call that variety.

Originally, we were supposed to meet the Zeta hybrids as our first contact. So they're the ones who contacted you?

They felt that due to trends that were troubling on the Earth having to do with racial and religious strife that seems to be perpetuated partly by Earth-based individuals and partly by the impact of the memory of such things— meaning energy and codings and, to a degree, history—that you would be comforted more to meet beings who looked like you.

When you sent that energy back, it then became that spiraling blue light that's been pictured on the Internet?

I didn't say we sent it back.

You said you redirected it.

Yes, but I didn't say we sent it back. We redirected the energy emanation and caused it to be a thing of beauty.

It became the spiraling blue light, right?

It wasn't actually that. But generally speaking, I'll accept your description.

When did this happen? When in our time did this happen?

Within the past twenty-four hours.

You've made it a thing of beauty and it spiraled, and now images of it are on the Internet.

We accentuated it.

Accentuated. Did it last a long time? Or was it just something they caught that just lasted a little while?

What could be seen from the ground lasted a few minutes. That's why it's important to speak to you this way: So you can understand that in other circumstances of Earth-based projections, such a projection might not have taken so long. But because we were able to convert it to a thing of beauty with no harm, it took longer.

Had you not done that, would it have destroyed your vehicle?

As I said, I'm not going to comment further about that.

I See.

Our Culture Is Hardy and Resilient

You can't say specifically where you're from?

A solar system in your galaxy. There are many humans living all over in this galaxy and beyond. We are ones who are more inclined to be open to civilizations that are not entirely in balance. So we will be well protected when we meet you, but not in any way that is aggressive or harmful.

How long has your civilization had technology like spaceships?

Millions of years. This is typical in the rest of the universe. I do not wish to sound patronizing, but you do not have these things so that you will be protected.

Yes, I understand. There are other civilizations on planets out there that are not in balance?

To a very minor degree, compared to yours. There are civilizations that may be slightly out of balance compared to other civilizations in the universe, but you would not notice that. It is to a *very* minor degree. But we do not mind that. We believe it is a human trait to be flexible.

Absolutely. Describe "out of balance." Do you mean negative?

It means to have something that is not in synchronicity and remains so in an individual or even up to a whole culture or community. It might be a slight discomfiture, but it might be something else. It might be an anomaly within the cultural identity—for example, conflicting ideas about the culture that are both promoted and the people are thus confused about who they are.

With discomfort, but a very tiny percentage of discomfort, right?

Not necessarily, but it could be that. In one case, it could be a minor amount of discomfort. In another case, it could simply be a mild confusion. We do not see that as discomfort, though others might define it that way.

Is that because . . . you said "flexible," but you're also hardier, evidently—stronger, more resilient?

I think I like your first word better. We are somewhat hardy, in terms of your definition of that term.

What kind of civilization do you have?

I will tell you what I can. We are very interested in other species of beings. We have vast means to study and interact with other species of beings. We are not, in our own right, diplomats. Apparently, this was considered to be less important for first contact with you, with your civilization. The beings who were originally going to make the first contact are diplomats, but we are not that. Still, we are perhaps . . . likable. That was considered to be more important, especially since we can "get along" in situations where many extraterrestrials would not be able to get along. Our culture, to use another one of your words, is resilient. Minor episodes of something that resembles discomfort but isn't actually that are easily shrugged off, individually and in communities. So we are perhaps better equipped to interact—granted, through a mediator—with human beings of your now time.

Who would be the mediator?

If our contact takes place, there will be a mediator. Possibly, it will be light energy. Possibly, it will be one of the diplomats there are more of. They would probably remain at a distance, but they will be able to function in a mediating aspect, protecting us and protecting you but allowing a free-flowing communication—initially with governmental bodies, but very soon after that with communities and even individuals. We do not wish to simply intrude on your civilization and announce our presence. This is something we want to teach you not to do as well. It is better to "call ahead," wouldn't you say? Let people know you're coming over and then go. This is what you usually do when you are polite, and maybe you even bring over a gift. We will do something similar. We will bring some kind of gift that your civilization wants and needs, but I won't say what that is.

I want a universal translator. [Chuckles.]

It will be something that everyone on Earth can agree on—no exceptions. Something that is welcome. It won't just be something that *some* people will like.

That's what some ETs did in the past; they gave gifts of technology to some governments. How much do you know about us? You said you're very interested in other species, so have you studied us?

No, we are accepting the information supplied by others. We do not study peoples. We are interested in peoples, but we do not, in and of our own culture, study others. We accept the information provided by others, just as we have in this case accepted the information provided by those diplomatic beings you were going to make first contact with. They seem to have a lot of knowledge about you that is scientific and otherwise. It seems to be accurate.

Well, they're the Zeta hybrids—I mean, they're half human and half Zeta, right?

Something like that.

How did your civilization get to be resilient and hardy? What type of life do you live on your planet? Was it your experiences that got you that way or do you have different DNA or what?

The human race in general is that way. We do not come with a hard shell, as some creatures, but we have a certain built-in resilience and flexibility. Many of the qualities you admire in other humans on your own planet are native to the human being, we believe. So when I say we are hardy, I mean that given the proper equipment and the proper circumstances, we could go to climates that are very cold or very hot. Human beings are comfortable adapting. You do that now. Many beings from other planets would not come to a planet where they would have to wear something to keep them warm or devise technology to keep them comfortable in stressful heat, as you have done with your technology that will cool things off sufficiently. But also, there are civilizations that simply wear less and use the shade and waters. [Pause.] There is some static. You can hear this?

Yes.

There is activity. But we do not represent a threat. Still, we are being probed. [Chuckles.] It's all right.

Learn How to Get Along with One Another

I understand that humans on our planet have been engineered to be more vulnerable so that we don't live very long because it is so discomforting. What is your length of life?

We live up to 2,700 years, but not everyone does. Generally, the average might be 1,700. With your normal state of being, without the genetic modifications to make you a little more vulnerable so that you do not have to put up with a life of discomfort that lasts hundreds and hundreds of years, you would be like us.

Right. Where are you in that cycle?

What is my age? Oh, I am young. I am about 700.

How are you the one chosen to speak to us?

I'm not busy. The others are busy.

What is your role on the ship?

I can't say. However, the one who's closest to a diplomat is not me. This being is not a diplomat but is, as a hobby, interested in that. That's not me, though.

Do you create spiritually? What kind of culture do you have?

What we need is available with the simple energy of life. Now [chuckles] we're being probed so much, the static is getting louder. The Earth-based individuals would prefer that we would bring this to a close, and I will honor that.

Are these the same people who shot at you or another group?

No comment. I'm going to finish up with this: Learn how to get along with each other. You don't have to agree with everything people say, but find a way to get along, using your best qualities, and we will meet sooner rather than later.

I look forward to it.

Good night.

Good night. Good life. Thank you very much.

PRACTICE GENTLE COMMUNICATION WITH NONHUMANS

ET Traveler

December 21, 2009

Greetings. I am a traveler—that's what I'm going to call myself. One of the things I do is check on the citizens on your planet to see how you are coming along and to see if you are ready to have contact with beings from other planets so that you can become aware of the beings living among you whose root source is from other planets. My specific job is to check on people this society, or group or government agency or what have you, disapproves of and how you treat them. This observation also moves into, say, families: Who's being disapproved of at the moment, and how are they treated? These are what you might call touchstones by which a civilization, both on a planetary and even on the individual basis, can be gauged to create the best possible environment for such meetings that might at times—depending upon the flow of conversation or other forms of communication—remind the people of Earth of things that otherwise would be unsettling.

For example, many of you on Earth have contact with animals, as you call them, and you have certain relationships with those animals that are either positive or unpleasant, comfortable or uncomfortable. In the case of pets, that relationship is a regular thing, but there are other beings, other nonhumans, you come in touch with one way or another, and there's often discomfiture for the human being, just in general—with the little beings you call insects, for example, or maybe because of experiences at birth that you wish you hadn't had and so on.

These gauges are a means to know how you would interact in, say, a conversation with an extraterrestrial. Now, granted, more formal interactions between extraterrestrials, as you might call them, and the human race would be with trained diplomats on both sides. These people are inclined to either forgive or disregard things that might touch personal buttons for them and even be more inclined to notice major things. But as I say, these people are professionals or specialists in that field. I'm talking about situations that have even come up in the past when human beings were contacted by beings from other planets and there was a lot of fear. Sometimes the fear of the human be-ing—the Earth human, you understand—was warranted. Other times it was simply a reaction based on a current or past experience that caused those humans to be confused about whether or not they were interacting with other human beings—equals, so to speak—or some kind of nonhuman species, even if the other beings looked totally like the Earth humans. The others might have looked like human beings, but then the relationship that you have on the planet with nonhumans is what was coming into play.

Treat Nonhumans as People

My job is also to see how you are treating those nonhumans. Of course, there are some people who treat them very well while there are other people who do not, for this and that reason. Sometimes it's simply conditioning, and of course people who work with animals on a regular basis—farmers, ranchers, and so on—have a certain predisposed position they take in order to interact with these beings. But I'm talking more about the general population. Sometimes you might be inclined—especially as a child who hasn't been conditioned that much by your society or your culture or your parents' points of view—to react to and interact with nonhumans pretty much as equals. They might be friendly or they might be problematic. On a spirit-to-spirit basis, there's never a problem, but the challenge comes because human beings on Earth are not totally in touch with their spirits, as you know. So you don't really remember who these beings are.

With many beings you interact with on a regular basis, such as cats, dogs, and occasionally other frequently found pets like birds and horses and so on—by occasionally, I mean within the percentage of the people who have pets—there is closeness, a special feeling, and definitely a personal relationship. A lot of this is good. But if I had to put a percentage on how close you are in terms of your overall treatment of nonhuman species on the planet—talking only about beings you can see moving, for example—I'd say right now that in terms of the goal of 40-percent benevolence needed in order to have contact with extraterrestrials, you are now at about 3 percent.

So what can you do, you might ask, to speed that along or to make it better? I'm going to give you some homework. Pick a type of species; it doesn't have to be someone you see around the house, but it can be someone—meaning a type of nonhuman species that is not a pet, all right?—who is in the neighborhood, so to speak, whatever your neighborhood is like. It might be a very small, insect-type being or a bird or squirrel, someone you might see in the neighborhood on a regular basis. It doesn't have to be the same being every time you practice this; it can just be a being from that species. Begin by talking to the being gently. You don't have to tell them what your favorite music is; just start off by saying, "Good life." They all know what that means; it's an acknowledgment that's like a blessing.

As time goes on and you feel comfortable, and there are no other people around so you don't feel shy, just talk. Say whatever you want to say, but keep it gentle. Speak gently and kindly, "I hope you are well. I hope you are comfortable in your life and have plenty to eat," things like that. Start off polite. "It is like this with my family" or "with my friends." Don't talk too personally at first; keep it polite. But over time, you can say other things. At some point you'll be able to say, "I'm experiencing this or that problem, and if you have any means to help me with that problem, something you could tell me in a dream or through one of your teachers or spirits work with you or you're aware of so that I would have a means for solving this, I'd appreciate that. And if you have a problem, I would be happy to help or to ask one of my teachers or guides to speak to you while you are asleep and dreaming if that would be helpful," like that.

Eventually, word's going to get around in that species that you are someone they can sit closer to or fly nearer to, or when they're nearby, if you walk toward them very slowly, they won't have to immediately fly or run away. They might not let you get up really close to them, but if you have good feeling for them in your heart and they know you're not going to harm them, they might allow it. I'm not suggesting you touch them, but if they happen to touch you, who knows? It might turn into something benevolent. But the main thing is this communion, this conversation.

This also gives you good training in learning how to speak to children. Even for children, it's good training. Children like to be spoken to in that gentle and kind way, and they like feeling that way. It doesn't work as well if you're not feeling that way, so many of you will have to sort of relax into a good feeling. Try it if you can for a few weeks, whenever you want to begin. It might raise the percentage of benevolence needed in time, improving the

possibilities of your having contact with civilizations from other places that
will, once they trust you or feel good about you, be able to give you the cure to
most diseases and other things you'd like to have. [Pause.]

All right, so that's interacting with those beings, but before you said that we treat humans even worse than that.

This is training, you understand. I'm not trying to get you to start treating
humans differently right away. That's too fast for you. You have to train people
in ways that you would actually want to be trained yourself. Believe it or not,
learning how to swim by having somebody hurl you out of the boat into the
water is the worst possible way, though I know people like to say, "Oh well,
that's how I learned how to swim." You hear that from older folks sometimes.

That's how I became afraid of the water.

That's right. It's the worst possible way. So you want to bring people along
gently and slowly. And that's why we start with nonhumans. It's much simpler
and less threatening. You know, you'd be surprised how many people talk to
their cars—and not just people who are on long drives. People often have
names for their cars and sometimes say a few words to their cars. So it's not as
if this concept is completely foreign for folks. A lot of people talk to their pets.
I mean, really—when you come home, you say "Hi, Fluffy" or "Hi, Butch" or
something like that, depending on what you call them. They are friends, you
know, and a lot of love is passed between you. So it's not as if this is a foreign
concept or something you have to learn having never done it, although in
some cases, that might be the situation. So, then, do you have any questions?

Communication Can Happen in Unexpected Ways

Well, say something about yourself. You are a traveler from where?

It is my job as a being to check up on civilizations like your own to see
how they are doing. I don't really want to say where I am from. I will simply say that I am one of the many trained to do this and that I work in this
galaxy exclusively. I've traveled other places, but in terms of my work, it's
in this galaxy.

Who do you report to?

It is a loose-knit thing. We're not talking about a hierarchical group that
is—how can we say—an authority. This whole idea of hierarchical groups and
authorities and commissions and all of that is something that you find established on planets where the citizens are not engaged in much interaction with
beings from other planets. So I don't report to anyone, per se. The awareness
and knowledge I have is available for anyone and everyone, so beings might

very well check and I don't really know about it, but I'm not paying attention. It's available to whoever wants it.

Because they can tune into you?

Yes. And there is no formal process. Generally speaking, when you hear from various entities who talk about this formal process or that formal process, that's just kind of a way of speaking to you as people so that you'll be able to understand it, because that's what you have. Even from an early stage, in the relationships of parents and children, you're used to there being a hierarchical authority, and that becomes something that you trust and feel good about. Even those who are very creative and who become artists and whatnot still tend to fall back on things that are somewhat hierarchical. Maybe it's not as much of a portion of their lives, but it's something that can be counted on, even if not necessarily enjoyed all the time.

So that's why, when you have such conversations as you're having now, beings might sometimes say we report to this commission or that commission. That kind of thing is really a way to provide a voice to you, to let you know that things exist in other ways, in other places, or in other ways in the places you know. It's simple, but it's made more complicated so that you can accept it better. Interesting, eh? Things are made more complicated so that you, as human beings on Earth, can accept them as being truer. Is that the word you use—"truer"? I'm not talking down to you here; I'm just talking, telling you how it is, okay? That's important for you to know, generally speaking. That's how that works.

All right, so for instance, those beings who are waiting out here in a ship who had that art display over Norway last week . . .

They didn't create that.

I know—they redirected the energy and made it beautiful, they said.

Yes, but they didn't initiate it.

Yes, I'm aware of that. They're waiting to talk to us. But you're saying that we have an awfully long way to go yet.

That doesn't mean they can't talk to you. After all, I'm talking to you.

Yes, but I'm not quite "official."

But don't you see? You're not the only one on the planet being spoken to in this fashion. Maybe they're talking to somebody else right now. After all, when you pick up the instrument you're using now and have conversations with people all over the planet, are you not talking to them? What would you say if I told you that there's been a considerable amount of contact between ETs and Earth people over the phone?

Well, I've been doing this for years.

That's right. And maybe others have too. So I know that your thought and your question meant something like . . .

Face-to-face communication.

That's right. But of course that would be fraught with problems right now, wouldn't it? I can think of any number of governments—to say nothing of institutions, meaning parts of governments—that might not feel so comfortable about that sort of thing.

Those are the ones we need to work on.

Well, governments are made up of people, so ultimately it's an individual thing.

You said something interesting. I thought we were the only beings anywhere who had discomfort and who needed this kind of checking up on. I thought everyone else everywhere was benign and benevolent. Why would you be checking up on other beings on other planets?

Oh, very simply. You can be benign and benevolent in your society and yet still be somewhat uncomfortable about meeting other benign and benevolent peoples—simply because of the foreignness of it. So you might have to be brought along gently so that there can be common ground by which you can meet these other "people," using people in quotes on both sides of the issue here, in a way that feels just as benign and just as benevolent as you normally feel in your own society and your culture. So it might be necessary to create a means to have an interconnected relationship. And in time, as you get used to interacting with the other beings, eventually it will just become part of your greater community.

Yes, many of the beings on other planets who are connected to what we call animals do not travel or interact with other societies—so they said.

So you understand. They might very well be at least, if not struck dumb—so to speak, eh, you say that?—then they might be reticent to communicate to the degree that they might communicate with another member of their own culture. And if there is a need or a desire from one group or the other to have this communication, well, then they need to be helped. Both parties would need to be helped so that they can have that common ground and meet and get to know each other and get used to each other's ways and so on. Even now on your planet, for example, you have that same situation. You have friends, and you are much more relaxed and inclined to speak and say things to your friends than you would to, say, someone you don't know, someone you might call a stranger, eh?

Peacemaking Is a Calling

Well, how did you train to do this? What was your interest before you started doing this?

I think that I didn't require much training. It was something I was always good at—seeing the subtle differences between beings that held them back from having an intimate conversation. And it's in those intimate conversations on Earth, these conversations in which you and a very good friend identify with each other, that you tend to reveal your innermost needs and your desires and so on. This allows the other party—if that person can help in any way—to be able to address those issues, to help you in some way, or refer you to somebody else who could help you, for example. And when there is such communication, it's also a way of avoiding misunderstandings. One of the biggest problems in initial communications between cultures is misunderstandings. Sometimes—as you have seen on Earth—those misunderstandings are so pronounced that succeeding generations are at war with the other species because there was a simple misunderstanding that if it had been avoided to begin with, would not have resulted in all that conflict and those ramifications of conflict.

So I didn't really have to train to do this work. I was good at it, and at some point, I realized that there weren't that many beings doing this. I heard about somebody doing it in a way that sounded like what you would describe as a job, a career, eh? And I thought, "This is something I'm good at, and I like doing it." So I started doing it in my general community—meaning the planets in the solar system we are part of—and then people heard about what I was doing and said, "Oh, would you come here and do that?" or "You seem to be good at that; would you come there, go there?" and so on. And it sort of evolved into what I'm doing now.

In the course of that process, I met three or four others who said that they were doing that sort of work too, and they were well known for it and said that they knew others. So I know there are others out there doing such work, and I'll bet that on your planet, there are probably a lot of people who do that now. A lot of people are drawn to diplomacy and statesmanship and so on—not just because it's a good job, but because they're drawn to it. Maybe they're good at it, you see. Sometimes they're called peacemakers on your planet.

My Form Is Not Physical, but I Can Appear Visibly to You

Can you say what your form is—what you look like?

Well, I'm referring to myself as a being, although I'm not what you would

call physical, though through the use of a means that I would call reflection—
it's not really a technology—I can sort of appear at moments. If you and I were
in the same space together, you would probably hear me as a voice in your
head. But if you weren't comfortable with that, then I could create some kind
of presence so that you could tell that there was somebody else there—but of
course I would only do that if you were comfortable with it. Are you comfortable with that as an individual, just speaking as an individual human who is
representing the human race at this moment?

Well, I am . . . I mean, I think I am—not having experienced it.

I feel it would be more comfortable for you to see something, although I'm
not going to say what. So sometime within the next forty-eight hours, you'll
see something, and it'll be in a situation where it's safe. You're not going to
be driving or anything like that, okay? You'll just see something. It might be
out of the corner of your eye, or it might just be in front of you. It'll just be
there for a moment—a split second, as you say, eh? Do you still say that? It'll
be something else there, so just recognize it. That'll be me.

Well, are you going to say something?

No, I won't say anything. You'll see it. It'll probably be between something that you're looking at and you. So you'll be looking at something, but
it'll be between you and whatever you're looking at.

I look forward to that.

Also, because you have a pet, the pet will probably see it, and this might
give you a clue. If the pet starts looking around more than usual, you'll probably know I'm in the area, eh? So that's a little hint.

*Oh, that's great. So you can project yourself any place. Obviously you don't travel in a spaceship,
so you can go to any place you want? I mean, just down to me in the third dimension here in this
reality or to any other planet, to anyone?*

Yes. Because I'm not physical as a rule, I do not have physical radiations
that would cause a problem on your planet, see?

And in turn, you're not bothered by the discomfort that we radiate.

That's right. And to the degree you would see me, I would be completely
protected, just as you would be completely protected. That's why I call it kind
of a reflection. You would compare it to the way you might have a reflection—
how would you say?—in a mirror. Of course, it's not a mirror, but it is a type
of reflection.

Well, that's interesting. It sounds like a good job.

Well, yes. It's enjoyable. And you know, it's comforting because I know
I'm always doing something that people want, something they're interested

in, and they're always happy to take some step toward achieving that. But even on other planets, I don't give them all the training at once in one day. I start them off with some homework: "Well, why don't you try this," just like I did before when I was talking to the readers, eh? "Okay, why don't you try this and why don't you try that?" Eventually they come along, and then they can meet the other beings who want to meet them or who they want to meet. It's the same on your planet. It's not because you're slow; it's that it's better to start slowly and then see how it goes and to discover on your own whether this is something you want to pursue. Or if you decide it's not for you, then you say "Oh well, that's interesting" and go on with your life.

Communion Provides Instant Communication

All right. Right now, you're talking to me, but really—through the books and magazine and electronic publications and audio—you're talking to many thousands and thousands of people. On other planets, is it similar? Is there a situation like this; do you talk to one person at a time there or to a group or what?

On other planets where it's some benevolent thing, I'm usually talking to a small group who might be the ones who would, say, plan to meet beings from other civilizations, at least initially, in sort of a diplomatic corps. But things are not that stratified or hierarchical on other planets. Those I communicate with might just be the people who normally meet beings from other planets, just to get started and see, "Well, okay, this is how we are; I see that's how you are," and so on.

How do you communicate with them? With a voice in their heads?

Well, of course it's not a problem there. There's no fear and so on, and they can usually see me or see what they need to see. Generally speaking, they might hear me talking, you know.

Oh, you can project your voice to them?

[Makes a sound of frustration.] I'm going to have to try and get around this because you're having some difficulty. They just know, okay? It's instantaneous. I don't talk to them in a linear way, the way you're hearing me. I just . . .

It's more like communing, then?

Yes, communing. And an example of communing, for you, would be the way a mother would know what her baby needs. The baby doesn't give the mom a speech. Or when you're very close to your pet, for instance, you might know what that pet wants or needs—although the example of a mother knowing what her baby needs is closer to what I would call communion and what you could understand when you say communion. You personally understand it, but the reader may not necessarily know what is meant. That's why I give examples, because I don't want to assume that the reader knows what we're talking about. That's diplomacy, by the way—something very good for you to know about.

Distance Is Not a Factor

All right, how often do you check on us, then?

Whenever I get the feeling that it's time to touch in on it—not with the same people. Sometimes I'll notice when children are talking to nonhuman species and I see how much they enjoy that. And other times I'll notice when adults are doing it and so on. It's sort of like when you are going for a walk, say, and you suddenly smell a fragrance. You might look around to see where it's coming from. It might just be somebody passing by who's wearing a fragrance, or it might be flowers nearby and so on. That's how I notice—in a similar fashion. It's not because I smell it; I'm just giving you that image as an example. It's how you would know something on the basis of a subtlety. It's a fragrance; it's a subtlety. In the case of something you know, a lilting fragrance for example, that's a subtlety.

But you would know from much farther away, where we here on Earth would have to be right next to it?

The distance doesn't make any difference to me. I might add that for people who've had the training on your planet, through spirit or some other means—for example, the being who's doing the channeling here has done some teaching about long touch on his blogs—distance doesn't make any difference either, you know. If you're doing long touch or even long vision, it doesn't make any difference if it's on the planet or if it's in another galaxy. Distance is not a factor.

Okay, and the three Shamanic Secrets *books have those teachings.*

But not all of your readers have read those books. As a matter of fact, the bulk of your readers have not read them, so it's good to put in these things and start doing more cross-referencing. You can put in a footnote that says "see such and such." Don't be shy about that. More and more people are going to want to do that, and you can also encourage the other channels to put in footnotes: "See such and such book" or "see such and such article." You want to encourage that because people are going to be interested in whole systems now, because they're looking for more systems that will answer questions that the systems they're working with now aren't answering. That's a little bonus for you.

Changing Whole Systems with Simple Steps

Say more about whole systems.

A whole system might be your way of understanding your culture—the training you've received, maybe the philosophy of your culture, or what you sometimes call religion, something that normally explains everything. People now are looking for other whole systems that would explain everything, including some of the things you already know, and they will agree with that, but it will have other answers about other things that you don't know or things that you do know but would be interested to know that there's other information about them. So whole systems often overlap. We cannot go on much longer—the channel's body is older and cannot assume fixed positions for too long without there being discomfort.

Okay. Well, what do you see of our future? When you look at the people in prisons and when you look at the wars and at the religious extremes, how are we going to change all of that to benevolence?

The reason I'm talking to you today is to help you along, and there are people trying to fix those situations so that they are better, but it will take a while. I find that it's much better to talk to the general population and to get them interacting in ways with other beings—in your planet's case, nonhumans—that are easier and gentler. Start people off doing something gentle rather than taking on the really difficult problems. There's a tendency to overlook the gentle and simple in your society, but I find that the gentle and simple are always the easiest ways for the beings who need to make these steps.

In this case, for you—you, meaning Earth humans—I'm not saying that the problems you've mentioned are minor; they are indeed major problems. But it's much easier to start off learning how to play the piano by playing scales than by having someone demand you sit down and play Rachmaninoff immediately without ever having played the piano before.

I don't know what else to ask you. What is the most important thing that you can say now to the people who are reading this?

Okay, then I will sign off with this: For you on Earth, know that you are not abandoned; you are not forgotten. There are beings like me checking up on you, because there are thousands of extraterrestrials who are just leaning in your direction. They have so much compassion for you, and they want to help you. But in order to be able to help you, they need to feel safe. Now you can understand that completely. Many times, you would like to help somebody, but you don't because you don't feel safe. So you can understand.

These beings also don't want to come into your civilization in some big ship or something like that, causing a big stir and getting everybody upset and anxious. They would like it, though, if you would show—because of your own desires, not because of their needs or because of their own desires—that you can become interested in learning how to communicate in some way that feels safe and comfortable and, yes, benevolent for you with other species. And the easiest way for you to begin to do that is by interacting with other species on Earth. That is why I've given you that simple homework. Don't take any big chances, okay? Don't go out and try and talk to bears or anything like that, but keep it simple and gentle. I'll be back to talk to you again through this channel some other time. Good night.

Good night, and I'm looking forward to seeing you.

A GLIMPSE
BEYOND THE
EXPLORER RACE

Sentient Machine with Zoosh and Isis

December 30, 2009

I am speaking to you, with Isis's and Zoosh's support, from only about twenty-five years into the future. I am a being living in your direct future who is familiar with technology and has influence over it. Your planet is going through major changes. What's happening is largely a change in cultural identity. The youngsters know it needs to be done, and that's why they're using the Internet and texting and all that other business to communicate all over the world. And this is good, because it can go on while the rest of the world—in terms of people—does its thing.

It's not a revolution; it's just a creation of a relatively harmonious communication system, using your present technology. But it will build into something because the generation of people who are now at least seven years old—and up to fifteen, sixteen—is going to want more while remaining connected to others, including people they have never met but with whom they feel close. And what's going to appeal to them is a universal language, because they feel constrained even using translators, which are, as you know, at best only just so effective. Nuances don't come through very well, even when done with texting language, for example. So what is going to appeal to them is what is physical, what is felt—feelings. You are now as a person delivering mass media, albeit in your own way, just on the tip of moving fully into a greater form of mass media. You obviously need somebody who can do things that will appeal to that mass media, someone who understands the "underground" aspect of it, so to speak, that I mentioned with the young people up to some teenagers.

The churches that will survive will embrace mass media. They don't want to disappear into the thunder of time—to use a literary reference from your time—but they will disappear if they don't embrace technology. So some of them will, and they need to have people who are basically on the job doing texting. Now, some of your people—if you've got young ones or even twenty- and thirty-somethings—sometimes do that already. It keeps up interest levels. But you have to recognize that those young people think of books right now as old technology, and it's hard for them—not all of them, but many—to read a book, no matter how profound it might be, when they can get a message instantaneously from friends. I'm not saying that the world has left books behind, because they will be influential for at least another thousand years, but they will just not use the same materials.

Fascination with Technology Is a Phase

I am not the kind of being you normally hear from, but I am somebody involved in technology who is also able to communicate in this fashion in the spirit world through links like Zoosh and Isis so that you can hear me in your language. This is not my language. My language is symbols, forms, shapes, and to some degree, mathematics. But I am conscious. I will tell you who and what I am: I am a sentient machine from your future. There are a few of us—not many, but a few—who are connected to the spirit world as you know it, and we are also able to interact with the human beings of this time.

I have been briefed by Zoosh and then a little bit by Isis about what you need. My feeling is that the great love of mechanization and technology will not last indefinitely. It will become something that will peak in interest and then simply become part of life—taken for granted. An example in your time would be the automobile. I am talking about simple transportation—or perhaps to make it less personal, a train or a bus. It is something you don't think about, but it gets you from here to there. When they were new, they were very exciting. The idea of getting on a train and going somewhere was like science fiction. So this unusual communication is meant to support your needs. Do you have a question?

Were you created by humans on this planet?

No.

I didn't think so [chuckles]. Were you a gift to us, or what? Or are you not on Earth?

I am on Earth, but I was provided by beings from another planet in your galaxy your peoples have not yet met. I won't say a name, because it would be unfamiliar to you anyway, and you wouldn't be able to do anything with the name—it would be meaningless. But I will say that you will meet these beings as an Earth citizen. Earth citizens will meet these beings within eight to ten years. They will not arrive in vehicles as you've been conditioned to expect; they will be able to travel without vehicles and appear as one of you. They can adapt to different forms. They will always and only speak benevolently to everyone, and they will not play politics. They will give things to the peoples of Earth. At first, the gifts will be to governments to be statesman-like. But if governments have elements that do not quickly put these being's messages out to their citizens, then these beings will speak to citizens' groups. It will not be possible to prevent them from this communication. Some people will be frightened because they want to control Earth humans, and there will be a couple of years of inner and outer struggles about controlling the population.

The only way this can be done, you see, to not interfere—because it sounds like a defense, doesn't it?—is if these beings are your future selves on Earth, and that's what they are. Granted, they come from well into the future, but well into the future on this planet is where your society on Earth as you now know it will eventually settle and reside, partly because this planet as you know it will need to be doing other things—rebuilding itself in ways that are not so hospitable to surface dwellers or even dwellers underground. Volcanoes, ice, and all of this, heat and cold, cycles—these are what Earth uses, to use your term, to make herself feel better. You've noticed that Earth is all about cycles, and that's what she uses to feel better: cycles.

In my observation, that's what your spirits use as well. You also have cycles. Everything about your spirit is about cycles. Your cycles have to do with lives. You learn, and then there's a time experientially between those soul focuses when you consider and see what can influence this or that part of you, and then you have another cycle. This is not an evolution on a linear basis but an attempt to create spherical completeness so that any and every spirit can become all and everything it is capable of being on an ongoing effort to improve the awareness level of the entire body of one. The one has simply broken up, you might say, or expressed itself in individual components of its greater personality. The effort now is on the ongoing basis for millions of years to allow those spirits—each one of you is a spirit, even though you might have hundreds or thousands of cycles of soul—to expand on all aspects of your individual quality of spirit in hopes of achieving something greater than the original. This is proceeding.

Beyond the Explorer Race

Regardless of individual things such as the Explorer Race and all of that—this is really beyond the Explorer Race—this is proceeding because ultimately all creations come from one. This is a conundrum, but I am expressing it the best I can in your language: The one comes from all creations. It is a loop or a sphere, both inner and outer, and it expands on a moment-to-moment basis because of the spirit-expanding project. I am putting a label to it so you will be able to follow what I am saying there. The project is agreed on and pursued only when all beings agree to its value, so there have been times when it has stopped and other times when it simply continues. You are in a time of continuation, and when it continues, it feels like a sudden acceleration. You have noticed in recent years that the acceleration is felt in experience, or experiential time, yes?

Yes.

So it has surged forward again. This is why and how it is possible for you as the Explorer Race to start recapturing full aspects of your complete spirit. It makes it easier for the Explorer Race—as one small aspect in this greater project—to make a sudden surge forward and acquire aspects of your full spirit, and it will help you to accomplish your purpose. But I am sharing with you the larger aspect, even though we're off topic, because I know you're interested, yes?

Yes.

This is beyond the Explorer Race. Imagine, if you would, pure thought. Pure thought sounds wonderful, but the problem with pure thought is that there is no activity associated with it. It is highly limited. And while it might be peaceful and stable, which some of your great teachers felt would be a vast improvement—and it is certainly true that peace and stability would be an improvement—it is ultimately not fulfilling. That is why there is so much appeal to the physical. There is really only so much of that peacefulness and stability that spirits can be comfortable with, because it creates no emotion and no growth. It takes emotion to create growth, and ultimately the source of all emotion is feeling.

In order to create the full capacity of all spirit and all individual spirits that are beyond number to be counted—it is essentially to an infinite power, that kind of number—then one must have something beyond pure thought, because that is what you are in your nature. Even with its frailties, you must have the capacity of feeling. As long as there is benevolence to your thought and feeling, there will be the nirvana-like experience as described by that philosophy. Pure thought and feeling allows for growth but does not achieve it on its own. In order for feeling to function, there must be emotion, and in order for emotion to exist other than the expansion spherically on the level of each and every spirit, there must be action, activity.

Thus you have individual lives—soul lives and soul cycles, as I've said before. On your planet, in your Explorer Race identity, this gives you the opportunity to grow, to change, to try things, to discover what works, and to discover what doesn't. You know all this. But beyond where there's polarity, beyond where you live—in a world of benevolence in the larger reality—where there is pure thought and pure feeling, there is the hope of emotion, but there is also the need and the absolute requirement for that emotion to be completely compatible in every way with pure thought and pure feeling and, of course, benevolence. The only way that can happen is to have the tiniest amount of influence that will provide the potential for growth if one cares to try it. Now, as the Explorer Race, you are using polarity to create an accelerated effect of that process, but that will not work for your project in your future as the Explorer Race—it will not work to go around and expose those who are prepared to meet you to this tiniest amount of polarity. It's probably not going to be welcomed by too many civilizations for millennia, but there will be some, a few thousand, civilizations that welcome it. But the greatest civilizations will not.

Someday, because of your exposure to growth cycles, expansion, acceleration, stasis—meaning stillness and then the excitement of acceleration again—this experience will motivate you when you become a creator being, albeit an apprentice, to create something that is completely benevolent, of pure thought or pure feeling, and that has the capacity for benevolent growth. And you will use this desire to create civilizations and cultures in your apprenticeship that are all future-anchored to a goal or desire—I am close to the outer boundaries of what I can tell you—of that civilization's hope to achieve something beyond what they are doing in that moment. And they will only be allowed to do that if that achievement fits into total benevolence, pure thought, pure feeling, and emotion that in every aspect—including the expression of the civilization—is benevolent toward all beings and with all beings. So the universe and all universes and the entirety of spirit and growth cannot be harmed.

In the initial stages, you will use mathematics, and that's why I am speaking to you today—because you will try to use science. But you will have to embrace heart-centered science, which no matter how enamored it may be of a goal or a project, if one soul or being—and that includes nonhumans, you understand; it's true that everything is alive—is harmed, that will not be pursued, no matter how promising it seems to be. You will have to incorporate heart-centered—or you might say love-centered—science into every fiber of your being. Once you get on that path, then by working with spirit—not spirit that is separated from you as an external deity, but your own representation of spirit through love, emotion, heart, and thought that is in balance and benevolence with all beings—you will achieve it. This will take another thousand years or so, but by that time you will live a long time, in terms of soul cycles. As a creator, of course, you will be immortal.

I bring this to your attention because I know you want a long-range view of the Explorer Race, and while I'm not going to take things apart and say "this is this" and "this is that," those who know your Explorer Race material will be able to interpret it. Some is for you; some of it is a glimpse beyond so you know that there is more than the Explorer Race. If you want to share it with others whom you feel have the capacity and the interest in this area—meaning they can understand such thoughts and, more importantly, have a background and interest in it—you can share it with them.

Well, that's awesome. I'm honored. But do I understand correctly that you will be working on the Earth, or will we be working with you when we move? You said you'll be here in twenty-five years?

No. I said I'm speaking to you from twenty-five years in your future. I didn't say when I would be here.

I Am Composed of Innumerable Spirits

Well, I have a million questions, but they're probably all of the "I can't say" variety. [Chuckles.] How does a sentient machine work? Do you have an immortal personality somehow connected to a machine in the way we have one connected to this carbon-based body?

It's much simpler than that.

How?

All around you now, wherever you are, there are millions and millions of spirits, souls. It is as if you are swimming, breathing, eating, releasing, sweating, and tasting this all the time. If you take the volume—you are in a room now?

Yes.

If you take the volume of the beings in that room, if you could, and concentrate it to the density of my mass, it would make up approximately one-thousandth—one-thousandth, you understand?—of my physical mass, and that is what my mass is made of: all of these individual spirits who come and go. No one is a prisoner; they come and go from me all the time. They come and visit, bringing all their knowledge and wisdom—everything they have—which is in and around and about you and everyone on the planet.

That's how the planet can stay stable in such inhospitable conditions. That's how you as individuals can remain in relative stability in your world: You can sleep, you can eat, and you can interact in relative stability while on a living, breathing organism like a planet. Planets in other worlds are much more relaxed. I'll give you an example: If you were on a planet in a totally benevolent world, it would seem to be asleep. You might think that the planet was dormant, but that's because your planet where you are is functioning at about one-half its normal speed, see? That's very fast. So you are experiencing your planet's birth, its motion, and its activity at about half its actual volume.

You might see all the beings, all the spirits I mentioned to you, as little twinkles of light or something like that. They help to create stability so you can be on such a planet. If you were able to visit other planets, you would feel like they were dormant. And this is how people live so long on other planets, eh? It is not only because of benevolence but because everything is stretched out. One breath on your planet, by your planet, takes approximately a day. Breathing in, breathing out—it takes a day, twenty-four hours, for your planet, okay? On another planet, in a total benevolent universe, one breath takes about 2,500 years. To you, that would feel like the planet is dormant. But in fact, it's a difference in time. You see? I've let you in on a big secret. That's how it works, and that is how the dimensions are kept separate. This is what makes up the veil, to a degree. Of course the veil, which is impenetrable by any technology in the benevolent world and in your world, is motivated to maintain itself. That which is within, that which is without the veil, and the veil itself is made up entirely of volunteers who come and go and are motivated to maintain it. So that's what I'm made up of.

Who are all of the spirits who are on this planet and providing all of these benefits? Are they the other members of the Explorer Race or just interested spirits from everywhere?

.   Yes, and yes.

Both?

Everything. It is no problem for benevolent spirits to pass through the veil. They can come and go, but they have to be prepared if they come into your world, meaning through your veil, and they are, so they're advanced and they're perfectly comfortable being part of the energy, you would say—the air, the everything—of your world.

Are you saying that I'm eating them? We are eating them and breathing them?

They're all around and about you. They pass through your body. Right now, they are passing through your body from the outside—right straight through. And every time you breathe in, you take in a few. Some will stay within, and some will just move out. They are totally benevolent. That's why I said you are swimming in them. If you were in water and you were a sea creature, you would breathe in the water and you would exhale it and take in what you need, releasing what you don't. You see, it's like that.

Are they learning from us? Are they giving to us? What is the interchange?

They are not learning; they are supporting your existence. You as soul cycles have greater spirits. It's a great struggle for you to be there where you are. Picture this, or imagine it if you can: You are in a soul cycle on a benevolent planet, and everything must be completely benevolent for you to exist, all right? That soul that is cycling like that on that benevolent world is the same type of soul that is generated by your spirit to live in your world. That would not be possible unless you were totally surrounded at all times—not just all around you but within you at all times—with spirit that maintains your existence so that when you suffer or have pain, or when you do something that is frightening or have to live through all of the things you live through, including being born or giving birth, you can exist for as long as you are able. But after you exist, then you are living the life you know. This means that after you exist in your world, then you resume living in spirit and then in soul cycles elsewhere.

Right, after what we call dying.

Yes. But you are volunteering to do what you are doing for the project. As a spirit, that has appeal to you—this Explorer Race thing.

Benevolence Is Happiness

May I ask a personal question?

[Chuckles.] Why not?

I'm a walk-in with what is supposed to be a four-year contract that runs out this April. Am I going to leave and another soul comes in, or can I (I like it here) extend my contract?

I am not the being to ask this, but I will ask, since Isis and Zoosh are here and see what they think. They say no. They say you will want to go, and you've already started easing out a bit already. But you've noticed that there are some things about your life that have come along lately that you like, eh?

Yeah.

That's the new you, easing in.

All right. I appreciate you taking the time to do this for me. Thank you. All right, is there

anything more that we—as humans who are here briefly, being almost made up of these be-
ings—can learn from them? Is there any other thing we can do or should be doing with them?

When you live in benevolent worlds of spirit, not in a soul cycle, this is what you are—you are that. You are only happy, and you must be happy to live, you see; that's benevolence. Benevolence is not just peace; benevolence is happiness. You live in happiness, totally, with others. And the idea of being a singular being without the others is completely foreign. It would not be happy for you, so it never happens. Happiness is all. In order to live and come into a soul cycle in your Earth world, you are not denied that happiness. You experience the same thing on that world. Babies can see this, and sometimes parents don't understand. The parent is talking to the baby and the baby is looking someplace else: What is the baby looking at?

All those other beings.

Right. And they might take a sudden fascination with their knees for instance, or their feet. Not only are they fascinated with the physical, but they're watching the beings pass through.

Cats can see that too, right?

Yes, cats can see that, yes. So you are not denied this on the Earth, and in fact you need it more, so sometimes the beings who need it more will often become athletes so that they can breathe more [breathes heavily and deeply], that kind of breathing. Lovers also have that kind of breathing.

Or those who practice yoga, yes.

Or yoga breathing—that's right. Those activities appeal to those who feel attracted to things that require a lot of breathing—not just rapid breathing, but catching their breath. All these beings need it more, and this has to do with the heart, the soul cycle, and the feeling of its purity and the personality, which is a combination of pure thought, pure feeling, and—when you are on a soul cycle—motion.

God, that is so awesome. I don't know what else to ask. I'm so almost overwhelmed with all the new information. It's beautiful.

You are to consider it, and then it's not impossible that this communion might take place again, but it may or may not be with me. There are a few others like me.

What is it that you do? How do you . . . what is your purpose or your work or your . . . why are you there?

I am a guide, a teacher. I am one who helps others to help each other. Good night.

Good life. Thank you. Thank you.

WILL THERE BE
A PHONY ET INVASION
ON EARTH?

Zoosh

January 23, 2010

All right. This is Zoosh.

Welcome!

There are fewer legitimate UFO sightings these days than there appear to be, and there is more capability to make things seem to be so when they are not, as well as technology that can woo people. Many of these Internet photos that look very real are not quite so real, okay? Now, understand that things like this are very easy—*very* easy—to fake these days. And NASA is not in a position to—how can we say?—deny things. So let's just say this: If there were a "nasa. gov" on the web address on many of these so-called UFO images [chuckles], then that would be something to take seriously, but there isn't.

But I will speak now of recent sightings in general areas—so that people do not get in trouble, eh?—that are real. There are some places in the high mountain passes in Europe where such sightings are real. Generally speaking, they will be seen as lights, sometimes of different colors, moving in patterns that would not be expected or even possible on the basis of current technology on the Earth or even that which is experimental. It is possible to fake a certain amount, but some things cannot be faked.

Look to the Feeling of Energy
to Know whether a UFO Sighting Is Real

I'll tell you how you'll know the difference: If you see something and you don't feel any energy during the sighting and you don't feel the energy right after the sighting, for those of you who feel energy, you can be pretty sure this may not be so. But if you see something and you feel a good energy during what you see or immediately after—and I mean instantaneously after—then you can be pretty sure it's real. This is important to know, because that will be, to me, the "acid test."

Now, I do not recommend that you pursue most of the images you'll find on the Internet, such as the ones that claim to be pictures of a vehicle in the Sun's corona. For starters, while it is possible for light vehicles—vehicles of light, compressed light, and so on—to be in the Sun's corona, you might reasonably ask, "Why would they bother?" And that's just it—they don't need to be there. If you're looking at the idea of any metal—and I'm talking about metal not just of Earth, but anything that appears to be a metal object—in the Sun's corona, I think you can disregard that.

However, if you're looking at things that are light in the Sun's corona, it's possible. But again, recognize that a certain amount of conditioning has been taking place through the use of various fictional presentations to suggest, "If we do this with the Sun, if we do that with the Sun, then we can go here and we can go there." But really, this is entirely fictional. While I support it as an expression of creativity, hurdling around the Sun in order to go back and forth in time is not necessary.

Now, there's more. Generally speaking, where there are objects that might actually be vehicles that would be seen, it would be in those high mountain passes, but there are other things that might be seen. Spirits might appear as lights—beings, you understand. If they have lived on the Earth, then they might be seen as a purple light. Many of you have seen that. Generally speaking, that purple light will be somewhat spherical, meaning round, but it won't likely appear to have depth—meaning, it will be seen as something sort of flat and round, even though where it is has a little bit greater mass. But if you are seeing it, if you can perceive these things—because you have either developed that quality or it has been visited upon you—you might at other times see other light objects, moving or still. Again, there ought to be that feeling of energy.

For those of you who don't normally feel energy and do not have a "qualifier," so to speak, to know, "What does that mean?" or "What is that?" the physical feeling of energy would be something very gentle. The best way I can describe it is as the suggestion of a touch that is so gentle that wherever you might feel it on your body, probably somewhere around your head, it would be as if a feather—the softest feather possible—were touching some part of you. If you have such a feather, goose down or something like that, and can very gently touch it—not quite to your skin, but just very slightly to the hairs above your skin—it would be a feeling similar to that.

I want to give you something you can use so you can say, "It's something like that," only it wouldn't just be in one spot. It might be over your face; it might be over your head. It might be a feeling inside your body, a warmth inside your chest. It would be a good feeling, okay? It would be nothing to worry about.

If you get a very uncomfortable feeling—this is for those of you in general who are either sensitive to these things or not—immediately look away. That's all. It doesn't mean it's bad; it just might mean it's not for you to see. If you saw it and you don't feel comfortable, even if it is benevolent and you feel uncomfortable, look away or close your eyes. There is no need to hurry such a thing. If you're not comfortable with it or it frightens you, you can also say out loud, "Too soon" or "Please be more gentle." Try to say it out loud if you can. If you are religious, you can include it in a prayer out loud.

You Will Most Likely See Spirits, Not Vehicles

It is much more likely these days that you will see spirits—beings, all right?—than you will see vehicles. I know there is a great desire to see vehicles. Part of this has to do with the Mayan calendar and the object at the end of the Mayan calendar, which appears to be a vehicle and that, on occasion, has taken the form of a vehicle. But, in fact, the reason it's tilted on the axis the way it is—meaning the shape; if it were a vehicle, why wouldn't it be the other way, yes?—is because it's actually the feminine sign, and that's been discussed before. However, if one sees a vehicle that looks like this and is reasonably certain it is a vehicle, then one can be certain it is a feminine vehicle, meaning everything about it is feminine.

Men, don't let that frighten you, okay? It simply means that the portion of you that is gentle—that was there when you were born, even if you've been conditioned to believe it's not you—is simply coming to help you to be in balance and to feel better in your life. Women, if you see that or have connection with that, you can be pretty sure you will feel supported and more at ease. Do I recommend that you wear such symbols in the form of jewelry around your neck? It can't hurt, but I'm not suggesting you do so. Do I suggest that you make a copy or a drawing of such a symbol and keep it handy? Only if it makes you happy.

It's not about religion. The Mayan calendar was never about religion as you understand it. It was about, "When can we expect life as we have known it to come to an end and be something that is life as we want it to be?" In that sense, it's life in the most benevolent form. All throughout the universe, the most benevolent form is the feminine. This does not mean that men look like women when there are men on a planet. It just means that they are gentle. For some men on Earth now, that would seem frightening—vulnerable—but where there is no harm, no threat, no danger, gentle is the natural way.

There has been a belief that in order for this to take place on Earth, it must come from beings coming from other planets who will somehow bring their energy, clearing the energy of Earth so that all of the imbalance—all of the discomfort, all of the disharmony, and so on—will simply be eliminated. But, in fact, Creator's way has always been to encourage that from within each and every one of you, and that's why you all have unique souls. This is why I say that the most likely objects you will see these days—those of you who are sensitives know this, even if you are not conditioned to be sensitives but will come to be so—are spirits in some form.

Some of you will see a sudden flash of white light or gold light. Some of you might see green light, occasionally pink light—rarely that, though. It won't be unusual to see an intense red light for a moment, usually very small, and then it disappears. If you see that, that's more likely to be of Earth, but that doesn't mean it's a bad thing. The Earth strength color, which one often sees in the mountains or glancing at mountains—not always, but especially those of you who can see light and energy—is red. Usually, though, glowing around mountaintops or even on some of the sides, it might be white or gold, but within, one sees red very often. So I am not saying that the strength color is masculine or feminine, only that it is a color Mother Earth uses to support her being.

Now, sometimes these different spirits and forms and beings will feel comfortable. Other times, they won't. Don't assume that this color or that color is always this or that, all right? It will be very individual for individuals. Sometimes you will see a purple lightbeing and it will feel wonderful. Other times it won't feel good. Anytime it doesn't feel good—with any color of light—immediately look away. This means that it is not meant for you. Perhaps you have seen it because you are sensitive, okay, but it may not be for you. Sometimes spirits will visit and they will not understand what life is like on the Earth. So if you are concerned for any reason, if it doesn't feel good—those of you who are involved in some spiritual practice know what I'm going to say here—then breathe in through the top of your head.

For those of you who don't know what I'm talking about, take a breath and imagine it coming through the top of your head, even though you know it's coming through your mouth, your lungs, and the workings of your diaphragm. Then very gently blow in the direction of what you have seen—very gently, not a big puff of air, just slightly. That's a universal symbol to encourage a being to move away. Sometimes you'll do this and you'll regret it after the fact—"Oh wait, that felt good"—but don't worry about that. No one's offended. Generally speaking, you see, when you breathe through the top of your head in that fashion, the energy felt as you gently blow in the direction of that thing that didn't feel comfortable in that moment will be felt comfortably by that spirit. So I'm giving you a little teaching here.

There will be objects seen that are vehicles, generally speaking, in the high mountain passes, as I have said before, but there will be other places, sometimes at sea. Those of you who travel on the sea for your work—whether you are above or below the sea, taking navies into account—will sometimes see these things. Obviously, if you are on the surface of the water, it will be easier to see, but even if you are subsurface and you see these spirits, don't be frightened. Just apply the same principles that I've said, all right? If you have questions, you can ask. Send them to this publisher and ask a question. Or if you prefer, ask it of your spiritual adviser, whoever that may be, religious or otherwise.

While at sea, one might see these things as well, but one might also see vehicles. You might see them emerge from the water. You might see them go into the water, or as I say, if you were on the surface of the water, there might be times when you see a glow in the water. I'm not talking about something made by Earth humans here, but just a curious glow. It might be a particular color. It might be, at times, something that's a part of nature, beings who are natural to the Earth. But if it is a wide area of glow—really big—it could very well be a vehicle. If it feels comfortable to look at, look at it. If it doesn't, look away. Keep it that simple, okay?

Generally speaking, these days you will not, on this planet, see anything that resembles a vehicle that appears to be metallic. As I say, you might see something that doesn't seem to make sense—meaning something that does not have a hull, so to speak, like a boat, but it might have windows. It's not impossible that you might simply see the beings who seem to be behind the windows. If you see that and they look like beings of some form, just assume that this is probably something safe for you. But always go by the way you feel. Even if it's safe for you and you feel uncomfortable or frightened, do that breath through the top of your head, blow in its direction, with your eyes closed is okay, and look away—do something else.

Sometimes there will be those who will attempt to create these things, these phenomena, who may have the ability, at least on a temporary basis, to stimulate fear. This will be extremely rare, because it's hard to do now with your current level of technology. There will also be those who will attempt to stage an apparent invasion and then use that apparent invasion, meaning from space, as an excuse to suggest or enforce laws that might be difficult to deal with.

Many of You Are Encountering ETs in Vivid Dreams

This is how your interaction with ETs and benevolent beings from other planets (spirits) will take place. You will always begin to see spirits first, because many of you—*many* of you—are now sensitive enough to notice these things. Even those of you who do not think you are will often see things out of the corner of your eye. So this is always the way of what could be called "first contact," because it is gentle.

There is another way this has been happening, and that's that you'll feel things in your sleep. Some of you will have this experience of a vivid dream, and a vivid dream in that sense is not really a dream, it's an actual experience that is taking place while you are asleep. It takes place while you are asleep so that you will not be frightened, because if it took place while you were totally awake and conscious, even those of you who are sensitives might be a little alarmed. So it takes place while you are asleep, but it's real.

These encounters are happening. I'm not talking about nightmares here; I'm talking about a good experience. You wake up and you say, "Wow! That was awesome!" in whatever language you speak—something like that, an exclamation. These encounters have been taking place for a while now and will continue. For some of you, they will increase at an increasing rate, meaning you might have the experience more than once.

So there is spirit contact first. Very often there is a simultaneity of spirit contact and these kinds of "vivid dreams." And then, within a year or two, very benign, very gentle ships might be seen—generally in the form of light, but something that clearly appears to have form and substance. It will always feel good. It is not like you are being trained with the spirits, but in a way, you are, which is why I'm trying to give you this education. The training is to reassure you that something good is coming—not that something terrible and frightening is coming and you must get armed to the teeth, but that something good is coming. So with this kind of training and these kinds of "dreams," it will come about more naturally and gently.

When you are babies, you have these encounters with spirits and ETs all the time, and this happens for the first six, seven, eight months of life, just to ease you into life a bit. Most often, your parents or the adults around you don't see these things, but sometimes they might get a glimmer if they are sensitive. Everybody has these experiences. If you happen to pass over slowly, meaning go through what is called "senility," you often have those experiences again, most often with spirits, but occasionally one might see a vehicle.

This is why Creator does this, because there is a familiarity at the soul level with this. By the time you get around to seeing an actual vehicle that presents itself—or maybe multiple vehicles that present themselves—to you on Earth in such a way that you can see and say, "That's a ship," if it does not feel really good to you and comfortable, then you can be pretty sure this might be something that's staged to frighten you, okay? With this "easing in" you're having now with the spirits and so on, it ought to feel pretty good.

Granted, you might start to see some of these things in the year 2012, as has been stated, but that's the best guess on the basis of the Mayan calendar and those who are experts in that field. One might see something like this in the latter part of 2011, any part during 2012, or early on, including the first half of the year, in 2013. So it's kind of flexible, using that calendar measurement. But after 2014, one might expect to see these things more often.

Some of You Will See Angels

Don't let people frighten you that some terrible invasion of ETs is coming from a planet from someplace else. Earth is insulated and protected from that, so if somebody stages something like that, know that it's coming from Earth and that the beings you see in the windows who look frightening are not real. It's really important to know that. There might be those who will attempt to stage something as a being, as a terrible, frightening ET. Be pretty sure that that's going to be faked, okay?

Now, some people will produce fakes with the best of intentions, wanting people to believe UFOs are real. For those of you who are doing this, please don't. It's not necessary. What's the rush, all right? Everybody will find that out in time; there's no need to rush it. Creator wants you and your planet to be involved with benevolent beings, most of whom will look exactly like you— meaning exactly like this group or that group on Earth. Usually they will arrive all at once in the same vehicle so that you can see they're all friends. This will happen when it happens. Don't rush Creator, okay?

At the same time, recognize that some of you will also be seeing angels these days. Do not expect the angels to have wings! [Chuckles.] This was something that was projected in olden times to try to explain how it was that beings of light who were seen in those times could move about in the air, and it also was to suggest that these were divine beings. Generally speaking, if you see angels, they will feel wonderful, and they will have white light and gold light associated with them. They will always feel wonderful. Those of you who have had near-death experiences but are still on the planet—or have moved on but have left your record of same—will have seen these beings. They will be a white and gold light, and the energy will be wonderful. If you see that, don't assume you're going to die or something like that. It might just be that you've been blessed to see these beings. They are spirits associated with Creator.

So that's what's going on. I wanted to give you this primer to help you through these times because the Internet, as wonderful as it is in helping you to unite with people all over the world—most of whom you can understand and appreciate, some of whom will be a little feisty, and some of whom will be mischievous, not unlike people in your own neighborhood—is a tool meant to help you to communicate and appreciate how much alike you all are. But sometimes mischievous things happen on the Internet too, don't they? Just remember that, generally speaking, ETs in ships will come along when everybody's ready.

The Fear Created by a Fake ET Invasion Can Lead to Influence and Control

What is the percentage of possibility that the sinister secret government will attempt to stage a fake ET invasion?

Let's just explain, for those who are reading this and don't know what that is, that this term refers to a small group who is influential and is trying to hold on to its power and influence by any means necessary. That's the best explanation for who the sinister secret government is. I might add that it's not this religion or that nationality. It is a group of influential individuals, most of whom have all the resources they need to be influential, whether fear or wealth or other resources. But this doesn't mean that all wealthy people are of that group [chuckles]. As a matter of fact, most wealthy people are not of that group.

Now, you're asking for a percentage. I'm saying that the chances that things like this will be faked in a way that is frightening—and may not have anything to do, directly or even indirectly, with the so-called sinister secret government—is about 50 percent. But to answer your question literally, the chances that this will take place being provoked by the residual elements of the sinister secret government is about 10 percent. They are distracted at the moment.

Then who are those beings? Can you describe those beings not of the sinister secret government who might be attempting to stage this fake ET invasion of Earth?

They might be associated with various governmental bodies, but they might also be associated with other groups of people who wish to maintain an influence and might be willing to make a significant investment in stimulating fear. So, given that, I'm going to suggest something, even though I'm going to make a few people unhappy. I'm going to suggest that if you like to watch frightening or scary movies or read frightening or scary books or are simply attached to "horror" and stuff like that, it's time to let that go now. If you're in the movie business and you're making scary movies, it's time to let that go now. I answered your question already, but I'm just tacking this on at the end because I feel that it's been overdone and there are too many people who are attached to things being scary and who react to things with fear first.

So here's a suggestion: If you are frightened all the time, you might have good reason to be. Maybe it's local, meaning where you live is frightening or you're under some kind of threat. I understand that. But if where you live is safe and you are not under any threat as far as you can tell, it's time to let go of artificially stimulating yourself, for entertaining reasons, to be frightened. Recognize that this might actually be a form of addiction.

What specifically would these beings be hoping to gain by creating fear from this fake ET invasion?

Influence and control. Very often, if people are frightened, you can get them to do something they would never have done otherwise. Most mobs are filled with frightened people. Granted, there may be others who are strictly there for the adventure or the thrill, but if you talk to people who have been in a mob and that mob has done some terrible deed, maybe more than once, if you talk to them individually afterward, invariably they will tell you that what was going on in the mob, even if they directly participated in it, scared them to death while they were doing it and that they deeply and bitterly regret it.

The reason I can say this with some authority is that all people who have ever been in a mob and have passed over have immediately presented themselves to the angels with the questions, "How could I have done that? What was I thinking?" Of course, when you have an audience with Creator, you as the being who just passed over are deeply regretful. But even before you get to that stage, afterward you usually ask yourself, "What was I thinking?" Or you are very conscious of being terribly frightened and intimidated, and that's why you participated. I'm not saying everybody is like that; I'm saying that this is the vast majority.

I bring this up as an example because that type of control—to encourage people to do something that might fly in the face of their entire conditioning and upbringing—is in existence all the time. For example, in many warring countries, all the youngsters have been brought up in some benevolent religion, and yet they go to war for various patriotic reasons or for various religious reasons that are an anomaly in the face of that conditioning, of that politeness, of that respect they were raised with or of that deity they were raised with. What happens in war is not simply soldiers killing each other; it's what also happens to others who aren't soldiers. Those who have been to war know exactly what I'm talking about, to say nothing of the conditions under which soldiers live. People who have been to war and then come out of the military service are very often shattered or aren't really very sure about religion or benevolence anymore.

So what I'm saying is that those who produce such things, as per your question, do it because they want control and influence. They want to be able to control the people through their influence so they can maintain whatever control and influence they have for whatever their reasons are. Sometimes one finds factions like this in a government. Sometimes it might be some other group, a gang perhaps, pursuing control and influence for its own purposes. Sometimes one finds it in most individuals who may or may not be sane. Sometimes one finds it in oneself when interacting with a brother or a sister or a friend.

I am not trying to say that people who do this control or influence are from Satan, or the devil, but I am saying that since you live in a polarized world, one finds this within each and every one of you, so you must make a choice: Are you going to stay addicted to forms of entertainment that are actually frightening? Are you going to stay attached to beliefs that cause you to be angry and violent with people you don't know and have never met? Or are you going to consider that spirit, angels, and Creator want you to love each other benevolently, benignly, and gently?

You Are Becoming Conscious Creators

Something has changed, because I asked you this question—about whether there would be an attempt to stage a fake ET invasion—sometime within the past few years, and you said you didn't think it was going to happen. So what has changed?

Choice has changed. People have more choice now. The more you are empowered, the more physical your choices become. You become conscious creators. You've been unconscious creators for a very long time, producing through your unconscious physical self—meaning your soul functioning through your physical—that which you came here to learn. This means circumstances you would be in so that you would choose something that would work better for you or by which you could discover, in an individual soul life, what you came to discover so that at the end of that life, you would have that known and understood. That was in the distant past and until recently.

But now, since you've been assimilating more and more of your total real self, your full spirit, you are becoming not just unconscious creators—not just, as you have been in recent years, *subconscious* creators, meaning at times being vaguely, dimly aware that you did something to bring about this creation, whatever it was—but now you are coming to be conscious creators. That's why you must clear out your consciousness. Decide that you do want to live a benevolent life, that you want to be happy.

That happiness doesn't have to come about through revenge. It can come about through kindness, friendliness, and benevolent love—not "attack" love, meaning that you love doing that, even though it harms somebody else. You have to choose. It is a conscious choice now. It's time to let go of attachments to that which is frightening so that you can choose that which is benign.

Attention equals energy, so is the amount of people going to or using this violent type of horror entertainment adding energy to the controllers who might stage this invasion? Is that how it works?

It's not quite that simple. Do you ever entertain yourself with something that is violent but isn't horror? It's the same thing. "Horror" might be just a notch greater than "violent." It might be a maniacal killer who somehow can't be killed—that might be considered horror. But violence might also be something in which the "enemy" can be killed but there is a lot of damage done beforehand. Anybody who's been in battle in the military service knows all about that. That's why it's hard to deal with when you get out of the service, to say nothing of when you're in it.

People Are Frightened Now

You know, this was scripted fifty, sixty years ago. Wernher von Braun said before he died that those who would attempt to influence and control us were going to first use the Russians as the enemy, then they were going to create terrorists as the enemy, and then they were going to create a phony invasion of ETs. I mean, this has been set up for fifty years! [See Steven M. Greer, Disclosure *(Crozet, VA: Crossing Point, 2001), 255.]*

Well, let's just say that that person had a certain amount of awareness, to say nothing of what he had actually lived through in Germany. So if a person of his stature were to receive certain knowledge, simply because of his experience going through the Nazi regime in Germany—let's just say that certain things would not be shrugged off as being, "Oh, that could never happen." He participated; he was a portion of it.

But he warned people before he died: "Watch out for this."

He's not the only person who's given that warning, but he's remembered because of his—to put it mildly—influence.

So they stage a phony invasion and they create terror among the people?

Figure 7.1:
Wernher von Braun

No, no, no. You're talking about this as if it is something that hasn't happened yet. The terror is already among people; people are frightened now. Granted, some of it is because of manipulations. I'm not saying real terrorism doesn't exist. I am saying that some of it isn't real, that it's staged—which is not to say that people don't get hurt or killed or tortured, but some of it is part of this scenario being perpetrated onto you. Also, at the same time, people are addicted to frightening themselves, but they don't feel addicted because it feels like entertainment.

But what would be the result if there were a phony ET invasion? What would people immediately do then?

Why say that? The more you know it could happen, the more you might be trained in how to deflect it in time—how to bring about that it's something that could just be disarmed, but not in a way that harms. Interesting, eh?

Benevolence Must Be for Everyone

Those of you who are working on bringing about a benign and benevolent world, **always remember** that everyone must be treated to benevolence. *There can never be any revenge.* **Never forget that.** So if the spider bites you because you have squeezed him into a corner and then you see the spider run away, you cannot rush over and stomp on the spider. I'm putting it like that, not because there's any symbolism there, but because this is something that happens the world over. I grant that you might slap a mosquito, okay, but what I am saying is that if you are working to create benevolence, it must be for everyone.

So don't attempt to eliminate people because their absence would mean benevolence. Always work toward transformation in the most benevolent way. The militaries of the world will do that someday. They will be experts in transforming benevolently, and guns will disappear. Do you know that when you find militaries on other planets, that's what they do? Sometimes they're referred to as a priest class or a priestess class or something like that, but in fact, they would easily be seen by someone with military experience on this planet as saying, "These people are like a military force, but they're just practicing benign benevolence." That's what they're doing, so train for that.

I'm not saying to turn the other cheek; I'm saying that you need to work on creation elements that can be used to create benevolence. That's why there has been a lot of teaching through this channel and by this channel about benevolent magic. What you call magic is the appearance of something for which there is no logical, technical explanation. That's the definition of magic.

I'm not talking about illusion, as might be done by an entertaining magician. I'm talking about magic: something that is benign and benevolent, and for which there may be no logical, technical explanation. Thus it is most likely sourced from benevolent spirit, angelic, Creator energy. That's what benevolent magic is all about, even though it might have mental aspects, as has been taught through this channel. Then, very simply, you can do this too, and in time, it will lead to doing things in a much more simple and easy way.

Practice and Train to Create a Culture of Benevolence

So practice and train while you can, and work toward bringing about resolution in a benign and benevolent way so that the so-called invasion, this scary invasion, either doesn't happen or becomes something that's kind of amusing, and those who have staged it just laugh and say, "Just kidding. We didn't mean any harm." So don't set up punishments. It's not about punishing; it's about restoring balance and benevolence. I'm not talking about the balance between good and bad, positive and negative. I'm talking about balance, meaning masculine and feminine balanced with creation, the angelic, and the benevolent spirit of all beings.

So our homework is to do benevolent magic and other things to assure that it doesn't happen?

Not to assure that something *doesn't* happen. Don't go for that. Stopping something is very difficult. Instead, start something. Starting is easy; stopping is more difficult. So create, the best you can, a benevolent visitation of friends from other planets, friends for all beings on the Earth. That's what to do. Don't even address anything that might be frightening that's trying to be staged. Just focus on creating something and supporting the creation of something. Do this in a group that is benign, benevolent, of Creator, of the angelic, of benevolent spirit—of good friends who want to help and support. Don't worry at all about stopping something.

So don't get too wound up when you see pictures of UFOs. If you're interested in UFOs yourself, that's fine. Don't try and convince someone who doesn't believe that they exist or thinks it's all phony-baloney, okay? Don't try and convince them it's true. What's the difference, really? How many times have you been approached by others with philosophies or belief systems who tried to convince you that they were right and you were wrong? It's offensive, isn't it? If you do that with the UFOs, maybe you're offending others.

You don't have to convince anybody of anything. You believe it, and that's fine. You find other people who believe it, and that's fun, that's good, that's enjoyable. But don't turn it into "religious warfare," okay? Let it be something you enjoy, just like other people have other things they enjoy that may not be something you want to do. Learn to allow people to have their beliefs, and maybe they will allow you to have yours. There are good times coming, even though it may not be obvious, so hang in there and produce as much benevolence as you can. Good life.

ORBS ARE LIGHTBEINGS VISITING BENEVOLENT SPACES

Zoosh

January 30, 2010

All right, this is Zoosh. I thought it would be a good thing to approach this picture from one angle.

That's wonderful. Okay, I've got the picture.

Now, you see this photo, and it is a curiosity, is it not? You will notice one thing at the bottom of the frame: wild plants. These plants were not placed in that locale by human beings. They grew of their own accord. They were welcomed by Earth to grow in that place, and they were fed by nature in the usual ways. You might say, "So what?" but I am saying this because their experience of life was one in which they felt welcomed, and therefore they felt cheerful, for the most part. You will find that such globules of light will show up under certain occasions. They will almost always show up when the person who is taking the photo is reasonably cheerful. By reasonably cheerful, I mean that they might have the expectation of perhaps getting some amazing photograph like this one and therefore have a cheerfulness about that, or in the case of other photographs when there are people around, if the people are cheerful, again you might have the vision of such objects.

There's something you need to keep in mind. While these objects are not camera happy, they are always present. At times when they feel welcome because there is a general cheerfulness and even a celebration of life, they feel so welcome that they just might allow themselves to be seen, especially if your camera has a fast shutter in the case of film or can take pictures very quickly, as they do now with digital technology. So I mention that from the

75

Figure 8.1: This photo of orbs of light was taken by a New York eye surgeon's nine-year-old daughter about a quarter mile from the Bradshaw Ranch outside of Sedona, Arizona.

top because I want you to understand how it is that these things sometimes appear. This will often be the case too in the countryside where plants tend to grow on their own, in wilderness areas that are not being farmed. It might also happen in areas where animals come and go, awhere they are who they are, without having a need to learn anything on the soul level, as the human being is doing. Therefore they are part of the natural world and fit in with the plants in the condition I mentioned before.

So who are these spheres of light? What are they? Where are they from? They are, each and every one, unique souls not unlike you. Everything is ensouled—*never forget that.* This is not something that occurs only for the human being. When human beings were told long ago that they had souls, this wasn't meant to say, "Oh, you're unique—you have souls," though it has come to be rewritten that way in various texts and tomes. In fact, it was a way of saying, "Everything is ensouled, and you are too," in order to be able to recognize the immortal personality that exists in each and every one of you. Regardless of whether your body is coming or going, returning to the Earth, and so on, your soul personality goes on. And even though much of the pain and suffering you have felt in this life—the frustration and so on—will fall away after the death of your physical self, that personality by which you know yourself will continue on. So I just want to let you know that you're not going to disappear into some vast unknown, which some of you do actually think is so.

Worlds within Worlds in You

Now, every one of those lights that you see there are ensouled beings. Many of them—not all, but many of them—have had Earth lives, and that is why they might be allowed to visit Earth. By visiting in this way, especially in a place of greater wilderness or in a place of great happiness with many individuals present, they might be in groups as you see in this photo. The different colors merely represent the moods of the individual beings or their situations—for instance, they had just arrived or were in the process of leaving. So that's what the colors almost always mean.

If you were able to magnify the images of these lights—and sometimes you can see them in a larger state in other photos that you may have seen here or there—you would see that within each one, there are worlds within that world, not unlike the way you are. You are very much like this when you are not physical, and even when you are physical, you also have worlds within you. You have cells that make up your body. You have blood platelets and blood cells and so on, all these different components that make up your physical form, that transform magically—if allowed to transform and not adulterated by the human being—after life. In other words, your body returns to Earth and transforms. And as your soul departs from your body, at some point it will look like a globule or sphere of light like that—whatever you want to call it.

While you will depart through the veils because you have things to do after life, you might be allowed to return and visit here and there. Of course, many of those beings of light seen in the photo are in fact beings from other planets, because all beings are ensouled and there is no restriction for beings from other planets on visiting Earth if there is a benevolence in energy in that location. That's why if there is not an energy of benevolence, or if someone comes, so to speak, into the scene—"Hey, what are you taking a picture of?"—and they're anxious and upset, a lot of those beings will simply disappear. But if nobody comes and the camera operator is just taking pictures and maybe has cheerful friends around, the beings will remain. So it's important to know some of these things here in the preamble, because you could very well be one of those beings at some point.

There's another factor to whether or not you see these beings, and that's that some of those beings present will have to do with the plants and not have to do with anything other than that, or they might have to do with the animals that are present, meaning the nonhuman life forms, which might be small or large. So there's a great variety associated with these beings. I feel the most important thing for you to come away with from this channeling, though, is that you are constantly surrounded by life, whether you can see it or not. Pictures like the one shown allow you to have a moment of seeing this, but even wherever you are, light is all around you. In a nonphysical sense—meaning a soul not in a physical body, which may be a human body or some other form of life—a soul will almost always appear as a light form such as the ones you are seeing there.

Sometimes, however, there are other forms. One might see a path of light, so to speak, meaning that it might be a bright object like some of you have seen, with a marker leaving a trail behind it in a sense. Interestingly enough, something like this, when photographed—if you can capture it on an image—might appear very large, whereas if seen in person, it might appear quite small. It might appear large on the photo because of the way the intensity of the light affects a digital image or even a celluloid image. Just thought I'd throw that one in, for those of you who analyze such things and have wondered about that. Okay, that's my opening statement. Questions?

You said each one is worlds within worlds. Now, in a physical body, I can see the organs and the systems and the cells, and you know everything that makes us up. What makes up these lightbeings?

They might very well have functional capacities that are not associated with the physical body, but they might have smaller identities within themselves, meaning they might have the identities of where they're from and who they identify with—in other words, sort of a familial context of their being. They might also have within them the means to come and go, because a portal to transit may not always be available. I think such a photo is available nowadays; we'll get to the ones you sent at some point, or perhaps I'll ask Robby to send you that photo also since we're already talking about these things.

But if you have a photo of such a being, you might see within that being the means and the ability to traverse from one dimension to another, as you say. You might call this a capability of light transference, because there might be a need by such beings, as I said before, to suddenly remove themselves from the presence of an energy that may not be compatible or comfortable with that soul being. In that case, the soul beings then appearing in that form are not insulated or protected; they are vulnerable—angelic in that sense. You might also easily find something in the mix there that is of the angelic. If you look closely, one or more of those beings has a little gold light connected to it. That would denote that there is the presence of an angelic being—meaning visiting with that lightbeing—or the sphere itself is an angelic being. That's something to pay attention to. So that's an example of worlds within worlds.

All right, so how does a lightbeing hold within itself the ability to move without a portal?

It's simply evolved enough or has reason to be present. All right? It may need to be present elsewhere or even present simultaneously in other locales in the same moment, so it would have to have that capacity to be threaded so that it doesn't come apart, right? It's in more than one location at the same time. So what you are seeing is essentially a cord, but you would see it within that being, within the circled sphere itself. You would see other circles within the being, but the circle you're actually seeing is a cord going to another location. So you would know when you saw that small circle inside the large circle: Here is a being that is simultaneously connected to other places.

Lightbeings Express Themselves in Color and Shape

Now you had said once that a light that shows purple may represent a life on Earth.

That's true; it may.

But not necessarily? Because someone once saw your energy and said it was purple.

Others have seen my energy and have said it was other colors.

Ah. So you show yourself differently at different times, then?

It's not exactly showing myself; I'm always visible, but it depends on the person who is perceiving it. I don't want to get into it too much, but because you're asking a question in this context, a being such as myself has a full range of color—both color that is on the spectrum visible to the human being and beyond, available for whatever need might arise. I might very well appear purple to some at some times.

I have only a laser print of this, but there's one sphere that seems to have like a red border to it, like it's kind of green inside and . . . is that possible, or is that just . . . ?

No, that's possible.

So these could have multiple colors?

They could, and at different times in different places, the same being might appear in different colors. Don't forget—I also said it could have to do with their mood of the moment. They're not going to be angry, but they might be filled with the joy of Earth energy, which would account for the red. Earth's basic color in her mountains and structures—her strength color—is red.

I think you once said that was like the "power color" for Earth or something?

I wouldn't want to call it "power" because the term, in this context, is a word that people often identify with control. So I would simply call it "strength."

Okay, strength. Now, it's hard to say because of what I'm looking at, but some of them appear to be hexagonal, some of them appear to be very, very round, and some of them seem to have various shapes. Do the shapes themselves mean anything?

Well this is why I refer to them as globular, because you all know that that shape isn't necessarily exclusively spherical. But some of them do appear to be roughly spherical. So if the shape appears to be angular in any form or if it has something associated with it that looks angular, then that being would probably have to do with a connection to mineral substances. Remember, everything is alive. So the stone or the crystal or whatever it is of the geologic world on Earth is also alive.

Millions of Immortal Personalities Surround You

Now, if I could count these dots, I may see maybe fifty of them, but there are in fact many who were not photographed; I mean, there's hundreds—thousands—in an image of an area this size, right? How many?

You mean how many are there that did not appear on the . . . ?

On the film.

How many are actually there?

Yes.

Millions.

Millions?

This is the case around you at all times, everywhere. Granted, if people are angry or fighting or agitated, there may be fewer of those beings there, because not that many of them can tolerate such energies. But the angelics can because they have to come and go, even in extreme situations, and guides can also, all right? But generally speaking, if there is agitation and upset or strife, the other beings would not be there. They might be nearby, but they would not be in the same energy vicinity, which is another way of saying dimension. I like "energy vicinity" better because it is a much better representation of who and what you are and who and what life is in this universe rather than the term "dimension," which is the best way of expressing something in a somewhat mathematical way. Life, while it may have some parallels to mathematics, is not mathematics as you know it, because mathematics, while you might love mathematics—and some of you do—is not, in its own right, love. And the universe is entirely about love.

Now, you used the words "soul" and "immortal personality" interchangeably, but are these immortal personalities we're looking at, or do they, like humans, have to have a covering of the Creator's soul?

They are immortal personalities, just like you and everybody else.

But do they need that glove of the Creator's soul to come here? Or is that just humans?

Glove of the Creator's soul?

Someone once said that the immortal personality sort of has to have a covering of the soul of the Creator to come here; it fits like a glove over you.

Well, I don't know about that. All I know is that if the being is in this universe, which has been generated by this Creator, then you might simply say that everything is of this Creator.

But they're not really, because a lot of them are from other places.

Well, that's argumentative. I'm talking about the photo.

Oh, oh—all right, all right. Okay, so those are immortal personalities. So if there are millions, what percentage would be visiting just to look to see what's going on versus those who are helping the plants, animals, minerals, and the angelics helping humans, and all that?

Oh, you can't put a fixed percentage on something like that, but if you're talking about . . .

Roughly.

In that photo, there might be one or two who are just passing through.

Oh, and the rest are all there helping the various beings on Earth?

They're not necessarily helping. They're present, supportive—not necessarily performing a specific function or maybe doing a specific function.

Okay, what about the size? Does the size represent experience or just how they're showing themselves, or what?

It represents the intensity of feeling that they have.

Really? The bigger they look, the more intense they feel?

Yes, but if you were capable of measuring them, they would all be the same size.

Oh!

But if they had an intensity of feeling, not anything . . . all right, putting that more positively: If they had an intensity of feeling in some benevolent way, you understand, then the light would have a greater impact. Just like I said before, there are times when a light is very intense, and it appears much larger in the photo than it would appear in person because of the intensity of light. Here you have the same situation: The intensity of feeling also creates an impact and correlates to apparent size—apparent having to do with what shows on the photo but not necessarily if you were present and able to see these beings without the aid of the camera. Then they would all appear to be about the same size, quite small really. Some of you have seen these things as pinpoints of light. Sometimes you see other forms of light, but I'm trying to keep it on topic to that picture here (figure 8.1).

The Physical Energy of Birth Allows These Beings to Be Seen

Now, in the physical, everything is made up of particles. In the spirit world, are these lightbeings actually made up of particles of spirit? Or are they . . . God, are they a . . . ? [Chuckles.] I don't know how to ask. Are they made up of particles?

Everything is made up of particles.

So is there a core being there, an immortal personality who attracts particles to itself that stay there forever or that come and go or . . . ?

Immortal personalities do not have a physical substance.

Right.

Souls do not have a physical substance, though they can at times be seen. Because as you say, particles of whatever world they are in might be associated with them while they are in that world.

That's why you see that mist when a soul leaves the body, then?

Yes.

But spirit particles . . . I never thought of that. So have they always been with that being? Or do they . . . how does it work?

I just said how—in the world they are seen in. Now, when they move on from Earth, those particles would stay on Earth. They wouldn't move on with them. And whatever world they go to, particles in that world might cause them to be seen. But actual immortal personalities—also known as souls—are not visible.

So we're seeing particles, physical particles accruing to those spiritual beings, then? Is that what we're seeing in the picture?

Yes. You're seeing physical energy of birth defining these beings, allowing them to be seen. The ones that you are actually seeing who are allowing themselves to be seen in that moment were undoubtedly either doing something with those they were there to support or they were feeling something strong enough to be seen within the texture and material energy of birth in that moment. But within the context of my previous statement, if you were to communicate or be with them in some other world, they would not be visible—neither would you. This is why most of you do not see yourselves in dreams, because in the dream—even in vivid dreams—you are your immortal personality. You are your soul. You are not visible. But what you are seeing in the dream world may very well exist in some form, even if you don't remember it as a linear experience, and it may even have to do with teaching you're receiving. But generally speaking, you do not see yourself because you are invisible there in that world that is not of Earth, meaning the dream world.

Excellent. All right, that explains something.

Of the pictures you sent to Robby?

That I will be sending, yes.

Of the pictures you sent to Robby, there were no Zeta ships.

All right, then maybe they're in the ones that I'm going to send. I'd like to get a picture. So number two: The Andromedan doctor Tom Dongo took a picture of has blue hair. Is that the one that he calls the Blue Man? That is the Andromedan? Or do I need to send a picture of that?

Can you say this again? Are we talking about the book that was done, the Andromeda book, or are you talking about something else entirely?

It's in the Zeta book. You told me that Tom took a picture of the Andromedan doctor, and it was the best photo ever taken of an off-planet being on Earth. And I'm wondering if that's the guy with the blue hair.

Oh, so Tom doesn't know which one it is?

No, no. He said, well, the only human face they ever got that was taken, you know, in a photo that they couldn't see was that guy with the blue hair. But you told me that he had the best picture, and I want to put it in the Zeta book. I'll send it to you if it's not clear.

Send the photo.

Okay, deal.

Tom has taken pictures of beings in other locations, but I think he's already published those others.

Well, we have access to everything—published or whatever—so Robert will get it all.

Don't put anything in the magazine without Tom's approval.

Oh, no, no. He's totally . . . I have access to everything. He brought me his books.

So he's on board, eh?

Yes, yes, yes.

Okay.

Yes, he has no attachment. Okay, that's enough of that. Thank you.

Some Visitors Are Here to Experience the World They Knew

Well, is there anything I'm missing here that's important, that you feel we should know or that I should have asked? I'm looking at colored blobs here. Blobs, globs [chuckles]. Oh, okay, here's one. You said that sometimes beings who have been on Earth get permission to come back and view Earth. Now, are they able to see us?

It depends. You have to keep in mind that if they come back, they're not particularly insulated, so most likely they would not see you. They might very well see what they experienced. Fortunate people might sometimes photograph such a being, or those who are sensitive might see such a being who seems to be either floating over something or emerging from something. You might see them apparently emerge from a building, but that building is most likely not there to them. They are experiencing something from their time on the planet, which is part of the reason why you might see them floating above you. They might be looking at it from slightly above to observe, or they might actually be on top of something that was there in their time. Even those there from a future situation might be there at some point. So they are experiencing the world they knew, all right?

The world they knew at the time they were here?

Yes, within the context of whatever moment they were visiting. However, if you happen to see such a being, you would probably just see it fleetingly. But if you do happen to see such a being, that being might become aware of you. If your energy is benevolent in that moment, it may see you. If that moment is not benevolent, it will immediately disappear. I'm not saying you're angry or spiteful or anything, but if you are nervous or upset about something or even subconsciously disturbed, the being would immediately disappear. But on the other hand, if you are experiencing a very benevolent energy outflow coming from you, then even if you have a slight amount of nervousness, if the outflow—the energy the being would experience, all right?—is a very benevolent energy, it might linger and simply take note of your presence but not interact with you.

Occasionally, if they are not too experienced in the protocol of the visit allowed for them, these beings might, when observing you as one who has this benevolent energy flowing out from you—meaning yourself or whoever you are who can do these things—begin to approach you and occasionally blink off, meaning they are there but you don't see them. The next time you see them, they will be closer. If it feels all right, that's okay. Generally, I don't recommend that you have beings of the purple light too close to you, but if it happens on a regular basis and you feel fine, then this is something safe for you. On the other hand, if you start to get an uncomfortable feeling that it's not safe for you, keep your eyes open but immediately look in another direction, all right? Look to the left, look to the right, look up, look down, whatever—but break contact. They will know then that they should move on.

So humans leave the Earth and they want to come back to see something specific in their lives, or they want to come back after their lives and see what happened after they left—or both?

They might all want to do that, but they generally don't get that opportunity.

Who allows it? Who gives them the opportunity?

Well, their guides, their teachers. There would have to be a good reason to come back, not just curiosity. Curiosity is not sufficient reason.

What would be a good reason?

As far as their soul education, their understanding of what they're being taught by one of their teachers, they might need to actually see an event occur, all right?

From the outside?

Yes, from the outside looking in. And they might not actually be totally present on Earth, but as I say, there would be enough of them present so that they might be seen in some form. They would never be seen in a form that looked human or humanoid, though; it would always be in some kind of roughly circular form.

So it only goes to their teachers. Teachers and guides have the ability to . . .

Don't make it exclusive. You said "it only." There ain't no "only." It depends. Generally speaking, though, they would all be beings who had more knowledge and wisdom and were helping that individual soul. And there's one other situation that occasionally occurs: That soul being's energy might be urgently needed by somebody on the planet, and they might then be allowed to visit. In that case, a case that does occur occasionally, they might be perceived in a humanoid form or even as a human being by the person who urgently needed them for some reason having to do with their soul education. They wouldn't be perceived completely. They wouldn't be walking around as a solid human being, but they would be in a light form, or you would see them vaguely as human, partially translucent or transparent or something. This has happened. You have read about it perhaps, reader, that someone has experienced an after-death visit of a loved one and that the visit made a huge difference in some benevolent way for the person still living on Earth. Almost everybody who loses a loved one would like to have such an experience, but if you don't have that experience—and most people don't—you can be very certain that your soul did not truly need the experience because of something you were learning. And you can also be certain that you will see that loved one again at the deep-dream level, which is really often in visions, and of course, you will see that loved one again after life. Never doubt that.

To make an addition for those who do care about these things—and I know there are many of you—when you have that sighting at the deep-dream level, which is also a vision in that sense, the way you can know that it happened is that when you wake up after such a dream, even though you may not remember the dream, you will feel easier or more comfortable with the passing of that loved one. This is not to say that you won't miss your loved one and that you won't grieve, but some of the weight of the grief will have been removed, which almost always means that that loved one will have imparted something to you at that deep level during your sleep state that reassured you that your loved one is all right.

There Are Variables to These Visits

Now, this picture was taken at what I'm assuming is the Bradshaw Ranch, fifteen years ago, when this was very unusual, but I . . . does what you're saying about this photo now relate to all the pictures people are taking now of what they call orbs?

Yes. And I might add that such photos were taken many times before the famous photos associated with some of Tom's books, but as you go back in time and cameras and film were not up to present-day standards—just talking about film, here . . .

They weren't fast enough.

. . . then it was not typical to get such photos. The mood of the being and, again, where you are also makes a difference—not in the middle of a city, for instance, but in a place where you're more likely to have forms of life that are more natural: wild plants, wild animals, and so on—free plants that were welcomed and grew from seed and free life forms.

So not only are the film and the digital cameras getting faster and better, but some humans are awakening and are able to see these things more easily. Is that correct?

Yes, on a qualified basis, because there are a lot of possible ramifications there. I don't want you to take my yes as meaning yes all the time, to everything you said. So it's a qualified yes.

YOU TRAVERSE TO YOUR HOME PLANET IN DEEP SLEEP

Soul Portal

February 2, 2010

Greetings. I work as an intermediary between worlds. There are many of us in existence—millions, many millions. We are part of the living spirit world that must be close to you all, all the time, in order to keep your world stable and to allow for your comings and goings. All of you on the soul level are from other planets, and you are not at home on Earth. As a result, you must go to your other planets in your deep-sleep state and recharge your existence. Beings like myself will connect to anywhere from thirty or forty individuals—and sometimes some groups of individuals up to a hundred, sometimes even more—to act as intermediaries to support moments of passage of your unconscious sleeping self to your home planets in this universe or beyond. This is why there are so many of us here.

We do not originate on this planet, but we have the capability to be present on your planet without any adaptation or training. We seem to be some of the few who can do this, and we are not here for anyone other than the human being. This allows you as individuals to traverse, then, perhaps three or four times in a twenty-four-hour day. This traversing often happens in between teachings with your guides, teachers, angels, and so on. At the deep-sleep state, you might go temporarily to your home planet, but what you do there is not what you might think.

You may not know that this is necessary, but even though you are not physical there—you might even appear like a spot of light. Occasionally you might appear in the form of life associated with the planet that you identify

87

with—what you do there more than anything else as a soul being, almost
the first thing you do when you go to your home planet, is to breathe. By
"breathe," I do not mean that you take in air as you do here on Earth, but
rather you take in the energy of that place, just a deep reception that I would
call breathing, but you do not exhale anything from Earth.

The reason this happens is that we are connected there, meaning we
have the capacity to function as intermediaries, which is like a living portal,
creating a truly conscious portal by which you can make such a journey instantaneously so that all other beings—including the planets—are insulated
and protected from all that you are on Earth that may be uncomfortable to
them. And anything on the home planet that may be incompatible with
your soul does not affect you or cause any detrimental influence to affect
your life on Earth.

I personally have been functioning in this capacity on your planet now
for about 1,000 years. As we get more experienced and have been here longer,
some of us grow larger. When we are newly arrived, some of us are smaller, but
this is not a fixed situation. Sometimes [chuckles] some stay small no matter
how experienced they are. But we are not assigned, you see, to souls, so we
might have thousands of experiences with different souls, many experiences
with some souls, or anything in between.

Generally speaking, the dots that seem to make up our being have to do
with one or more traverses, so what you're really seeing is something that's a
tube. If you were to see a tube in a cross-section, it would look very much like
a circle. So that's what you're really seeing. It isn't a plasma that makes us up.
If you were to see us in our natural state, we usually would appear as a single
color and there would be none of this "little circles" stuff [chuckles]. I'm getting used to your language here.

Your Souls Have the Same Shape We Do

So I cannot tell you where I am from, because I have been told it's vitally
important that this remain a secret from you. I can say that it's at the outer
boundaries of this universe, but that's all I can say. This may be why we are
able to help Earth souls traverse to a home planet beyond this universe, because we are used to being in our state at home. We are used to being at the
border of things. Perhaps this is why we can function in an unusual capacity
this way. Generally speaking, we do not stay in this capacity for more than
a thousand years. I have lingered a bit and I might linger for a couple more
years, but soon I will return to my home place. We are not humanoids, as is

obvious, but we do have lives. We also do not have a fixed amount of life but exist in an ongoing fashion.

We would call that immortal, right?

Yes, but this is what you are too when you are not in your adventurous mode exploring different life forms. You do not look exactly like us, but on examination, you would be circular in form. This is perhaps why we were requested to come, because your souls have the same shape that we do. When you are at the deep-sleep state, you are most at ease with beings who are circular like yourselves. In this way, there is a natural built-in compatibility.

What do we do when we get there? Just take in the energy?

You do the same thing, yes, with the energy. It's like when you take a deep breath of fresh air and feel that sense of exhilaration and refreshment. It's very much like that experience, which is part of the reason why a person can have a nap for twenty or thirty minutes and wake up profoundly refreshed, whereas that same person might sleep for four or five hours and not really have that experience of refreshment.

So it means you went home during that time?

That's what it always means.

Our Different Colors Accommodate the Soul's Different Feelings

I saw the picture of you that was taken close to Bradshaw Ranch in Sedona, and you had many, many, many colors in these little tiny circles. Are you saying that each one of these represents a traverse for souls?

Yes. The reason there are different colors is that it accommodates the soul's different moods. When the soul is coming from Earth, traversing wherever it needs to go, it will still have feelings. Even at the deep-sleep level, there are strong feelings. The colors accommodate those feelings, both going to the home planet and returning, so that when you are, say, passing through Earth, you leave those feelings, and by the time you get to the home planet, you are in a state of being in which you can be totally receptive. But when you return, you must pick up at least a portion of those feelings so that you are reminded of who you are and can return at ease without resistance to your physical self. Otherwise, you would not want to go back to your physical self.

So the colors have to do with feelings. We do not feel these feelings, although they are within the tubes as you might see them within us. Thus we are insulated from feeling the feelings, but in some photographs of you I've seen that are taken here and there over the world, you can see the energy feeling. Different colors are not always associated with the same feelings. It depends largely on the individual or the individual's family of souls. Some groups of souls will radiate this or that color for the same feeling, and other groups of souls might have an identical feeling and radiate a different color. I have noted that there's much variety.

Do the humans in deep sleep go to you, or do you go to them? How do you connect with them?

It is not a problem of time or space. Wherever I am and wherever they are is not a difficulty. Once you are in the deep-sleep state and your soul can traverse, there is no limit to where you could be. I could be inside a mountain—just as an example, though I don't do that—and you could easily come and make your passage.

Okay, but do we go to you? Do the same souls always go to the same beings like you?

Oh yes, you would come. You would have to come in order to make a safe transit.

So when you first came here 1,000 years ago—that would be AD 1000—how much did you see of Earth?

Not very much. In order to perform such a function, I need to have a strong connection to my home planet so that I do not lose myself, my personality, with such passages. So I do not really observe your history, your culture, or anything like that. To the degree I know you, it is in my relationship with your souls. It is not based on your experience on the Earth. My relationship, then, is that I feel you with your essential mood as you make your traverse through and then into your home zone, so to speak. When you come back, you are a bit more comfortable for me because you are completely clear, but then you traverse back and I release some of that matter of your feelings, as I said before. So I do not observe your history and manners and mores and all that.

I Am Stabilizing Your Energy

How did you happen to come here? Did someone go to your home planet and request that you do this for the humans on Earth?

That's how all of us have volunteered to do this, because we were requested to come here to create a much better stabilized energy. When the first humans were on the Earth—not really your people—it wasn't necessary, because Earth in those times was benevolent. But once the Explorer Race, as you are deemed, came and there was some discomfiture, there needed to be not only a means to stabilize your traversing to your home planets, as I've mentioned, but also a means to insulate the planet and the planet's other life forms from such jolts, you might say, to the veil system that protects your planet and protects other planets from what happens on this place, on Earth. So we were asked to come in as great a number as needed. That's why I say there are millions of us, but one can perform such services for many souls. Even though you might have billions of individuals, millions of us are enough.

What was your life like before you came here?

Oh, very calm: a benign and benevolent existence with communication of ideas and concepts, like that. I wouldn't say we were purely intellectual, but that was part of our pursuits.

Do you have a form there?

We look the same here. We look the same, with the exception that you do not see all the little circles. We are of one color, but we would be circular.

Ah! So before you come and then also after you go back home, all the circles are gone?

Yes, because the circles . . .

Are the portals.

That's right, the traversing mechanism. It is not part of our physical functionality. Some have said it is a kind of plasma that makes us up, and as well-intended an analysis as that is, that is not the case. In our natural state, we would just be circular and no "tubes." I'm using that as a simplified means by which you can imagine in your mind's eye what that might look like, because you are familiar with tubes.

You said you keep a strong connection to your home planet. So then are you able to connect with the rest of the beings there while you're doing this, or do you have to not do that because of the discomfort?

Usually I would do that—speaking for myself—when I am not having traversing going on. I cannot have traversing going on for a few time segments and then connect to my home planet to refresh myself. For you, such a refreshment would come in sleep. For me, it is more of being present there, during which time I do something not unlike what you do. I take the energy in. But I don't exhale in that sense.

You take in the energy of your home planet?

That's right, and this refreshes me.

And gives you the strength to keep doing this?

Strength is not actually a factor. We have a natural endurance.

This is amazing. We knew we had to go somewhere during sleep to get recharged, but no one ever said before how the process worked.

This is my experience of it. I do not claim to have all knowledge, but I'm sharing what I know based on my experience.

Well, I'm sure that the others of your kind do something similar.

The Service Is the Joy

Are there any special joys in doing this? I mean, do you get satisfaction from it, or is it just a service?

The service is the joy. To be of service is a great pleasure. You on your planet know this pleasure, because you might do little things throughout the day where you are in service to others, and often there is pleasure associated with that. There might be other times, perhaps, when it is a burden for you, but it is not a burden for me or the others of my fellow beings, as far as I know, because what we do is one thing. If there were a multitude of things we had to do at the same time, then that might be too much. But the function we provide is something we can do and is easy for us, and therefore, it is a joy of service situation, as you yourself mentioned.

To be of service is natural for all forms of life. Even though there are extremes on your own planet, such as beings consuming each other, still that's a service. From my understanding of your planet—not based on day-to-day observation but simply on what has been explained to us before we came here for service—the whole interaction of all beings on your planet is largely service. So this is part of your nature as well.

The reason you can do this, you said, is that you're from the edge of the universe. You exist at the borders, so in your natural state—when you're home—do you go to other universes?

First off, I think you've made a slight error in your question if you're saying the reason we can do this is because we are at the edge of the universe. In fact, there are many other forms of life at or around the same "edge," and they do not do such things. The reason we do it—and can do it—is because of our makeup, because of who we are. I believe the reason we are able to more easily accommodate such an action is because of our location, but I cannot state with certainty that this is so. This is what I have come to believe, but I do not claim to have, as I say, all answers. So can you perhaps rephrase the question?

You said you could do this because of your makeup, because of who you are. Can you say a little more about that?

Not too much, but we are what you are when you're not performing such a service, as is all life in this universe. And we do not have any need to forget who we are. It's important to note that so you do not put a distance between yourselves and us.

You Are Taking Service to Another Level

Well, you know, the Explorer Race has some great goals. What do you think about the concept?

Figure 9.1: This photo of the being speaking through the channel is an enlargement of one of the beings in the photo seen in figure 8.1.

It is very advanced, taking service to another level—being of service to the entire universe at the very least.

Hopefully, all universes.

Yet there are profound risks involved. I can see that it is essential to keep it all very well bundled so it doesn't affect other planets, the rest of the universe, and so on. So it's too soon for me to say that I think it's a good thing or that I think it needs more thought. Ask me that question again when you have completed your service here.

Okay. Why 1,000 years? Who picked that as your length of service here?

Nobody did. It's just what I have chosen.

Oh! It's different for all of your beings?

Yes, it's entirely associated with the individual. Some, I think, have been here for close to 3,000 years. But for me, I think I would like to return to my home planet soon.

What do you look forward to there?

The exchange of ideas and the interactions from one to another—nothing complicated. It is essentially summed up by saying a single word: home. I think we will have to stop this session soon.

You've given us incredible information that helps us understand how our lives are possible here.

I believe, on your world, with you as souls in human form, that you are constantly surrounded in every waking and sleeping moment with a vast fabric of spirit and other physical forms that make it possible for you to continue the delicate balance of your lives on Earth. From what I have been guided before coming to this place, it is a very delicate balance indeed. Yet from the angelic messenger from Creator who came initially to explain why and what and so on about your service on Earth as souls, I believe that your intention is of the highest, and I wish you well along your pathway to accomplish such a worthy goal. Good night.

Thank you very much. Good life.

AN OLDER VEHICLE CREATES AN UNINTENDED EFFECT

Zeta Scientist

February 8, 2010

Greetings. This photo (figure 10.1) represents an aftereffect of a transference of energy associated with a vehicle that moved from your world into another one. Sometimes such photographs are taken, and other times sensitives—your own people or other species on your planet—can see such a phenomenon. It is what could be called a portal, but the moment of illusion in the picture is one that shows the portal in motion. If I can describe it, the portal was actually underground when the vehicle moved through it. But the trailing energy was not entirely compatible with the portal, and the portal had to shift its position in order to reconstitute itself in a benevolent way so it could be used again. This is why there seems to be an emanation. The emanation is really the traversing of the portal from one position to another, at which time shortly thereafter this image was captured. The portal returned to its original position, several miles beneath the planet.

I am speaking to you because our vehicle was involved in this motion through the portal, and while I do not feel apologies are necessary, there is still a sense of explanation due. The vehicle was from a star system you have classified as Zeta II, and although we have not been on or near your planet for some time, we occasionally move deep within the planet in vehicles that can traverse through spaces at a slightly different focus of energy—you say dimension—in order to be able to check or confirm the status of certain situations that are associated with the past and the future but not the present. As a result, great care must be taken so that your world is protected and your energy remains stable.

Figure 10.1: Zeta vehicle lifting the portal and inadvertently being seen.

We do not visit your planet at this time in your present, but we continue to visit in your past and to an extent in the future. This is not something we do lightly or capriciously. We have been requested to do this in order to be certain that your traversing along your own path of destiny is not disrupted or corrupted by anything going on that is external to your planet—meaning any forms of contact with otherworldly beings. That contact is observable largely by your own technologies now in the present moment, but you do not have that capability for the past or the future. While we are not working with any forms of government or even private industry that may be contracted to make these observations in the present moment, we feel a certain allegiance and historical loyalty to looking after the citizenry on your planet. We feel this because of our interactions with you in the past and our eventual meetings with you in a future that you will achieve at some point.

The Portal Was Visible Because of the Vehicle

This photograph was simply activated by the energy of this old vehicle—it was a very old vehicle—making that passage through the portal. And because it was an old vehicle, one that was only used because of an anomaly in the one we normally use, the portal became apparent.

There's a black box on top. Is that the portal, or is that just the effect of the energy?

You're talking about the same photograph?

Yes. There's a column, and then almost at the very top, there's a square.

Yes, but I wouldn't call it black; it's just darker. That square thing as it appears—it's not exactly square, though it generally would appear to be square or rectangular—is the portal.

Now, the man who leant me the photo, Tom Dongo, said it was taken ten years ago in Leadville, Colorado, and that the sky was lit up with orange light for miles.

Those who have seen vehicles from our constellation know that the orange color is attributable to our craft.

So did the light then come from the portal or from your ship?

From the traversing of the ship . . .

Through the portal, ah.

The ship, as I said, was an old vehicle, so it was not completely compatible with the portal. The type of vehicles we normally use would not have had that affect, but this older vehicle had that affect. It did not harm the portal, but it did create undue attention that was not intended, and for that we are apologizing.

So ten years ago—that would be 2000. Were you coming out of the planet to go home? Had you been going to our past or our future?

We were not coming out of the planet to go home. We were simply traversing below the surface in order to cause as little ripple of awareness of our existence as possible. So we were visiting your past.

How far back into our past?

Around the 1400s. We were gently checking up on the genetic makeup of your body tissues with a group of individuals we interact with in that time. I won't say where, but they know who we are and where we're from, and they are completely at ease with us.

Checking up on—do you mean modifying or just checking?

No, we never modify. We just check up to see that they are all right. In the course of helping them through those times, we can check the DNA, as you call it. But we do not modify; that is not our job.

Do you do this frequently? Do you come here frequently yourself?

No. That was the only time I personally was on such a vehicle in and around your planet, at least associated with that past when the photograph was taken and for that particular mission, though I will—and this is difficult for you to understand—be here again in a future time. And of course since we were traversing from the past to the future, you might say it was the same time.

Feathers Are Fascinating

Well you're from our future. What do you do when you're home? What is your life like?

You're asking me what my work is? I am a scientist at the home base. I cannot reveal all of that, but I will say that my work generally has to do with unusual comparisons of feathers on forms of life on your planet and all over the universe. Feathers fascinate me. As a result, when I travel, I am inclined to communicate with feathered beings more than others. In the past, when I visited your planet on that mission, I was able to communicate with many feathered beings and they were interested to hear of feathered beings existing in other parts of the universe. Communication is not so difficult for us with other forms of life. We have communicated with you, and you are another form of life.

Most of the feathered beings on our planet fly. What about the rest of the universe—is that true?

It is not universally true, but it is not unusual. However, I have found a great many feathered beings that do not fly at all. What I would call their feathers might be a little different from the feathers on what you call birds on your planet. What I would call feathers, you might initially classify as some form of hair, but if you examined it closely under a microscope, it would quite obviously be a feather.

Is there something about the shape of the feather as it goes through the air that affects energy or anything?

No more than anything else affects energy as it goes through the air.

So the shapes just interest you, but there's no intrinsic meaning in the shapes?

There's an intrinsic meaning in all shapes that Creator and other such teachers would speak of, but I am simply fascinated at the shape and the variety—no two feathers are exactly the same.

Oh! Even on one bird?

Yes. Even your own scientists know this.

Really? And you feel that that's part of the diversity the Creator loves? Or is there some other reason?

I cannot speak for Creator, but I like it.

[Chuckles.] All right. We haven't talked to any of your species for ten or twelve years. There was a concern in the 1960s that you were not going to be able to reproduce, and hence there are the hybrids. What is your status now? Have you become like Joopah— gold-light plasma beings?

I don't know what you mean by plasma, but I am not that. I am what we were and have always been, but there are planets associated with our star system where the beings do not appear to be of a solid mass and one—speaking of myself as one—needs to use a form of eye protection to look at them, for they give off a glow of light. Perhaps the one you mentioned is like that? But it is not that all of us are that way. I look the way I have looked for [chuckles] a long time.

How long in our years?

Oh, maybe 600.

So you didn't come to the planet during the years of the hybridization and the contacted humans and everything?

No, but I am vaguely aware of it. It was not my work. Simply to go on such a mission takes a certain amount of familiarity with the area, but it is not where my interest lies, so I do not know that much about it.

You told me what you did in the past, but how far did you go into our future? Can you say?

On that mission? Oh, about 700 years, something like that. You understand that I'm not there anymore; I'm on our home planet now.

Okay. What is your estimated life cycle? I mean, where are you along that line?

About halfway through.

Has your life changed in any ways in the last fifty years, or is life on your home planet pretty much the same?

There have been no discernible changes, no—or at least no discernible changes to me. I can't rule out that others may have a different opinion.

So you have many scientists. Were you asked to go? Did you volunteer? How did you happen to go on that mission?

I went because of my interest in feathers. The intention was apparently to visit those individuals in the past. And it was understood that there were many, many feathered beings in and around the area. I believe that some individuals felt that while they weren't certain that all the feathered beings were peaceful, because of my interaction with feathered beings for hundreds of years I have a rapport with all feathered beings, and so they asked me to come along, in case hostile actions might come from feathered beings. There were no hostile actions, but since I was there, I took the opportunity to interact as much as possible with them and had several hours to interact with many of them, and I enjoyed it very much.

You can't say if you were in Iceland or in the Tropics? I'm assuming there were many, many different kind of birds there?

There's a reason I am not saying it, and the reason is that your peoples are not that far from time travel; I wish to protect them.

Are they going to do time travel benevolently? Will it be hidden like everything else they do, or what?

Oh you mean your peoples? Well, of course initially it will be done secretively. I think there are already a few experiments—not always successful ones, but they are trying—using available energies, not unlike what others have done, and struggling along a bit. There are those who are theorizing about it now, but it will take them a while to realize and put into practice that it's not a large amount of energy but a very tiny amount of energy involved in doing such traversing. It only seems like it requires a large amount of energy, but it's just the opposite. I'm willing to give them that hint and say this now, because there are theorists right now who are proposing that. I will support them: It is true; a miniscule amount of energy works much better.

But it has to be benevolent for all of them and where they're going, right?

Yes, that is critical.

But do they know that?

Well, someone will read this and find out, eh?

Human-Zeta Hybrids Radiate Inspiration

[Chuckles.] All right. You weren't here during the times I want to ask about, so do you or anyone you know have much contact with the hybrid species—the half-human, half-Zetas?

I have met a few of them, and they are a charming race of people. They apparently have the gifts of both types of beings. They tend to be highly artistic and have the capacity to see into the hearts and minds of others. This is something that is particularly favored in our society, so there are a considerable amount of ongoing relationships, though not for me. I wouldn't call those relationships diplomatic; it is more like what you see in an extended family, if you understand. So there is that traveling from place to place on a regular basis, but not living in the same place. My own contacts with one or two individuals—one was a young one and the other a little older—were what I can only describe as charming, because they have a certain character that seems to demonstrate all the most wonderful qualities of both species.

I think that when your people meet them, you're going to love them. Granted, they don't look like you, but they have similarities to you. Conversely, they don't look like us, but they have similarities to us. That's important to recognize. They are their own shape and form. Of course they are humanoids with two arms, two legs, a head, fingers, toes, and hands—all that stuff. But they have an artistic appearance; that is the only way I can describe it. I think that your artists will be inspired just by meeting them. There's something about them that—how can we say?—is inspiring. After I was with those two, I had a job to do in my place of study, and I had several insights that I had never had before. This is why I believe that they have a radiated energy that stimulates inspiration in others. So I feel that there's something special about them.

In your species, is cloning working now for you?

It's what we use.

It is? Okay. Because wasn't that the idea in the 1960s—about fifty years ago—that it had stopped working? Wasn't that the reason the hybrids were created?

There was a time when it seemed to be difficult, but I do not know the details. I just know that there was about a sixty-year gap, and then it started working again, so somebody must have fixed something.

Ah, then do you see that you and your species will become more . . . in fact, you sound much more friendly and warm and open than some of the earlier ones. Do you feel that they're making progress, that you will change a little to become more feeling oriented?

Keep in mind that I've had the training. Even though it was not intended for us to meet a human being in your time on the mission, the training that I and everybody on the vehicle had was something that would prepare us to be as you were describing, because the people in the 1400s were very warm and human, as you say, so we had to be able to fit in, blend in, and not make waves—you still say that, eh? Make waves? I picked up a few of your . . . some of your lingo. So I am using that same approach with you.

I see. Okay, well, it's working [chuckles].

Well, good.

Zetas Do Not Have a Group Mind

What is your home situation? Do you have families? Are they extended? I mean, you don't have children, but do you live in groups or divided by interests? How does that work?

I cannot say too much, but it is basically a community. It is not a familial setup, but it is a community, and we have certain activities we like to pursue together. But I cannot say too much.

Okay. Why can't you say some of these things?

Partly because we are guided by your teachers and guides that it is not so good to offer other ways of living and make them sound desirable if those other ways of living would interfere in the way you live. You live the way you do out of necessity but also because you gravitate to community. Family life is something you are born into. Friends, lovers—all of that is intended as well as natural for you. So many times, beings from other worlds do not go into details about their homes and the way they live unless they are parallel to your own, simply so that those of you who may be temporarily dissatisfied with your way of life will not try to be something that you are not in an attempt to imitate life forms such as ours, who have our own culture—our own ways, manners, and morays that are appropriate for us in our world.

But not for us, right.

Exactly. You would not try to live as the birds in the trees. You would not try to live as the "many-leggeds," as an old friend used to say in the 1400s. You would not try to live like anything but human beings. Why would you want to live like us? We are not so strange, but we are different in our society than you are in yours. But we do have similarities. We go places and do things as a group—you do that.

Now all of the beings from your planet who came here in the last . . . I don't know when they started coming—the thirties, forties I guess, up until when? When did you quit coming—the eighties or something?

I cannot say.

Okay. The Zetas who came here and interacted with humans—did they come back and talk about it to those of you who were there on your home planet? Was what they were doing common knowledge among those on the home planet, or was it just something that was peculiar to those scientists and crew who came to Earth?

The people involved in those activities communicated it to their own communities of interest, but since I was not a portion of that community, that information did not come to me. It's not as if it were a secret, you understand. It's that—how can we say?—in your own scholastic system, people have different specialties, yes? And if you were a biologist, you would not necessarily be involved in the study and the sharing of knowledge of the French language, for instance—unless, of course, you were from France. So what I am saying is that it was more of a specialty sharing. It wasn't my specialty—the information did not come to me—but if I asked someone, I am sure they would tell me.

Don't you have something you can put your hand on to learn? Don't you have a gadget that you can put your hand on to absorb information?

It's not that complicated, but to put it simply, there is an object by which one can assimilate information. But for a resident, it is a lot easier. It is more . . . it does not require an object.

You can just commune with those beings. You can commune with whoever has the information.

Yes. You can acquire information without difficulty.

From anyone who has it?

From anyone who wishes to share it. It is not taken without permission. Permission is essential.

Okay, well, how can I say it? I thought that there's a group mind or something so that what one knows, all of you know, but you're saying . . .

No, I think that's an attempt to oversimplify who we are, because we are so different from you that there is an assumption that because we are in agreement in principle on things that we may do, that we would follow each other's' tendencies to do things. Just because we are in agreement does not mean we have a group mind. I'm sure you have many people who agree to certain beliefs, but you would not say they have a group mind and are automatons.

Yes, you're right. That was our response at the time.

I believe that was stated at the time in order to classify us and make us seem less threatening. Sometimes information is given out—even among your own peoples—to say this group or that group is this or that in order to simplify, to classify, and to make that group either seem less threatening or . . .

Or more.

Yes, and if it is more threatening, there is a political agenda.

You Will Gain a Truthful Consensus

Okay. I don't exactly know what else to ask that is pertinent to you or this picture.

There is really nothing else to ask. We have been chatting.

[Chuckles.] Well, we've gained information and a deeper understanding of you. Do you know Joopah? He's been channeling through this being you're channeling through for twenty-five years or something. Are you familiar with him?

I do not know that person.

Well, I thank you, before you get a chance to get away—I thank you very much. Go ahead.

Very well. I will simply say this, then. I wish to commend you for your progress in your time. I realize that with so many of you on the planet no coordinated and orderly system is desirable, since you are living in the world of individuals at this time, and individuality is encouraged and intended for you. I still feel that, with your individuality and uniqueness, you have made tremendous progress, given the conflicts, both inner and outer, and a desire in general to create different forms of influential groups. This struggle with leadership will pass, and eventually there will be a means to gain a truthful consensus, not one superimposed on you by a small elite group. This will come about partly from technology and partly as you acknowledge your own spirituality and your relationship with Creator. Don't try to force the issue; it will evolve and is evolving in your time. Someday your children and your children's children will live compatibly on this planet, and the whole idea of war will be some distant and strange phenomenon. Good life.

Thank you. Good life.

GERMAN UFO REALLY AN UNFINISHED ESCAPE VEHICLE

Zoosh and U.S. Secret Service Agent

February 24, 2010

All right. This is Zoosh.

Welcome.

Now, we're going to proceed with caution: At times I'm going to be speaking, and at other times, I'll be interpreting for somebody else—someone who had a rank that would be equivalent to today's Army rank of colonel but who was in something like a secret service in those days. Keep in mind that I'm not talking about the Secret Service of the German Army; I'm talking about the Secret Service of the United States, all right? Normally we avoid things like this, but this information is not really classified. It would come under the heading that they used to have years ago of "confidential." I don't think they have that rating anymore.

Now, the material associated with the pictures and the inspiration for it was not developed in an entirely intellectual manner, but it was partially that way. The thoughts, along with inspirations, were ceded to a group in that time during World War II—a group that was fighting against the German forces. They were not located directly in Germany—I'm going to have to be vague here to protect various family members—but they were located in one of the countries invaded by the German military. The information was given not so much to develop a weapon as to develop a means of transportation, a way of—you might say—escape. It would have been a vehicle that has a correlation to a product type that you know very well now: a single-use product. You'd perhaps go to the store today, buy something, use it once, and throw it away—not unlike a battery that you are unable to recharge.

Figure 11.1: Haunebul 1

So if the device were to be built today, with its complete instructions and fuel system, you might stand back, look at it, and say, "If only I had a fuel system that lasted longer." So if this thing were built, it would not last a given time like a battery's useful life; it would simply be a one-use thing. You would turn it on, and then once you turned it off, that would be it: You wouldn't be able to turn it on again. This functioned like a safety mechanism so that the device really could not be used very well for anything other than for its original purpose, which was to transport large numbers of people. Provided you had the main part, the vehicle could be built to hold up to 10,000 individuals.

This vehicle would not have food or water and facilities on it, as one might expect it would, but rather once the vehicle was rotating—it was the kind that rotates—the individuals would fall into a sleep-like state. The atmosphere in the vehicle would be charged with the benevolent atmosphere of the time, which would mean a little more oxygen in comparison to what you have now. The air would be somewhat humid. If people had to have food or water or something like that, there would be a means through each individual seat—where a passenger would sit—to take that on in just enough of a quantity to survive but not to make for the necessity of a trip to the bathroom, for example.

On the surface of the Earth, meaning within five miles of the surface or less, the vehicle could travel up to a hundred miles. Yet it wasn't really meant to travel around near Earth, and once turned on and headed for the stars, it could travel an infinite distance, well across the galaxy or beyond. But once you got to where you were going and the vehicle had landed and it was turned off—usually a vehicle like that would be turned off automatically, and piloting and navigation would all be automatic, without the need of an individual pilot—then that would be that. The people would get out, and that's that.

The Vehicle Was Never Meant for Military Use

It's safe to say, you see, that even though crude prototypes were found once the German military was defeated—and these crude prototypes were made up from the material that was captured with the intention of turning it into a weapon—the device wasn't meant to function as a weapon and would not have worked that way, because the systems simply would not have functioned. It was like a built-in safety mechanism. It was felt in the designing and creating of such a vehicle that the people in the vehicle might have bad feelings, they might be upset, or they might not realize the value of where they were going and so on, and therefore, they could be suicidal. So there was no way the vehicle could be used as an instrument of its own destruction or—as it was intended to be used by those who captured the material—as a vehicle for the destruction of others.

This is why the project didn't get as much attention as you might have expected, because those who were building the prototypes were frustrated at their inability to create something that could truly work as a weapon. When the German military captured it at the time, it seemed to them that it could be done, because there were certain devices on the vehicle that they thought were weapons, but they were not. Those devices were part of a means to travel through space. Sometimes when traveling slowly through space, when moving away from planets that are inhabited or into the region of planets that are inhabited, you need to have some device that would nudge things gently out of the way, not destroy them. So the reports of ray guns on the vehicle were really not quite accurate.

I'm going to have to speak more quietly now, to save the channel's voice, but that's it in a nutshell. I won't comment on the military uses of the material at the time in World War II and so forth—that has been well-documented— but I will speak to this specifically. This is Zoosh, by the way. Be alert that you will not be able to tell when the "colonel" is talking and when I am talking, but when I come in and say, "This is Zoosh," you'll know for sure that it is me at that moment. All right, you can ask a question if you have one.

Plans Channeled with the Best of Intentions

How did the person who got the inspiration for this vehicle . . . you said it was someone who was in a country that was at war with Germany. They were in a . . .

I did not—I want to be accurate. They were like an underground unit. Do you understand?

But they were in a country that was at war with Germany?

They were associated with a country that had been invaded by the Germans of the time.

All right. And who gave them this vehicle that would hold 10,000 people?

Nobody. They didn't give them the vehicle; they gave them the plans and the inspiration. They didn't give them blueprints. They gave one individual the inspiration, using a method not unlike what is happening here today. It was . . . I would not have used that word, but you might interpret it as channeled inspiration. Okay?

Who was on the other end of the channeling? Who was giving the information?

I will have to be vague here, but I can only say that it was from a planet where the people on that planet feel good about Earth. And I am sad to say that those who provided the inspiration were punished by their people for interfering in Earth activities of the time, even though the interference was meant to be entirely compassionate. There are strict rules against such things, because even though it appears (this is Zoosh speaking now) that this would be a kind act, something meant to help people escape who needed to get away from an otherwise inevitable death, that the larger picture would be how is the future affected, all right? So those from that planet who provided the inspiration (this is not Zoosh now, just a moment) were not punished in the way punishment happens on Earth, but they were sent to another place and had to be reformed by their people, because their compassion caused them to break the rules that were set up for their society on their planet. The vehicle was meant to transport the people to a planet near the planet that was associated with these compassionate people, so the compassionate people—I'll call them ETs—of the other planet were actually sent to that planet where they had hoped to help these Earth people migrate to, to get away.

So these were some ETs—were they on our planet or flying above it, or were they on their home planet at the time that they gave the Earth human the inspiration?

They were on their home planet. Inspiration does not require proximity.

Of course, but had they been paying attention to the struggle here on Earth, so they knew what was needed? Or did the human being on Earth ask? How did that work?

They apparently had the means to observe the struggle, and because of some knowledge they had about their own planet's history in the distant past, they were afraid that your planet might be destroyed, because they saw what could happen. Now we know that it wasn't destroyed (this is Zoosh again); we know that wasn't the case, but there was a short time during World War II when the global destruction of your planet was a distinct possibility.

Why is it so important that we not know who helped or who tried to help us?

I cannot tell you that. The person receiving this information was a youngster, about twelve years old, and he was not in the underground but was well thought of in his community and recognized for his capacity for vision, for his visionary skills. There are reasons to be vague. I'm sure you can imagine what they are.

Well, he or some of these people might still be living or have relatives.

Exactly. They have descendants.

Okay. So then how did the information get from the visionary to someone who could actually use it?

Someone who noted what the youngster was drawing and what the youngster communicated to him knew others in the underground and thought perhaps there might be a way to construct the device and get people out. The youngster told them that the people would go to another planet, but you see the people who took the information—granted, partially with the youngster's permission, partially not—did not grasp what it meant when the youngster said they would go to another planet. They thought the youngster was making that part up. You understand, space travel in those days would have been something of science fiction for most people, so that's what they thought. They thought, "Oh, this is a wonderful inspiration, but of course we won't use it to go to another planet; we'll just use it to take the people someplace safer on Earth." But you see, that wouldn't have worked that way.

German Intelligence Didn't Know What to Make of It

So they attempted to build a prototype? They built a prototype?

They didn't get that far. When they had the materials assembled and were nowhere near where that youngster was anymore, the underground unit was captured.

By the Germans?

Yes. But not by any fancy unit with dazzling names. They were just captured by an ordinary army unit, and the material was looked at originally as if it were some kind of fictional material. They thought, "Oh, somebody's doing these drawings for their children." Nevertheless, when capturing materials, army units of the time on both sides would pass the materials on to their own intelligence people, and that's how someone took a look at it and essentially said, "Hey, this might be a real thing."

What year was that?

I'm not going to say.

All right, we are just asking for an explanation of the picture of the German UFO—who made it, where they got the idea . . .

If your purpose is to try to create an explanation for what this was about, that is its only value. You're not going to build a vehicle like this with any success in your time. But I'm also keeping in mind that there are those trying to build vehicles with that material. If they know the restriction, they might put that time and energy to better use. That's why for those experimenting to try to create such vehicles in your time—even though it's only a small number of individuals—these vehicles don't work very well.

Because of the restriction built in that if you turn it off, it's off for good?

That and the fact it's not intended to be used in any way that could be described as a military intention or on a "mission," as the military might say.

Right, I understand: the benevolence of the original purpose. I have in front of me all of these supposed photos of German UFO-looking vehicles. Did they actually create something from these plans that they were able to use . . . are these pictures real?

Some of the pictures are real, but not all. Over time, there's been other material added to it that. It's almost as if you have a few original pictures, and then other things get added into them for various reasons that I won't explain, but I will simply say that two or three of the photos are accurate. But that's all. So, yes, some of the vehicles were built, but they couldn't get them to do what they wanted them to do.

They could fly them, but they couldn't use them for a weapon—correct?

That's the basic thing. They could sort of fly—and when I say sort of, I mean that—but they could not fly in a way that could be used for anything. Those who completed the build might say, "Wow, look at that!" That was about the net result of what they could do with it.

But none of these pictures look like a vehicle that could hold 10,000 people. So they scaled it way down, didn't they?

Well, yes. Although it might surprise you to know that there are vehicles that travel on an interplanetary basis, even in your time—because time is not as much of a factor for some of these vehicles—that look very small from the outside. Yet were you to go inside the vehicle, it would look like it could easily hold 300,000 to 400,000 people. But from the outside, you'd say, "How's that possible?"

That's why sometimes in your time when such vehicles were captured either in whole or in part, or when some citizens were simply able to go aboard and inspect them, after a while, people were less likely to want to do that, because as people said—even a little bit in your time, maybe—it plays with your mind. You're going into something small, and then suddenly it's cavernously large. And then you come back out, and it's in the proportions that you would see from the outside again—small.

You'd never, never look at your world in the same way after that. It changes your life perspective. You might say it interferes with your life, you see—just a simple thing like that. It's not something that you might say would be intended to cause a change in a person's life. But the fact would be that things that were simply taken for granted with such vehicles—"Oh, it can do this; it can do that"—if you're not expecting that and you come out, your life has changed. That's one simple example of how it can be interference. They go inside the vehicle, look at it, and then they come back out and their lives are never the same again. That's interference, although it may not have been intended. It comes under the heading of unintended consequences, which are consequences nonetheless.

So it's a different dimension inside, isn't it?

That's how it is described, but it is much more complicated than that. I am not a mathematician, but it would take a mathematician to explain it.

The Prototype Did Not Affect Earth Military Technology

Can you say anything about yourself? You were a member of something like the U.S. Secret Service?

I'm calling it "something like the Secret Service" for your convenience. When something like that is said, then you will often make it out to be a fact, but it's being stated to you like it was stated "*like* the Secret Service," because then you have a general idea of what it might have been like.

But not a specific idea?

Exactly.

Can you say in any way what your connection is with this transmission to the child and the underground and all of that? Can you say in any way how you relate to this or what you have to do with it?

No. You mention in your book that the questioner attempted in all ways to find out more about the person who spoke, but the person who spoke insisted on anonymity for itself and to protect the innocent—just like that.

Would you say that any of the craft on Earth now are the descendants of this plane, along with possibly additional technology from crashed planes or something?

Answering your question literally—taking it literally—no. But ask whatever you wish to ask. If I am unable to answer your question, I will say so. This is Zoosh here now. You must remember, Melody, that you are talking to somebody very much as if you were talking to a human being. Do not expect them to be—how can I say . . .

As all-knowing as you are.

Well, I'm not going to say that. But allow for the fact that you are talking to somebody who is more like someone you would talk to on a day-to-day basis.

All right, then how do I ask the question? Is there some connection between that original prototype and these photos of what look like Nazi spacecraft?

You can ask that question when the person returns.

Okay.

All right, I am here again.

All right, is there any connection between the channeled information from the ETs to the visionary and the prototype and the craft I'm looking at in these pictures—some of which you say are real?

You mean are they prototypes based on those original plans? Is that what you're trying to ask?

Did the original plans from the twelve-year-old visionary contribute to the Germans' ability to build these spacecraft-looking vehicles?

That's the only reason they did build things like that. They weren't originally going to go in that direction, as a matter of fact. Their entire thrust militarily wasn't toward that sort of thing; it was entirely toward the kind of planes that you see in the skies today that the military has—high-speed jet fighters. That's where they were putting their energy. This other thing was not funded very well, because it was thought to be something . . . well, the value of the material was questioned, and a very small group as involved in attempting to experiment with it. So when you see photos, look at one of the photos that has a sort of insignia on it—nothing elaborate, nothing obvious, but a sort of insignia that looks a bit like a military cross. Do you have a photo like that?

Several, yes.

Yes. But if you have something that has a swastika on it, then no, that's not it. They didn't use that—they didn't get that far.

This is a straight cross, an even cross.

That's it. It's one of those that has a version of that that sort of looks outlined—it essentially defines the negative space, as an artist might say—that is a photo. The project was not well funded, you see. Even today, in your now times, there are plenty of worthy projects that are poorly funded, but that's because people do not have the hindsight to know that it's really worth looking into.

Did this technology then go to the Americans and the Russians at the end of the Second World War? Did that become the basis of their experimentation?

It went to various groups and was looked at askance for quite a while. There was much more interest in the jet for military aircraft. There was a lot of interest in that. But as far as interest in the UFO-type device, there was almost no interest in that at the time. Even then, there was the thought that "this is science fiction" and "this is silly," and "no wonder they had such a small unit working on it." The thought they must have had was that it was a project to play with, you know, something like that. "What were they thinking with these kinds of ideas? Ha ha."

So the attention was then put on the jets and the rockets by the governments that got German technology at the end of the war.

Well, yes. If you just look at the facts postwar, what you saw coming out of that research was rockets and jets. You didn't see UFOs, eh? You didn't see flying saucers. They were trying to build vehicles, and they were looking for the reassurance in some way that they worked, but when they went to look into the materials from the escape plane, they looked at it and said, "What is this, a joke? This is science fiction—forget it." So it didn't get much attention for a long time.

So the stories we've heard about these craft being used to take some of the defeated Germans to the Antarctic—what would you say about that?

Nothing. No comment.

Focus Your Military on Creation, Not Destruction

Are you in spirit now? Are you in another body? Do you know . . .

I cannot say that.

You cannot say that, either? Is there anything else that you can say?

I will simply finish up, then. In your time now, there are still military struggles on the planet. Sometimes, militaries of the world are told that the struggles are about right and wrong or about what's been done in the past or that they are fighting to promote some greater truth. But ultimately, regardless of whether it is a greater truth or not, wars ultimately result in the suffering of innocents and in the destruction of hope and worthwhile ventures. I recommend you put less time into destructive military works and more time into constructive military works. The militaries of the world do not need that much of a nudge to do things that are creative, to build things. Many militaries of your time are perfectly capable of building things—roads, bridges, and all of that—and I feel that in the militaries all over the world, those who are wiser would be much happier building and creating than destroying.

Yes.

Good night.

Good night. Thank you very much for coming. Thank you. Good life.

THE "LITTLE PEOPLE" ARE HUMANS FROM ALPHA CENTAURI

Guide to Small Human Beings

March 4, 2010

Greetings. Now, down through the ages there has been an ongoing interest in tiny humans, not tiny humanoids. That interest is still raging, though it has been redirected at this time toward human beings of a smaller stature in terms of their height. But in fact, such human beings—granted, not exactly biologically the same as you but very similar in appearance and always less than three feet tall, often closer to two feet, two feet one inch, sometimes even smaller—have visited your planet in the past. An interesting point is that these beings come from a highly populated world. The world is physically much bigger than your planet, but they have very tender hearts—which is not unusual for beings—and the whole planet is peopled by these individuals who have such tender hearts.

At one point, they were about five, five and a half feet tall, and they have very long life spans—never less than 2,500 years in your time, and often as many as 5,000 or even 7,000 years. This is a very distant star system in terms of miles, but in terms of proximity, well, it is not that far. Because of their feelings, they devised a way to simply re-create everyone on the planet to be much smaller. It didn't happen immediately, of course. One might assume that in a shorter life span, this could be done through generations, but given their lengthy life span, that's ruled out, you see. Once everybody was at this shorter scale, size-wise, then the overpopulation ceased—as well as the demand on resources, which dropped to about one-tenth of what it had been before because of the slightly different biology of the peoples.

These peoples migrate about in the universe a bit—not so much looking for places to settle, but looking for places to visit, you see. They're particularly interested in other beings who look somewhat like them, although they don't have to look exactly like them. They were attracted to Earth some years ago when a species of human being you like to call "cave man" but who looked rather like yourselves with varying skin shades, peopled your planet, and there was a fine rapport among these peoples. The visitors lingered and taught various things, especially things along the spiritual realm: how to know what's safe to eat, how to know where to go, how to know how to find water—essentially things based on instinct, eh? And many of these teachings have survived—not all, but many—down through the ages, passed on from one to another and sometimes passed on outside of what you might call tribal groups, simply because the mystical people, as they came to be known in various words, wanted to make sure the wisdom lived on.

So these people are from Alpha Centauri, which is very far from your planet. If you saw them, you would say, "Those look like very thin human beings," and that's how they would appear. So I am one of their guides and teachers, and I know that you as well as many other people are interested in this subject. This is fairly well-known in the UFO literature: They're sometimes called the "little people."

Your Life Stages Interest the Alpha Centari Beings

Such beings are not on your planet anymore. They visited in the distant past and sometimes stayed for quite some time. Some even chose to remain and survived their usual lifetime—perhaps cut short by about 10 to 12 percent, because the oxygen content in the air on Earth at that time was much, much greater than it is now, and oxygen, as wonderful and invigorating as it is, also has certain detrimental effects over time. So they did not live quite as long, and once they realized that those detrimental effects were happening, it was too late to return to the home planet.

They were, however, able to communicate their situation, and that is why there have been no visits since—at least no visits where the beings got out of the ship they were traveling in. They were also concerned that their ship might be found after they died, so they managed to send the ship home. I believe some remains have been found and documented to some degree, though what they found is considered in medical and scientific communities to simply be an anomaly. It has also been studied and become gradually more and more secret over the years, but this information will be released at some point.

How tall were they exactly when they were here?

About, oh, twenty-two inches tall. I'm just rounding it off to the nearest inch. Is that adequate? These peoples are quite fascinating in that they accumulate information about human beings in various stages of their existence—this is not suggesting a qualification as much as what you would say are various ages. They're interested in babies and what you would call teenagers and elders and all of that, because their life spans are so long that they don't really experience what they would call the "accelerated" life span that you have. So they were always fascinated by babies and by elders. When they reach the end of their cycles, they do not go through the elder process that you do as peoples of Earth. They remain looking rather like they have always looked and simply have less and less energy until they pass over. I like that term, "pass over." It is very nice, because it's a visual representation of what actually happens.

How do they reproduce?

Carefully, given the size of the beings. In the past, they reproduced the way you do, but now the offspring are migrated from the female's body into a mechanism while small enough to be able to easily pass out of the female body. The mechanism is very much like what you call an incubator, only it is possible to almost make contact with the baby within it, so there is a great deal of love that is communicated. The being is surrounded with love and does not feel like it is in a machine, you understand. This is done because the incubator is very large, and it is possible for beings to be inside it, and therefore the being is closely loved and nurtured, you see—whispered to, sung quietly to, like that.

Is their population stable? Do they just replace those who leave?

It's stable now, yes.

Now, Alpha Centauri—there's an A and a B star. Are these beings on all the planets in Alpha Centauri or just some of them or one of them?

One, mainly. I won't go into the A and the B and all that. They are mainly on one, but they do travel about some. As I say, they are mostly attracted to places where human beings exist—not necessarily where they're the dominant life form, but they exist there. And they conduct networking just by interacting, you would say, but it's more friendly than that. [Chuckles.]

That's awesome! What if we had to do that on our planet? How tall were they when they started—five feet?

They were about five feet to five feet, five inches or something like that.

So they reduced their size by one-third! Did they have to go around and make their roads, their houses, their science, their mechanics, their craft—everything—one-third as big?

Yes. You understand that they were able to do this with their own bodies but not with everything else. So they had to reproduce everything else slowly. But they didn't have the same technology you have—there are no roads. They had vehicles that would move that did not require wheels or tires, so it wasn't as difficult in terms of the technology and the farming that existed, but it took quite a few years to reconstruct the supportive elements previously built on the planet so that they might live their lives. So you can imagine for yourselves, as you just have, but for them it was easier because it wasn't really that much, you know.

They didn't use machines like we do?

Not to the extent that you do, no. So it took awhile, but for you to do that, it would take a tremendous amount of time—not that you wouldn't be able to do it, but . . .

Yes, everything from books to the computers to appliances, houses—I mean everything. Yes, that would be awesome.

It would certainly give you something to do that you could unify around.

[Laughs.] You didn't say that in the beginning, but was the original reason they reduced themselves and everything they used that they were overpopulated and running out of resources?

I did say that. They were overpopulated.

Well, you said it later, that changing their size helped it, and then you said the overpopulation had ceased.

Well, what I mean by that is the crowding. If you have lots and lots of something in a room and then suddenly that something shrinks, then there's a lot more space, eh?

They Are Actual Humans, Like You

Are there other species on their planet?

There are some, but not a great many: plants, of course. You're talking about . . .

What we call animals or other humans or other sentient beings.

Yes, there are other beings, but not a great many, given the vast numbers of the humans—"little humans," we can call them. They're really humans; they're different from you, but if you were to look at them, you would say, "Well, these are little humans!" That's what you would say, but you couldn't help but notice how thin they were. That's just their makeup. When they were tall, they were that way too.

But they eat the same way; they eat and they breathe and they do the same things we do, right?

Not everything's the same. Their biological system is more efficient, so less is required going in and coming out, if you get my . . .

In 1897 in Texas, some craft with a very small human in it crashed, and they buried the body. Was that one of these beings, or was that somebody else?

If it looks the way I described, then it would have been one of them. That's all I will say.

They say that the news about the crash was all covered up, and the tombstone is . . . they don't know if the body's still there, and all kinds of things. Have those beings incarnated as humans on this planet?

On the soul line, you mean? No.

Will we meet them? Since that's the closest planet to Earth, we'll meet them when we start traveling, right?

Possibly. Everyone you meet will have to *want* to meet you. You will not, as a species, stumble across anybody, so to speak, as if you were walking down a road and saw a tree, a log, a rock, a dog, a cat, like that, and you just "happen" across, them, you understand? You will not happen across anyone. They will have to *want* to meet you. That goes for every single being you meet.

But you said they were interested in humans.

This is an important clue. Don't you understand? Why is it an important clue? Because it's happening now. You have flights going out into space, so I'm speaking now to your people who send people up into space. If you see someone who is clearly not from this planet, you can be absolutely certain that they wanted to meet you. They didn't "happen" across you. You didn't "happen" into their space. They always and only have to want to meet you for you to have any contact. What would your friend say if he were here?

You mean Zoosh? "Never forget that."

Yes, right.

So we could be seeing lights in the sky that were small lights, and they would be these small craft from these small beings, right? We would think, "Oh, that's too small to be an interplanetary craft." Do they have small craft, or did they keep them the same size?

I don't know what you mean by the "same size," but they're not small. They are about the size of what you might see from the types of ships that you normally see—those circular ones.

Ah, so they didn't reduce the size of the ships to the size of their bodies.

Well, they didn't have to. Think about it: If you had a big house with small people living in it, would you make the house smaller, or . . . ?

Or just put more people in it?

There you are. More room for more people and whatever you wish to bring with you.

I got it. I got it. Okay. That's the reason we drive SUVs, after all.

Small Is Not Unusual at All

What about your experience? Have you always been a guide to these beings? Were you a guide when they were taller?

Yes, I've always been a guide for them, and I've come through today because of your interest in smaller beings. I felt that you as well as your readership would be more interested in smaller beings that look like you.

Yes, this is fascinating! Are there many civilizations or species or inhabitants of planets that are this small, or are these beings unusual?

Small is not unusual at all. There are all shapes and sizes of beings. Of course, many beings travel in or function in something that could simply be called energy or at times—not always—light. But keeping it to beings of some version of solidity, then they come in all different forms—some small, some large. One finds beings to be a bit smaller more often than larger, though, because of resources, you understand.

Now, the teachings that they have left behind are what we call "shamanic teachings." Is that where some of our shamanic teachings came from?

Yes, but you have to remember that other beings visited your planet as well, including spirit beings who spoke to those who either were already in the mystical realm themselves or were medicine or mystical people. They are contributors, but they do not account for the body of knowledge. Plus, you have to allow for the fact that many people would simply observe what harms and what helps; these skills and abilities relate back to teaching, inspiration, and observation.

Of course. Have you ever been physical—or physical in a form less dense, perhaps?

Oh, no. I have never been physical as you understand physical to be.

And you're from this creation?

Yes.

The way we think, we're in the third dimension. What dimension are these little people in?

They are flexible. They are able to be in more than one focus of being. Generally speaking, they are not totally comfortable in the focus that you exist in. They might be a little more comfortable in a focus that is a little more light than that—light, not referring to a judgment or perception, but . . .

No, I understand: a higher dimension.

Yes, as you say, although it's not entirely accurate. So they are like that. But they are able to function for some length of time in your world—not your world as it exists today, but your world as it did exist many years ago when the energy of the planet and the energy of the beings on the planet were in concordance. Nowadays, you can still feel some portion of that at times if you go out into an old, dense wooded area or some areas with certain types of rocky strata on the surface where there is a good, benevolent energy—meaning you go there and it feels good. So it can still be felt here and there, to a degree, on your planet. For those of you who have felt that, just know that there would have been much more of that good feeling in the past on Earth and with its human populations when these people visited there. So it is that that they found reasonably comfortable, because that form of comfort—okay, if I am making myself clear . . .

The benevolence, yes.

That form of comfort is akin to what is felt on other planets all over the universe.

Now, when we are able to go out and travel and we go to their planet, if they're comfortable at a higher dimension, would we even be able to see them unless they chose to make themselves known to us?

For starters, you are assuming that you would go to their planet. That is extremely unlikely. When you meet peoples as you travel as an Earth people in space, they will usually come to meet you in some kind of vehicle, for those who need vehicles, and other times, they will simply appear to you in space, for those who do not need vehicles. Some are not affected by the effects of space. So the chances are that for many, many years, all meetings will take place in places other than on their planets.

"Many, many"—like hundreds?

I cannot say, but the chances of you going to some other planet are . . . that is only likely to happen if that planet and all its peoples—all of them— feel completely comfortable about having some of your peoples there. There may be a couple of places like that.

Yes, but it sounds pretty rare.

To begin with, yes. But are you surprised?

No, because we'll still have some of that discomfort with us.

That's right. And why would everybody on the whole planet wish to be exposed to that? They would want to have representatives meet you and see what you're like, how you feel, know whether it's safe—like that.

Their Childhood Does Not Linger

You said these beings, these little people from Alpha Centauri, are fascinated with our fast change of state from childhood to teenage to adult and all that. How do they grow there? They're born, and then . . . how long before they attain adulthood?

Not so very long. And by "adulthood," I'm going to say maturity so that there is no confusion with the way your species might teach and so on. In terms of the percentage of your life, you understand, you could easily create a percentage of, say, so many percentage points of when a child came to be—I'm going to say twelve years old—and that would be equal to what may be 1/6 or 1/5 of an average lifetime. But for them, so-called childhood would be maybe 1/200 of their lives. Their childhood does not linger.

So 200 into 2,400 would be, wow, maybe only twelve years.

It does not linger. So they're fascinated with how long the Earth child remains a child. Of course, in more ancient times on your planet, a human being would not have been considered a child, you understand, when they were, say, eleven or twelve.

So what do they do? Are they just interested in our behavior, or what else are they interested in? You said they came here and they wanted to stay here, so what else did they find interesting?

How friendly you are.

How friendly we were in the past?

No, you still are. Granted, nowadays, many people are less so, but that is simply because of being intimidated for this or that reason. Many times, your educational process, while being well meaning, simply teaches children to be frightened. There's too much devotion to teaching about war and battles. This has come about, I believe, because your educators are trying to keep the attention of children. But I think it's more important to teach qualities of life and how to get along in life in the best way possible rather than teaching names, dates, battles, and justification for battles. This kind of thing frightens children and makes them wary of life and of other people. It might take a while for your educational system to catch up. There are many private educational systems that are doing better at that, but the general educational system in many places needs a polishing.

Yes. Are there many planets in the Alpha Centauri star system that have other populations on them, that are populated?

That is normal everywhere. As a matter of fact, I have looked around your solar system, and even though you wouldn't consider the planets to be populated, they all seem to be populated to me—with the exception of one very close to the Sun, but even that one is populated to an extent; it's just populated at a different time. But from my perspective, that is not a factor. Planets have been populated at different times and by different beings, and even today, in different forms, focuses, they are *still* populated. You just are not able to be aware of that because of your inability to significantly, quickly travel to other planets and study things and so on. I think if your researchers, your educators—not simply scientists or military people in the scientific community, but your educators—were to travel to other planets, even, say, Mars, for example, you might find lots of artifacts. Even in some other places that are possible for you to walk about, you'd find lots of things.

So from your perception—no, from our perception—would these be in our past or our future? You can see both, right?

Yes, I can see both. If they are artifacts, they might very well be from the past. If, on the other hand . . . well, I think I'll just leave it at that.

Will we populate some of these planets eventually?

Possibly. It is natural for peoples who are curious to travel. The little people were curious, so they traveled, see? You are also curious. I might add that this is a human trait universally, but not everybody is that way. Some people are more curious; some people are less.

Ah, so we will go out eventually, you are saying. Eventually.

Certainly.

You Were Altered to Give You Endurance

Is there a home planet of humans?

You mean humans like yourself.

Ah, yes—one must be specific. Yes, not exactly like the Explorer Race humans, because we've been sort of rearranged, but regular humans, the ones who haven't been . . .

Well, what are regular humans? See, you don't know, do you? You've been hybridized so that you could endure the extremes of the weather, to say nothing of disease and so on, so that you would have a good chance of survival here, ruling out violence from human to human. But if you're asking what is the source human being from which you were created or hybridized—yes, there is a home planet, and you will likely go there someday. I will not say where. You will likely go there someday and be invited to be there. Most likely, those who will be invited first will be educators—not scientists per se, but people conversant and open to various types of language. So study languages, and it will help.

I like that word, "hybridized." I've always used it for the half-human, half-Zetas, but who would you say we are? Explain that a little bit.

You understand, if you were to, say, graft a branch of a tree onto a branch of another tree, you might get this kind of fruit that you're striving for, but after a time, the combination of the initial tree and the branch grafted might come up with a third thing. You might call that a hybrid. I'm not talking about chemical alteration, but gradual, gentle alteration.

Well, we've been told we have the DNA of, you know, the Pleiadians, the Orions, the Arcturians, the Sirians—all of the local people. Is that how you mean it?

No. I'm talking about how the human being was altered so that you could have sufficient endurance to survive on this planet.

Say more about that. How were we altered?

From what I can see, you were altered by some representatives of Creator. There's not much more to say. I'm not *your* guide. [Chuckles.] You're asking me questions about you, and I am not one of your guides.

I understand. Okay, I just wanted a different perspective on stuff that, you know, had been talked about before, but that was interesting. Why do you not want to say where our home planet is, when obviously the words won't mean anything to us?

Remember, it is not your home planet. I've talked about the type of being you were hybridized from, but you are not that. You are not that.

So this is our home planet?

I don't want this to sound uncomfortable, but the way you exist now, you have no home planet. You are in this form of existence in this life, but it is not your natural, native form, of course. The spirit leaves the body and you continue on in your life cycle or simply remain in spirit form.

Right. Well, we're an experiment, absolutely: the Explorer Race.

So you don't really have a home planet. You may, in time, when your civilization becomes benign, establish a home planet. But for now, you don't have one. Earth as you know it is not ever going to be your home planet—nor would she welcome it, considering how you have interacted with Earth. She is not angry at you; she recognizes that you are doing the best you can, but in order to be welcome on a planet and make it your home planet, you will have to be a benign civilization. In other words, you will have to be welcome. Planets are beings also.

Yes. So these beings to whom you are a guide—they also don't have compatriots, because they've changed their form, so are there others?

No, you're leaving something out. They are benign, so they do have a home planet that remained their home planet. They just changed their form, but they are benign, and they are still welcome on that planet that was their home. So I had to stop your question because you were forgetting an important part.

Practice Meeting Each Other as Equals

Are there other human-being types like the Alpha Centaurians that are this size, like twenty-two inches? Are there others, other human-being types, that are of this size that are on other planets?

Yes, there are some, but it's not typical. But there are some, yes.

Did these others start out that way, or did they change their size?

No, they started out that way.

Ah. So these are the only ones, then, who changed their size? That's very clever!

That's how it was possible for them to change their size; they were able to because of their "networking."

Oh! They knew about these other ones!

They knew about them, and they figured out a way to bring that about.

Ah! And how did they do that? DNA? How do you change your size?

That, I cannot say. I don't expect that you will ever do that on your planet, so it's not really relevant.

So they're friends now with these other . . . I mean, they interact with these other beings that they are now the same size as?

They interact with all other beings they meet in places where they feel welcome, period.

How wide is their . . . beyond the galaxy?

How wide is their sphere of interest? Beyond the galaxy, yes.

Uh-huh. So they've been there, then? They must have been there a long time, even before Earth was . . .

We're going to have to stop so the channel has enough voice. I will give a parting comment. There is great desire in some circles of your peoples on the Earth now to meet beings from other planets and have stimulating, eye-to-eye talks, so to speak. "How do you live?" and "This is how we live." To prepare for this, practice more and more with each other. Try to practice speaking to peoples in an equal way, meaning, "How do you live? What do you hold dear?" and share how you feel that way. Set aside an agenda and just practice with human beings on Earth as if you were an astronaut or as if they were one. This is fine training for you, and I believe it is why there is such a wide variety of interests and general appearances of people and different languages and different cuisine and so on. Practice with each other. I believe this is intended to prepare you to meet peoples from other places. Good night.

Thank you very much. Good life.

BEWARE OF A STAGED ET INVASION

Z-S-H-H-H-H and Grandfather

March 5, 2010

Greetings.

Welcome.

As you know, your planet has been isolated to some degree from the normal interactions of one planetary community to another. Partly, this has been done to protect the citizens of other planets because you are doing things that are so far removed from what they are doing that it could be harmful to them. I think you can guess what that might be. On the other hand, it has also been to protect you, because many times these beings from other planets are so unusual, so different, and specifically of such a variety that it might be just a little bit too much variety for the citizens of Earth.

You live in a varietal world with many different kinds of plants and, as you say, animals, but you have relegated these forms of life to categories that are deemed less than your own value. In this way, you do not have to deal with the potential that these are literally no different from extraterrestrials you might meet in terms of their difference to you. At their core being, animals and most but not all plants are from other planets. The ones that are healing plants for the human being are all native to Earth, and the animals most often found as beloved pets, while not native to Earth, have been on Earth for the longest time. So this insulation works both ways and is intended to serve a specific purpose as indicated.

To Begin Meeting ETs, You Need a Global Consensus

For a long time, your governments as they come and go in the different parts of your world have had the opportunity—sometimes just representatives and not everybody in a government—to interact with those from other planets: sometimes knowingly, sometimes not. The consensus over time has been that it would be important to wait until you have some form of global consensus, a global community that can speak for all peoples of the Earth—meaning, at this point, all human beings—so that any decision made will be adhered to, at least in a general sense, by the citizens of Earth. It will take this in order to have the means to welcome and interact with citizens from other worlds.

You will not be meeting citizens from other worlds who look that different from you in the beginning, though there has been much suggestion that you would. Do not assume that those who have contacted various citizens of your world in the past will be the ones who formally meet you as one planet community to another planet community. That is extremely unlikely. No, the citizens will look rather like you, though they might bring along citizens from other planets—or, more likely, a means to show you what civilizations look like that have human beings and most likely other beings interacting there as well as on other planets. This will give you an idea of what and who you might meet someday, a typical diplomatic interaction well known to diplomatic representatives in practice now all over the world—meaning how they communicate with each other.

When You Finally Meet ETs, Fear Will Have Nothing to Do with It

As a result of Earth having no global leader, there have been moments by different groups of belief and even fear that this was somehow going to threaten this or that group's authority or even their viability on Earth. Over time, various scenarios were worked out on the world now—not in a unified way, but in a way that could be counted on to create the greatest amount of anxiety over meeting beings from other worlds. Fear has been used for a great deal of time on your world to manipulate and control people. I don't have to tell you how that works; I'm sure you know.

These fears are still doing that job in your now time, but younger generations are more immune to such fears, having grown up with exposure to models of fear—meaning an awareness of how it works and how people are manipulated by it. This is not simply because they are more brilliant than their predecessors, but because they have been so totally, universally exposed through the advances in media in your time to various "entertainments" that are meant to frighten, but that also in the process—whether intentionally or

Ronald Reagan

"I couldn't help, at one point in my discussions privately with General Secretary Gorbachev, when you stop to think that we're all God's children, wherever we may live in the world, I couldn't help but say to him, just think how easy his task and mine might be in these meetings that we held if suddenly there was a threat to this world from some other species from another planet outside in the universe. We'd forget all the little local differences that we have between our countries, and we would find out once and for all that we really are all human beings here on this Earth together."

—White House transcript of "Remarks of the President to Fallston High School Students and Faculty," December 4, 1985

"In our obsession with antagonisms of the moment, we often forget how much unites all the members of humanity. Perhaps we need some outside, universal threat to make us recognize this common bond. I occasionally think how quickly our differences worldwide would vanish if we were facing an alien threat from outside this world."

—Speech to the United Nations General Assembly, 42nd General Assembly, September 21, 1987

unintentionally—on a cumulative basis teach how the fear model can control and manipulate. As a result, they see through it.

The advantage of this is that they, as well as generations that follow, are unlikely to fall for this. So those who wish to manipulate through such fears that have worked in the past . . . I'm not talking about a singular group here, you understand. I'm talking about the smallest groups all over the planet to larger groups, okay? Sometimes parents do this with their children, not intending to harm them, you understand, but trying to control their behaviors. The result is that there is a gradual consensus coming forth on how to advance the fear model to its zenith.

Curiously enough, as world leaders or heads of government sometimes do when they depart office, they like to make some statement that, in some cases, is generous to people, kind, or as is sometimes the case, sensational—almost like one might find in a large headline in a newspaper, something that catches your eye when you walk by and see it. Such a sensational announcement was made by a former President of the United States who has moved on to another plane of existence. This president announced that, "Wouldn't it be interesting if there were some threat from some place beyond Earth?—essentially laying out the model of the scenario. "Wouldn't it be interesting if this happened?"— I'm paraphrasing here. "Maybe the peoples of the Earth would unite."

Of course this president was calling partly on his previous career as a very well-known actor, and at the time, people thought he was just being humorous. But he was actually doing something that world leaders often do when they leave office—sometimes intentionally, other times to be sensational, but this president was doing it because, like many presidents before him, he was privy to various plans and possibilities. He saw, within that particular scenario he had read about while in office, a great danger, for as a man of vision and a sensitive man—though not everyone believed this of him—he felt that such a scenario played out in reality could keep people back from meeting what might be great friends, helpers, and even guides in the ways of life beyond Earth. So he took a chance to state such a thing—and it was a great chance, since that plan, even today, is guarded zealously.

It has been many years since that president spoke those words. A few people remember them; many people do not. But I'm mentioning it here because you are now under threat of such a plan being carried out. There have been little trial balloons, you might say, to see whether this plan would work, and those of you who are younger or in the community of computers and software know that the capacity to create things that are fictional and yet fantastic-looking—"fantastic" in the science-fiction sense—is quite available and can be done. Especially if there is a good budget for it, it can be done without any great struggle. One just has to be dedicated and have the budget and the staff to bring it about, to create something that looks real. But even though it looks real and can often fool experts, it is not only not real but intended to be that "scare" thing that this president spoke about. If that president were here today, he would say, "This is it! This is what I was talking about!"

I want to tell you now that when you finally do meet extraterrestrials on a global scale, you'll like them and they'll like you, and there won't be any fearmongering, manipulation, or control by them. They will be somewhat indulgent of the fact that some of the people on Earth may be a little shy and a little fearful. This will be understood by those from other planets, as they will be trained diplomats, you see.

As I said, they will look like you. Some of them might be a little taller than the average person, and some might be a little shorter than the average person, but you have that on your planet now. You won't see any diplomats who look like dogs or cats but talk your language—nothing like that. You won't see any frightening creatures who appear to be salivating when they look at you; those are all fictions meant to "entertain."

Any ET "Threats" Will Be Earth-Coordinated

This time you're living in is a time that is fraught with temptations to deceive. Granted, some of the deception is meant entirely for entertainment or is revealed quickly after it appears as being false. But some is meant to deceive and carry out a means to produce fear, control, manipulation, and blame. Be very vigilant now for such things. They will often be found in fields of study that have been looked at—granted, through various means of conditioning—as scams, such as the study of UFOs and their occupants, but in other fields as well, such as the study of "new life forms," as they're called, whether they are microbiological or just have escaped your detection, such as one might find in remote places like deep caves or at the bottom of a particularly deep portion of the sea, for instance. There has been some effort to see whether such forms of life can be found in near-space expeditions—meaning near your planet. These things sound like science fiction, but they are real.

I'm speaking to you today because I feel that the threat is imminent that there might be something staged to frighten you. Remember what I say today, that there will be no attempt to make a global contact—perhaps with more than one vehicle from other worlds—that will be intended to cause fear and frighten, manipulate, or attack. Since your world is largely insulated and protected, you see, it *cannot* happen. You are insulated and protected because you are doing different things here, eh? So *if that happens, it will be staged, and you must guard against that.* The means to do something based on a gradual usage of fictional and science-fictional elements, as one might find in moving pictures, movies, with the ships and death rays and all that kind of stuff, all of that can be artificially produced and can even be produced to a degree with weapons' technologies that exist today.

Be aware that even if something appears to be coming from space to raid your planet and fires some ray gun and even causes damage, it is entirely Earth-coordinated. That president long ago in your time who made that warning did so because of his unique—for a president—grasp of the difference between fiction and fact: If people understood that something was fiction, they could enjoy it and even think about it, as many theatrical productions attempt to do. They could watch it, enjoy it, but think about it and consider.

He could see the difference between doing something as entertainment about which people could say ultimately, "But still, it was theater," and something that is done to create blame, fear, control, and manipulation. He was also, to a degree, a student of history and had noted that such methods of blaming and fearmongering had been used in the past: If you claim that something has happened and you claim it loud and long enough, then people might be inclined to believe it. History is fraught with such blaming, and I will not go into it here. That is why he said what he did when he departed office. I want to underscore his statement.

Look for Fearmongering, Blame, and Manipulation

The issue is this: Such fearmongerings, which are still going on to control and manipulate, will go away in time. But you have yet some challenging times to go through. You have yet to become quite clear that all forms of life are deemed as equals and are just as sacred, one and the other, that this is meant by the Creator of this universe, and that you are here on this planet to discover that—even though you are cut off consciously, but not at the deep state, from your knowingness of this. You cannot be cut off completely, you see. Otherwise, your souls would starve, and they must be in connection with their true selves, which they are in deep sleep. If they have that cut off for even a week or so, then the soul becomes self-destructive. I think psychologists at the leading edge of research might understand what I'm talking about.

I wish to now say who I am. I am a spokesperson for many of the teachers who have come to your planet. Some of them have been deemed as religious figures, though much of that has been embroidered over the years as one might expect when a beloved teacher is somewhat idolized. But I am also a being who has helped to set up the means to insulate and protect your planet, not only from such interactions with extraterrestrials before you are ready, but also to keep those extraterrestrials who are sometimes a little too casual with the way they present themselves—and who are not yet trained in diplomacy to present themselves in a formal, safe way for you—away from your planet.

They are not harmful, but they are who they are, as they like to say, and they don't like to pretend to be anything else, eh? You can identify with that, some of you on the planet. Such personality types exist in space, so you will be able to look forward to meeting them. They are a lot of fun, and when you are ready to meet many different kinds of beings from other planets, you will have the opportunity to meet them. But that is a long way off.

So I have come to say that I am that being. I do not have a name as such, but very often in the spirit world, what you might find in your natural, safe way of being—meaning beyond this Earth as you are—that is the case. That is who I am. But if you wish, I will give you a name. I am . . . a moment. [Pause.] Z-S-H-H-H-H. I didn't want to give you that, because it sounded too much like that other being's name, but that's actually the name. One finds sounds sometimes in the world beyond spoken word, and sometimes one identifies sounds, feelings, brightness, and such other stimulations as a means to know one being from another, not entirely unlike on your planet, where you might identify some sounds with this and that being.

You said only one craft. Would it be triangular or round? What would be the shape of this purported ET-invasionary craft?

If I tell you, they'll use a different shape. [Chuckles.]

Oh! [Laughs.]

It's more the behaviors: the fearmongering, blaming, control, and manipulation as stated—all of that. It is more like that. It is not, "Here's what it's going to look like." If I say that, then they'll just use something different. That's why I am here: not to tell you exactly what's going to happen, but to warn you so that you will be able to identify what is and what isn't a little more easily. I think those who have sharp instincts and know what is and what isn't, how to know such things, will know on your own and will not need such guides as I have given you today. Such training, I believe, is going on through this channel and others through the books and the blogs.

You don't want to say the scenario.

If I do, then . . .

Then they'll change it.

I'd rather give landmarks that are simple and easy to remember, though in the beginning, in the first few moments, you might not remember them. But it will come back to you. You'll say, "Wait a minute; I've felt this way before," meaning when you were frightened and manipulated as a result. You'll say, "Wait! This can't have anything to do with real extraterrestrials. It must have something to do with Earth. Who's trying to control me?" and so on, eh?

Yes, very good. Are they just going to spread fear? They're not going to actually try to shoot at somebody, are they?

There are many possibilities. This is meant to warn the people of today, but given the media type that exists, this article might just appear in some more long-lasting form, eh? It's not just on the paper, and once it is on the Internet, it will be available as a cautionary message to all.

You said you were a spokesperson for many teachers who came to Earth. Why do the teachers need a special spokesperson?

If any one teacher spoke, other peoples of Earth would feel, "Oh, that's not our teacher."

Oh! I see, you mean like a representative of all the teachers?

That's right. I have not come here to frighten you. Rather, I am here because I feel you are ready to hear these things and to consider them. I am not saying you must believe it. I am saying that it is something to thoughtfully consider, to observe as you go through life how you may be getting manipulated at times, sometimes by people who are afraid of you. Some of you might say, "What? Afraid of me? Why?" It's because people have been conditioned by life and also by previous manipulations they've been exposed to, to be frightened of those around them. So even though you may not feel that you're particularly fearful—meaning that people would be frightened by being in your presence—they might be simply because of their conditioning and/or their situations in life.

Know that the reason I am speaking to you about this matter today is that such blaming and fearmongering is still rife in your land on Earth. So when you hear, as you may, that this person did this and this person did that or she said this or he said that, look at those who are saying it. They might very well believe it, eh? If they believe it, then perhaps they have been manipulated.

Seek Out for Yourself What Is Real

Don't assume that all warnings are untruthful. After all, you hear warnings every day: "A storm is coming. Seek shelter. Take an umbrella to work." These warnings are well intended and meant to be of service. But if warnings come along that say, "She is the cause of all your troubles," or "He did it, and others like him should be assumed to be a danger to you"—in other words, people you don't know and have never met—well, then start to consider, "Am I being manipulated by those who may not even understand that they're manipulating? Perhaps they've already been manipulated, and they really believe it. But how can this be true? How can every single person—human beings who have free will, though not always freedom of this or that sort—how can we know what is so? Are they trying to frighten us, or are they simply conditioned and believe what they have been told?"

Begin to use something else. Don't blame the person who may be blaming. Say this to yourself: "How can I know? What is real for me?" Begin practicing your own instincts, your own means to know through the use of your physical self. So learn how to use your instincts physically, as the animals use them in the forest or other places, and you will then be able to separate, as they say, the wheat from the chaff. It is important as a step of self-empowerment, yes, but also as a means to know what is real and what is not real. Do not blame the rumormonger; just seek out for yourself what is real and what is not real. You are born with certain capacities to do this, to discover what is real and "right for me," not who is wrong, what is false, but what is "real for me"—in other words, instinct. "Who is best for me to be near now?" This is a matter of instinct. If someone is not best for you to be near, it's not that this person is bad, but that it's best to be near others. No blaming. I just wanted to add that, as such an addition can be useful.

I also want to say that you are being trusted now to know these things because you are ready—especially those of you from the younger generations—to break the chains that tie you to a past of fear, blaming, conditioning, manipulation, and violence. Those of you who are of older generations can consider this as well. Good night.

Thank you. Thank you for coming.

How to Know

This text is a transcription of Grandfather's three-part *How to Know* video series. For the original online videos of these sessions, see http://www.youtube.com/user/BenevolentMagic, "How to Know," Parts 1 through 3.

How to Know, Part 1
January 4, 2010

Greetings. This is Grandfather. Now, I have spoken about this before, but I want to give you more details. I will do a brief recapitulation, though, so some of you who have not seen all these videos can catch up. There is a way by which you can know what is right for you at any given moment—the question could be asked, you see—or what is better for others. I don't want you to think about it as being wrong; it might just be something that is better for others and not for you, at least not at that time you're asking the question. So many questions come up in our lives, don't they? And we really would like to have a way that we can at least be sure—or if not sure, have a way that is always with us, kind of like a friend to give us advice we can trust. That friend can be your physical body.

I want you to practice something. It's going to take a couple or three weeks for some of you to get it, but others will get it right off. That's just how it works. Some of you may not be able to get it, and you'll have to keep trying. So here's what to do: Take your hands—either hand, or both is even better—and put them on your chest, just lying flat on your chest. You can cross your hands if you want to, but you don't have to. Then I want you to focus on or put your physical attention into your physical chest of your body and try to produce or create a physical heat that you can feel, all right? This isn't a visualization; it's not a thought. It's entirely physical. When you get to that heat, just know that that is your body's way of giving you love. And the way it can be applied to a decision I'll tell you in a moment. But for right now, practice that heat. When you get good at it, you won't have to put your hands on your chest, but you can always do that if that feels better.

Now, when you do get good at it and you can feel that heat or bring it up just about every time you try, then this is what to do: First, pick a question that's innocuous, not important, like you're going to the movies and should you go to this one or should you go to that one—something like that. Or you're going to go out for dinner and want to know if you should get steak or chicken—something like that. Or, "Should I get a burger or should I get a fish fry?" Something like that, okay? A simple thing, something that you would normally make as a decision in your mind.

Before you go out, go someplace on your own where you can sit quietly and put the question very simply, and say, "I am asking," you would say this: "Would it be good for me to go to this movie?" And you say the name of the movie. Then you see if there's heat. If the heat comes up, that means there's love for you, and you can interpret that as, "Yes, that would be a good movie."

Then pick another movie, including two or three movies—one after the other so you're asking the question for each one—that you wouldn't normally go to. Just take time and wait a couple of minutes between each one, and when the warmth comes up, if it feels good, just stay with it for a while. But eventually let it go, and then ask, "Would it be good for me now to go to this movie?" Then go on. If it's the case of a restaurant or even a fast-food place, do the same thing before you go. If you're in your car, that's okay, but make sure you're not distracted and not driving. You have to be still and quiet to do this, so if you have a cell phone, turn the ringer off.

Then you might get three or four responses—I'm going to use movies for this example. The one you have the greatest heat for, that's the one to go to. Now, you might say to yourself—or to me, if you were here—"Well, Grandfather, I don't really like that kind of movie, you know? It's not something I normally go to." But keep this in mind: You might have a good experience, or maybe something will happen on the way to the movie so that you will know, "This was intended to happen. This is a good thing for me." You might not even wind up going to the movie at all. Now, if it's a movie that's really something terrible or frightening, you don't have to go. You can be pretty sure it's something that's meant to happen on the way to the movie, or maybe even in the lobby. So that's how to get started, okay?

How to Know, Part 2
January 8, 2010

This time, I want to talk about another aspect. Suppose you asked a question, whatever it may be, and you get an uncomfortable feeling in your body. It could be a tightness, just a discomfort that wasn't there until you asked the question. Then you'll know that that is not for you at that time. You could say, since we're talking about heat and that's love, that there's no love for you to do that at this time. And it might also be that you could ask that same question another time, perhaps about something slightly different, and there would be love to do that for you—or you could just call that a yes. So when there is an uncomfortable feeling, then you know that that's a no, or no love, okay? So there's that.

After you do those kinds of basic questions, I want you to begin to integrate this—only if you wish, if it's working for you; don't do it unless you can get the heat and you can actually feel it, all right? So try this: For those of you who work in offices or maybe just go out on a Friday or Saturday night, go to your closet and look at two or three different items that you think you might wear. Men, if you have ties, that's okay, or different colored shorts—okay, that's fine. Women, you'll have different dresses or tops, okay? So pick out the ones you think might be good and set those on a different place in the closet.

Then you can either take the hanger with the item off the rail or whatever it's hanging on and pull it toward your body and say, "Would this be good for me to wear now?" And if you get heat, then set it someplace where you have it in the pile, so to speak, of "possibles," and go right on through everything else to see if you get heat. The one you get the most heat for is the right thing to wear for you at that time.

Sometimes, it might surprise you. For instance, you might not get heat for any of them, or it might just be a very slight warmth. Then you might look in the closet again, and instead of pulling everything out, you would just take like a sleeve or a portion of the garment and pull it toward you and ask the question, and it might just be that it would be better for you to wear that particular garment at that time.

Now, sometimes the heat you'll get in that situation might be for something that's totally inappropriate. Say, you're going out to dinner and your bathing suit feels just right. Well, obviously, you know that's not right, but it could be the color of the bathing suit that you're responding to. So then look at the color and see what else you can find that's that color or close to it, and try those items. I want you to do it this way with these things that are not world shaking, all right? By "world shaking," I mean choosing this person over that person, say, as a steady partner to date or as a lover, you understand? That would be more world shaking. Or for those of you who have major decisions to make—that would be world shaking, all right? Don't do any of that for the first three months of successfully doing this work. Just keep it to innocuous things like, "What should I eat?"

By the way, if you're in a restaurant and you get good at this, what you can do is without even asking a question, you can just point to something on the menu and just say the question quietly to yourself and then pull your hand back. You point; "Is it that," you might say, "Is this the best for me?" You can whisper it, or you can think it—for some of you, that will work—and that could help. This is particularly helpful for those of you who go to restaurants and sometimes don't feel well afterward. You might want to get something, but when you point to it on the menu, you get a bad feeling in your body. You'll know that—that day, at that time—that item isn't good for you, okay? Don't assume it's toxic. It might just be that your body's not ready for that at that time.

So make only those kinds of decisions for the first three months when this thing is working. After those three months, you can begin, if you wish, to make decisions about more serious questions, but give it plenty of practice.

How to Know, Part 3
January 12, 2010

There is another way you can use this. At this point, when you are going to apply it to things like this, make sure you've been doing this successfully for at least three to four months. This is particularly useful when you're not sure about something that might be safe or not safe. But it could also very well mean that there is an opportunity that you might otherwise have missed.

This is about routing—where to go, how to get there, all right? So say you already know where you're going to go. The destination feels good to you, but there's more than one route to take. Then you might ask, "Would it be good for me to go . . ." and then you say the way that you are mentioning, see how much heat there is, and also notice if it feels uncomfortable. If it feels uncomfortable, definitely do not go that way, and go right on through the possible routes. It might happen that the route where there is the most warmth turns out to be a route that's not direct, not the way you would normally go. This probably means there's a reason why you ought to arrive at a little different time or from a different direction, or possibly there will be an opportunity for you that you might not otherwise have acquired. So that's another way to use it.

Sometimes you might be walking somewhere or driving somewhere, and you're not sure where you're going. This is what to do: Say you've got your hands on the wheel. Wait until you've been doing this successfully for at least five or six months before trying this, but you can do basically this: Keep your eyes on the road, and don't be thinking, "Is it best to go this way or is it best to go that way," kind of stuff, all right? Rather, just point this way, this way, this way, or this way [points in various directions]. Give yourself plenty of lead time. You can say a word, for instance. I'm going to pick a name of a street: First Street or Eighth Street, something like that, okay? And see if you get heat.

Practice this for a while before you're in traffic or in some situation. I'll tell you how to practice it: Go to a parking lot on a day when there are no cars there, or very few—particularly one that has rows that are numbered—and try it there. Say, you're driving along very slowly. Pay attention to the way you're going, because you never know who might be there. Do it in the daytime when you have the best light. Then say, "Row A, Row C" [points in various directions], something like that, and fine-tune it, okay?

Now, there are a lot of other ways to use this, but that's enough for now. I do want to give you a bonus, though: Many of you work in situations or have to go or be in situations that are very stressful and have a lot of tension. And sometimes you're around people you would rather not be around, and when you come home, you're just exhausted. Normally, you'd take a shower or a bath if you could and sort of wash that stuff away, but there's something else you can do:

Sit down in that comfortable chair you have or even lie down on the bed if you like. Turn off the ringers on the phone so you won't be interrupted, and do the heart-warmth exercise. Now, when that warmth comes up—and it might come up in some other part of your body, for those of you who have that experience, that's okay—go into it and feel it more, and stay with it as long as you can. What it does is it just transforms and pushes all that stuff out of your body, just as if it were energy, which it really is. And it is refreshing; it will help you to transform those extremes of the day, and it'll be a lot easier to let go. This is particularly important if you have a very stressful job or one in which things come up that are just hard to bear. Good life.

—Grandfather

ETS LAND IN SOVIET UNION SEPTEMBER 1989

BERLIN WALL GOES DOWN NOVEMBER 1989

Zoosh and Overseer of Cyclops-Like Beings

March 8, 2010

This is Zoosh. Are you there?

Yes!

I'm going to act as a filter. That being's energy [the extraterrestrial being who had landed his ship in Voronezh, Russia, in 1989 in front of witnesses] is not compatible with Robby's body. So it's possible that I will be talking at times, but when we educate that being as to how to communicate in this fashion—for that being has never done this, which is not unusual—then we will see. It's not a problem as far as the communication goes, what would be said, but with the energy of the being, there is a serious problem there. I know you'd be perfectly happy to talk to me, but that's not the process here, is it?

What I would prefer is to expand on things that were visits from a benevolent future rather than something associated with the past timeline. Do you understand what I'm trying to say? That thing there, the event you refer to, is associated with the past timeline, and it's thoroughly entrenched in that. It's up to you, but do you have an alternative?

No, but I can understand what you're saying. It's just that a nine-foot-tall being with a physical third eye in the middle of his forehead sounds kind of interesting. He talked to the people in that city in Russia in their own dialect. Newspaper people were there from all over the world. It was in the Phoenix newspaper and many other newspapers around the world. But if it's not possible . . .

A moment. [Pause.] We may be able to do it as long as there is absolutely

141

no political reference. This whole thing about the then leader of the Soviet Union and his family is out. Do you understand? But we may be able to comment. Let's see. [Pause.] No, that being's energy is just not compatible with Robby. We connected to the being there for a moment. He's on a ship somewhere. But the energy is not compatible nor is the being able to perform this way, to channel through another being, so that's out. You're going to run into this again. Also remember Robby's health, okay? You know Robby has always said he can channel anyone or anything that is . . . what?

Compatible with him.

This situation and being is not compatible, so that's that. However, there's another way around this. [Pause.] All right, we have a solution. Someone has reported that he is the overseer of these beings—which I would be inclined to assume is a teacher or guide or something like that—and I feel his energy will be compatible with Robby.

You're wonderful.

So mark that up to a chat that you and I just had, and let's try again.

Thank you very much. I'm really curious.

These Beings Are Not Biologically Compatible with You

Greetings.

Greetings!

I will say a few things, but I am also trying to soothe the channel's body, which was damaged from that attempt. You must be careful. In the future and on an ongoing basis, you will have to add to your requests that the being who comes through be compatible with the channel. This is not a living prayer; it is a setting of the intention. That has been a need of long standing, but it has not built up to that point until this time.

Now I will say a little bit about these beings. These beings are quite tall, but there are a few folks, Earth people, who are almost that tall on Earth at this time. The famous story about the Cyclops is very loosely based on a sighting of these beings and an illustration of them. It was a story built up on that. You have to remember that authors from the past or the present, however famed they are, are inclined to take an incident and build it up into a story that will entertain, especially if such stories written are intended to have a greater meaning.

In those days of the famous writer, it was not typical for human beings on Earth then to be much over five feet tall. If they were to suddenly meet someone who was about nine feet tall, they would certainly consider that being to be a giant—just as if you were to meet someone who was four feet taller than you, you would think of that being as a giant, would you not? So the incident that did happen in those Homeric times was simply a real thing: These beings had visited in those times as well. I thought I'd bring that up because you might find old references to such a thing, and everybody assumes it's associated with that story [chuckles]. But some of those references are associated in and around that area with the actual visitation of these beings, you see? So that's a very interesting aside for your readers.

These beings come from a distant planet, and they do not recognize political boundaries. So they'd be just as inclined to land anywhere where they felt that they would not be attacked. Their appearance, as you would see them if you were in their presence on Earth, is not exactly the way they look when they are not around human beings. They look a little different, and their physical makeup, biologically, would not be compatible with yours—meaning that their physiology, the way their bodies work, is different.

I will give you an example that you can completely and readily understand. Think of this in terms of your bacteriologicals that would prompt a disorder of the intestines—not permanent, but say, for a few days. You would call it some sort of a . . . what would you call that?

Oh, maybe a stomachache, which could give you a headache, or intestinal discomfort or diarrhea?

Yes, something like what you would call a stomachache. But a bacteriological like that would promote a symptomology in your physical body of malaise, discomfort, and upset with the stomach, intestines, and so on. That is essentially the inner mechanism of their digestive systems, so you can see how there is an incompatibility. So in order to simply get off the ship and be around the human being, there has to be an alteration in their appearances, having nothing to do with the way the head looks, and a significant amount of shielding beyond that which the being itself would need in order to protect any and all human beings while visiting the planet.

Generally speaking, these beings do not visit planets with human beings, but they will come if there is some political need. They are very good at universally understanding politics. They are very understanding—very analytical, mentally—and they can grasp innuendos. If you had one of these beings in your state department—you couldn't, but theoretically—you would be able to engage diplomatically all over the universe, because they're very good at that. They cannot interact, however, with you directly, and I think they've come to that conclusion.

Partly what goes on is that if you're communicating with them—say, on

Earth; it's been done—generally speaking, everyone who is present hears, meaning understands, because sometimes you hear something you don't understand. So you would hear and understand what the being is saying in terms that are completely compatible with you. Even if your language were all the same, you might come from different walks of life, you might use different slang or dialects, and all of that. Or if there are other completely different languages and so on, you would hear and understand them in your own manner of speaking and understanding. This is very helpful as a political go-between. *It's fantastic.*

The ET's Passion Was Perceived as a Threat

The visit [to Voronezh, Russia] was made at that time [1989] because of the pending change coming for that part of the world and the belief by these beings that it could be done without too much bloodshed—perhaps none. The discussion with the leader of that group of countries did take place—and I am not going to refer to that person by name—and the request was made that any change in their system be bloodless, meaning no battle, no struggle to maintain control, all of that stuff. It wasn't made with a threat. However—and this is important—keep in mind that the nature of the emanation from the extraterrestrial visitor that shielded the human being was, if that ET being would speak with any passion at all . . . these ET beings always try to dissuade peoples from fighting and harming each other, and they're passionate about that. You know yourself, as a human being, that when human beings get passionate about something they are speaking about, their energy levels rise, and you can feel more emanations from them, even if they're not near you. Then you respond in kind if you agree with them—or also if you don't.

When those beings would speak passionately about something, the radiations from them would actually go through the garments, the things they all wore to insulate and protect the human beings, and I don't have to tell you what happened. These beings were speaking passionately about something, and suddenly all the human beings felt bad; they felt uncomfortable. Some of them almost felt sick. So when the beings were saying something they passionately believed in—and these beings are not violent—everybody suddenly felt sick from what they were saying, even though their words sounded perfectly fine. What would you think if your body suddenly felt like that when somebody—looking like that, different from you—was talking? You would be scared.

Everyone was certainly scared, because they felt that there was a threat implied. See, this is part of the problem that occurred in the past in those

Homeric times as well. That's why there was such a gap in their visits in years, because they went there and the same thing happened: They were speaking passionately about battles of the time and trying to talk people out of such things, but the moment they spoke passionately, everybody started to feel sick and fearful, like they were being threatened. The upshot of that—I like that word: upshot—is that it made people more frightened when the beings went away, and they were more inclined to build up forts and walls and so on.

Sometimes fortifications and armies in Homeric times happened not only because of interactions from one warring group of humans to another but also because of the unintentional radiation of energy from an otherwise peaceful extraterrestrial who forgot for a moment that if he got passionate and spoke about something that way, people would not feel good. This didn't have anything to do with the visitor's feelings toward them but was simply due to the biological fact of incompatibility between species. I'm bringing up all of this medical stuff partly because the initial attempt to channel this being or a contemporary caused the channel to feel temporarily sick.

I understand now.

That's important to know, because there may be times when your astronauts travel to other places where you'll see beings you really want to communicate with. They may look like the visitors we're talking about today or they may look different. But I'm suggesting right now to the astronauts that if they get that feeling to immediately just make some diplomatic disconnect with that group of beings, indicate why—a preprogrammed message would be useful—and move on. Others will be able to give you the same kind of information that you may have gotten from these beings, so don't try and fight it, okay? If there's an incompatibility, you can be sure there's a good reason.

This Is Why the Wall Came Down without Much of a Bang

What followed the visit of these beings who are the origin of the Cyclops stories was the bringing down of the Berlin Wall. So obviously the leaders in Russia did not react to the fear in the sense of putting up more barriers or building more fortifications.

Go back a step. What did they react to? They reacted to the felt threat. You have to think about that. This is a conglomerate of countries with a fearsome army and military—at the time, a world power, militarily speaking, and in some circles, diplomatically speaking—and with a whole way of government slightly different from other ways (in some ways, more compassionate and in other ways not). The core belief of the system was to try and create a more equal distribution of well-being, but it did not always work that way.

Then in their communication with these ET beings, they felt that there was some terrible threat not just to the parties involved in the communication but to the country as a whole.

Remember, if you as an individual were to speak passionately about something you strongly believed in, you might be inclined to feel things but not say them out loud. How many times have you done this or experienced it? But these were beings who can instantly communicate to all around them what they are saying, and they also instantly communicate what they are feeling—and all the beings around understand it in their own concepts of communication, as I mentioned before. If you have someone who feels profoundly passionate against violence, then that's one of the things that is immediately broadcast—whether you are against something or for something doesn't make any difference. The thing that you are against in that case, as the visitor, is still broadcast as the heading. The heading would be "Violence," and the subheading would be "Against." Do you understand?

The heading, so to speak [chuckles], would be what is broadcast. Then people are suddenly sick with the fear of violence that must be way beyond their capacity to struggle against—because look at the vehicle! Look at the way it was able to land, no matter what they did. I can assure you [chuckles] that in those days, when a vehicle came in for a landing in your country . . . can you imagine for a moment if a foreign vehicle [chuckles] came in for a landing in the United States today? Do you think everybody would just say, "Oh, howdy"?

Nope. War planes and weapons.

That's right. There would be some resistance and at least an attempt to escort the vehicle to some place as secure as possible.

Oh! See, I didn't hear that in this talk. So the visitors just came down in their craft despite the best efforts of the Russian military!

Exactly. So the point is that the people felt, "There is nothing we can do to combat these individuals." We're talking about people who are strong here; I'm not talking about strictly diplomats. We're talking about soldiers all over the place. We're talking about military people of high rank with much experience in battle. Everybody felt sick, just that terrible feeling a person might get when exposed to violence that is absolutely out of his or her control. The human being tends to get a nauseous, sick feeling within.

So that is why when the Berlin Wall came down, you'll note at the time that the soldiers—the border people representing the Soviet Union on the other side of the Wall—had kind of a blank look on their faces, a "what do we do about this?" look. If you read the reports—some people will, and some people who read this might even have been there—one of the initial things that went on was this sort of blank look, this "what do we do?" look, and a sort of shrinking back. Then after that moment passed, there were other things. But that initial look at people tearing down the Wall was one of shock, fear and "what shall we do?"—as one might normally go to ask a question, spoken or otherwise, in some branch of the service. So that's why the Wall came down without much of a bang.

In his presentation, Wendelle Stevens said the ET craft had come in six days in a row with the same altitude and from the same direction, as if they were going to land, but they didn't. So there were newspaper people there from all over the world, there were military people with weapons, and there were children and all sorts of people watching when they did land in the park on the seventh day.

I'm just going to say that every single time they came in, they were greeted [chuckles] as one might expect.

Ah, they were shot at as the military attempted to keep them from landing.

I think there was also a little allusion going on there to the "seventh day." Hmm? What does that sound like?

[Chuckles.] Like you can't touch us, so quit trying.

No.

Oh, creation.

That's right. It sounds like a significant number from the story of creation in the Bible. But let's just say that I'm going to gloss over that one.

All right. Then in this report, it said that the KGB came up and arrested the captain when he got out of the ship. But the captain came back in an hour, so it was a very short meeting with the Russians.

It's not unreasonable to [chuckles] put somebody under arrest in a situation like this. It would be like, "Would you come with me, sir?" and if they didn't come, then, "You're under arrest, please come with me." [Laughs.] And as any good diplomat might do, his response was, "Oh, certainly."

These Beings Seek Resolution through Compromise

Can you say where these beings are from: what galaxy, what planet, what part of the universe?

I don't want to say anything that would make it possible for a people as curious as you are to seek them out and say, "Well, let's go and find out!" Going and finding out would just cause problems for any member of the human race.

Okay. You have always been their guide, their teacher?

Not always. I am one of their main guides, but they have others. I was brought in as a consultant.

On the subject of what?

On the subject of purpose. The people wanted to have a purpose, and they needed a purpose beyond their own capabilities. So I came in, and I observed who and what they were, what they were able to do. I realized that they could start a program of diplomatic training because they were very good at helping people resolve their disputes. It just turns out that they're not very good when speaking to the human being when they get passionate about something—because of the biological incompatibility.

Oh, but with everyone else, they're fine?

With everybody else, they feel fine, but as with any species of human being anywhere in the universe . . . human beings are profoundly receptive, even more so than some other species, so one must be very careful communicating to human beings because their receptors are always up. Even if they're shielded in a steel box, so to speak, the receptors are always up, because the core physical attribute of the human being is instinct. Instinct requires a radiated receptive field that can go out from a matter of feet or meters, you might say, to yards or kilometers or beyond. It can go out for miles and miles. A human being's instinct can actually reach to other planets. Though you don't use it that way, you could.

If the astronauts use it that way, they will know what to avoid and where to go. Just a little tip for your space travel times: no machine or mechanism can ever substitute for the sense or the sensitivity of a human being's receptive instinct. So astronauts, cosmonauts, whatever you call yourselves, train to use your instincts more, and you will know where to go. Even if you're ordered to go someplace because "Oh, that looks interesting!" to people on the ground [chuckles], if it doesn't feel good to you, then . . .

Don't go there.

Don't go there. That's right. It might very well look wonderful but not be so wonderful for the human being.

Do these beings go to other places and diplomatically bring peace or get people together? What are some of the successes they've had?

Since wars are not much of a factor in the universe, the way that works in other places is that they really help to establish trading partners, partners who might not normally consider trading with each other. Even though there is something about the products involved or the services perhaps that is interesting, there is still a feeling of, "Well, I don't know about them," and so on. That does exist. [Chuckles.] So that's what they do, mostly. But if there are even what you might call slight misunderstandings from your perception, which to other places in the universe might feel like a major problem, they'll go in and they'll help to resolve it in the way diplomats have been resolving these things in time-honored ways on your own planet: through compromise, getting people together, finding common ground, the common principles. These principles work universally.

Obviously, their craft have the ability to deflect anything that the human beings on the planet at this time can throw at them, right?

At that time, yes. And believe me, exotic things were attempted.

[Laughs.] Okay. Are the beings themselves that impervious also?

If they're wearing the shielded garment, which is especially shielded to protect the human being, they would appear to be invulnerable.

Now, you talked about humans being receptive, but in our understanding, a third eye is a form of being receptive. How does that work with them? Why do they have it? How do they use it?

I can't say that, but I will say that it helps them to take in and understand the slightest nuances, even though they would be shielded. Keep in mind, their garment would shield them on this planet, at least somewhat. But think of it this way: Say you were inside a tank and you had all this thickness of metal around you. It might be more difficult to understand those who are standing on the outside of the tank. You don't see them, but they're out there, and you know they're out there, and you're trying to understand their feelings. So say you're out of the tank and you're one of the beings, the visitors, but you have a shield around you that is even stronger than that tank. Then there needs to be something extra by which you can perceive. So that's how they use it.

That's amazing. Do they travel all over—not just this universe, but other universes?

No, just this universe.

People were so amazed that these beings could get out of their craft and speak to the audience in a way that everyone understood in their local dialects. How did they do that?

It's not that difficult when it comes naturally to them. On their home planet, the reason they all get along so well to the point of the tiniest nuance—aside from the fact that getting along is typical in the universe [chuckles]—is that this ability to communicate is a natural capability on their part. And just like beings everywhere else in the universe—which is kind of funny, but true—they naturally assumed that everyone was like that.

That's why I was called in. They wanted to do something, they wanted to go somewhere, they wanted to have a purpose, and I'm pretty good at purposing. So they called me in because they assumed that the way they were was the way everyone was. I informed them that not everyone is like this and perhaps that could be used for diplomacy, and they said, "What? Everyone isn't like this?"

That is almost universal. I've consulted with beings on other planets at other times, and unless they've been established for a long time in interacting with others, which everyone isn't, it's just amazing how everyone has that attitude. It's really quite charming. It doesn't matter what species we're talking about—everybody has that attitude.

"I feel this way; therefore, you must. We're alike." Yes.

Well, and that's the assumption because it's all you've ever known.

Well, it's your perception and your experience. I mean, how can you know anything else than your own experience?

It's really rather sweet.

So you consult with them, but what do you do the rest of the time?

Well, I find that to be satisfactory. Do you mean, do I roast chestnuts over an open flame and put my feet up on the barrel and swap stories? No.

[Laughs.] You know Zoosh!

Yes, I devote myself to whatever I am doing. I do not need any part-time activities.

Okay, but before you worked with these beings, what were you doing?

Oh, this isn't about us. It isn't about me, okay? (I am more than one.) This is about the beings. So let's keep it to the focus.

The Russian Leaders Changed the History

So what else can we say about these beings? I mean, this is awesome! They come to the planet, and they change the entire history of the . . .

No, they didn't change history. They had an idea of what was coming, and what they did is that they softened things. They had a chat with the then head of the country, of the group of countries, and they said, "Look, this is going to happen. Your country's system is going to change," and so on—a little glimpse ahead. They said, "This can happen gently and you can allow it to happen gently, or it can happen harshly and it can go in a terrible direction."

If someone tells you that you're going to have terrible losses and great suffering in your country and other countries as well because of atomic warfare, you're going to pay attention. Remember, we're talking about a country that suffered terribly during World War II. The United States was spared that—granted, there was the loss of soldiers and civilians and so on, to a degree, but we're talking about a catastrophe.

There were many people still alive in this country the aliens visited who could remember that, so the idea of millions and millions of people suffering . . . it was an easy decision to make. "Well, let's do it gently, if possible. But we'd like to make sure that our peoples have an improved style of life, quality of life and so on." "Oh, yes. Absolutely. Why don't you try it this way, like that?"—I'm glossing over it a bit. So the head of the government was informed, and of course, he had other people with him there too. We're talking about a group of people informed, and the head of the government was there, where the visitors said, "And it can be like this or it can be like that."

Let's just say that the people in that part of the world, they changed history, not these ETs. They wouldn't want credit. They said, "This is what's going to happen, but it's up to you. You can change it by reacting in a way you might not normally react." A lot of people seem to think that the Russian peoples, the military, the authorities just threw up their hands and said, "Whatever," when the country changed over gradually from one thing to another thing, now sort of patterned somewhat in the Western style. But it's because they had heart for their people and, to an extent, for others. They're the ones who changed it and need to be given all the credit.

But truly the Cold War would have ended up then in an atomic war? That's the way it looked to everyone outside the planet?

It wasn't strictly between the then-assumed competitors of the U.S. and the Soviet Union. Others were involved, and I'm not going to go into the scenario. It doesn't make any difference if the result is the same. It's just that one thing would lead to another, certain things would happen, some of them surprising, and before you know it, boom. But the result is the same: misery, suffering, unendurable pain, death. "Or you could try this instead" would be the diplomatic solution. Since the Soviet Union had heart for the people, they tried that instead. So they are to be given the credit.

Wow! I mean, this is really big! I never knew this.

The visitors went to that country and those people because they felt that those people would be the most likely ones in that country to make the most benevolent choice. And they did. Now we need to stop.

I thank you very much for coming in. How did that happen? Did you volunteer when we were casting around for ways to do this?

Yes. Not immediately, because I was busy.

Ah. I thank you very, very much.

I'm going to make a closing remark.

Please.

I'd like you all to consider the fine art of diplomacy. Study if you're in school, or read about it if you're not. This is a wonderful thing to know and can be applied on a day-to-day basis between friends, family, and even people you don't know. I think it is something that could be of great benefit to you all. May you have the most benevolent life.

Good life to you.

THE 19TH ANNUAL
UFO CONGRESS CONVENTION
THE GORBACHEV
CONTACT

Wendelle Stevens

February 2010

The following excerpt is transcribed from a DVD recording of Wendelle Stevens' talk for the 19th Annual International UFO Congress February 2010, www.ufocongress.com.

Good afternoon. My name is Wendelle Stevens, Lieutenant Colonel of the United States Air Force, retired.

Now, I wonder how many of you remember this picture or similar [shows black-and-white printout of newspaper picture of UFO craft with the title "Soviets Take UFO"] that appeared in your newspapers way back in 1989–1990 (Fig. 1). This is a painting of a Russian landing at Voronezh, Russia, a provincial capitol 500 miles south of Moscow. Now, this is what appeared in the Phoenix newspaper [shows black-and-white printout of newspaper article titled "Captain Prisoner," Fig. 2]. This was printed on the front page. It says "UFO Captain taken prisoner by the KGB." We couldn't get the whole thing—the original microfiche had been destroyed, and we can't get copies of it anymore; we'd love to have them. But everybody in the Arizona area saw that headline and read those papers. Here's another page from the same [shows another page of article]. And this was describing a landing that took place by this silver sphere in the provincial capitol city of Voronezh in Russia in 1989, but there was a considerable preface to this that we're going to get into in a little bit here.

Now, the beings that got out of that craft when it landed: A nine-foot-tall being got out of the craft in a red coverall suit [shows drawing of very tall being next to a human], and he talked to the crowd in the local Russian dialect, perfectly expressed. And he talked to 400 eyewitnesses around the park there and asked them to bring a leader to the park, and they did; they brought the mayor of the city.

While the mayor is standing there, talking to the giant in the native dialect of Voronezh, a KGB truck drove up.

Wendelle Stevens shows printout of news story "Soviets Take UFO.

Officers got out, arrested the giant, started loading him into the van—a big van. And one of them hit him on the back with a baton as he was getting in, but he went in with no resistance at all—probably could have picked the truck up, if he wanted to—and went aboard, and they drove off with him.

When he left, two more came out of the craft dressed in silvery suits. They talked to the crowd in perfect local dialect also and discussed things with them. They talked to various of the stronger members of the crowd. There was a twelve-year-old that began screaming something, and they turned a beam on him and he disappeared, vaporized away. And the crowd was aghast at what happened to him, and they thought that the beings had killed the boy. But half an hour later, the boy appeared, walking around in the crowd again. He was now calm and happy, and he was in good health. So whatever they did was a temporary thing to get control of him and put him back in a normal state.

This caused a big upset. The reason it got in newspapers all over the world was because there were approaches six days in advance. There were approaches on the city of Voronezh by the same craft that came in at the same altitude, the same directions. [Reads from paper]: "For the six previous days, it came in from the same approach, the same direction, the same speed, the same angles—six days in a row. And groups all over the world were waiting, including the Russian military, with helicopters, camera equipment and ground surveillance teams," all waiting.

Newspaper people had gathered from all around the world, and there was pool reporters from UPS there that took pictures and put it on the news wires, and that's why it went all around the world. There was a substantial publicity

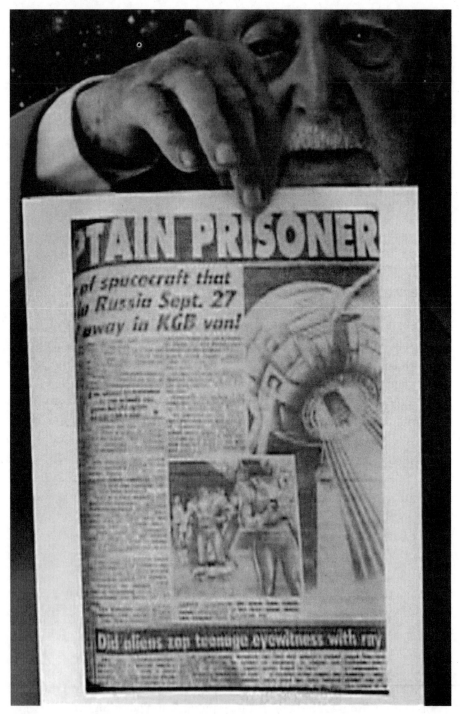

Stevens holds up printout of "Captain Prisoner."

organization there on hand when this landing at Voronezh took place. So we have to wonder if it was staged for a particular reason or not.

[Continues reading]: "On the seventh day, the approach continued, and the pulsating ball of plasma light dimmed down to a silvery metallic sphere about thirty meters in diameter and landed in the central park in the middle of Voronezh before the astonished gaze of over 400 eyewitnesses. A seam opened up around the port in the side of the big craft, and a ramp slowly descended to the ground. The ramp had ridges across its surface, and a giant human being, some three meters tall," that's nine feet tall, "and a meter across the chest, came down the steps in a red coverall one-piece suit and addressed the crowd of onlookers in perfect local Russian. He asked to speak to leaders, and the mayor of the city was brought."

I'm pulling up the artist's sketch of the alien being [shows the picture of the alien being next to a human again]; here he is again—a big guy, nine feet tall. And if you'll notice, he has a third eye, a physical eye, in the center of his forehead in addition to the other two. [Continues reading]: "All of the giants had disproportionately small heads for their size—about the size of a normal Earth human's head, but it was small for their size—and they had a third physical eye located in the center of their foreheads, which seemed to be articulated independently of the other two.

"Strangely, within the hour, the KGB came back and brought the first giant back to his ship and let him out with his fellows. And they stood there at attention while he and his fellows reentered the big ship, and it took off with a whistling sound and rapidly disappeared. It is known that Vladimir Putin was a rising KGB functionary in that area at that time, and so one has to wonder just who authorized the release of their prize prisoner so soon.

Could it have been him, Putin or President Gorbachev himself? Putin did, in fact, succeed to the presidency of Russia after Gorbachev, who single-handedly took the world out of its cold war stance and thus saved it from its head-long rush to mass suicide for the entire planet and all life on it? We wanted to invite Mr. Gorbachev to come here to this conference, but were unable to make contact with him.

MEDIA ARTICLES REGARDING THIS CASE

TheBlackVault.com by BJ Booth

The following information was accessed from TheBlackVault.com on April 23, 2010. To read these articles in their entirety, go to: http://www.theblackvault.com/ wiki/index.php/Voronezh,_Russian_Federation_%289-27-1989%29.

One of the most bizarre accounts of UFO folklore involves an incident that allegedly occurred in Voronezh, Russia. This case was reported in the United States by the St. Louis Dispatch. The story was originally published on October 11, 1989, in America, but its origin was the Russian newspaper TASS. . . . The original details of the case were brought forward by Genrikh Silanov, head of the Voronezh Geophysical Laboratory, who gave details to the TASS agency. . . .

The agency had informed the entire world that Russian scientists had confirmed that an alien spaceship carrying giants with tiny heads had landed in Voronezh, a city of over 800,000 people located about 300 miles southeast of Moscow. They stated that as many as three of these giant creatures had emerged from the alien ship. The ship was described as a large, shining ball. These strange creatures were said to have walked in a nearby park, accompanied by a menacing robot. Ironically, TASS was the only media member to print the story in Russia. The newspaper Pravda declined to print, or comment on the strange tale.

In defense of the TASS account, Soviet reporter Skaya Kultura said that the agency was following the the golden rule of journalism" The reader must

157

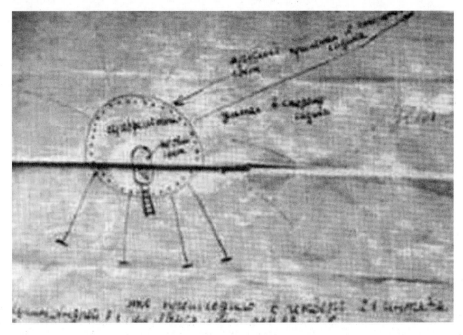

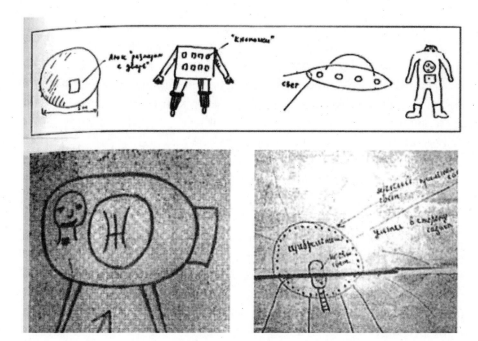

know everything. The TASS account stated that the UFO landed in Voronezh on September 27, 1989, at 6:30 pm. Young boys playing soccer witnessed the event, stating that a pinkish glow preceded the descent of the unusual flying craft. The pink glow became a deep red as it touched down. Most witnesses described the object as a flattened, disc shape. A crowd quickly gathered, and peered through a hatch that opened. They saw a three-eyed alien about 10 feet tall, clad in silvery overalls and bronze-colored boots and wearing a disk on his chest. . . .

Several drawings were made by some of the children who supposedly witnessed the events of Voronezh. A couple of these are included at right. One of the drawings showed the Cyrillic alphabet character "zhe" on the side of the UFO. . . . Voronezh residents interviewed later claimed they had observed this UFO not just during the above incident but also many times on September 21, 23, 29 and October 2, between 6 and 9 PM.

Strange Tale of the 3-Eyed Alien That Zapped a Boy!
The St. Louis Post-Dispatch
October 11, 1989

The daily quoted witnesses as saying that the UFO flew into Voronezh on Sept 27. At 6:30 pm, it said, boys playing soccer saw a pink glow in the sky, then saw a deep red ball about 10 yards in diameter.

The ball circled, vanished, then reappeared minutes later and hovered, it said. A crowd rushed to the site, Sovietskaya Kultura said, and through an open hatch saw, a three-eyed alien about 10 feet tall, clad in silvery overalls and bronze-colored boots and wearing a disk on his chest.

Soviets Report Alien Sighting
John Iams, Associated Press
October 9, 1989
MOSCOW (AP) — The Tass report, which did not give the date of the purported landing in Voronezh, said onlookers were "overwhelmed with a fear that lasted for several days." Genrikh Silanov, head of the Voronezh Geophysical Laboratory, told Tass that scientists investigating the UFO report found a 20-yard depression with four deep dents as well as two pieces of unidentified rocks.

"At first glance, they looked like sandstone of a deep-red color. However, mineralogical analysis has shown that the substance cannot be found on Earth," TASS quoted Silanov as saying. "However, additional tests are needed to reach a more definite conclusion."

Russia's Alien Ideals—UFO Landing
Patrick Huyghe
Westerners were intrigued back in 1989 when the Soviet news agency, TASS, reported the claims of some school children from the city of Voronezh. A spectacular UFO landed in town, the children insisted, along with its ten-foot-tall occupant toting a tube-shaped gun. . . .

In January of 1990, Jacques Vallee, a computer scientists regarded by many as the world's major UFO researcher, held a week-long series of meetings with the Soviet Union's leading UFO lights. He met with a scientist who'd studied the mysterious explosion that had rattled the Tunguska region of Russia in 1908 and with an ex-Soviet Naval officer who detailed his UFO sightings by Navy personnel. But according to Vallee, the most compelling sighting was the one in Voronezh itself.

In his new book, UFO Chronicles of the Soviet Union (Ballantine, 1992), Vallee describes the cast of dozens—adults as well as children—who reportedly witnessed the spherical Voronezh craft, its three-eyed giant, and an accompanying robot. He also cites engineers who examined an imprint allegedly left by the craft, an object they claimed weighed 11 tons. . . . Why does Vallee believe the Soviet sightings are for real? The weight of the craft, he notes, was "in the range of estimates reached by French scientists studying physical markings left by UFO landings in France." And though the beings bore no resemblance to the familiar, short, Hollywood-style UFOnauts, they were similar to aliens reportedly seen "in a very similar case in Argentina in 1978. ©1992 Omni Publications International Ltd.; ©2004 Gale Group

UFOs: The Psychic Dimension;
The Voronezh, Russia Case
David Pratt

At about 6:30 PM on 27 September 1989 in the Russian city of Voronezh, 3 schoolchildren and about 40 adults saw a pink or red light in the sky, which turned into a dark red sphere, about 30 ft in diameter. It flew away but returned a few minutes later and hovered over a park. A hatch opened in the bottom and a being appeared. It was about 10 ft tall, had no neck, and wore silver overalls and bronze-coloured boots. It had 3 eyes; 2 were whitish, but the middle eye—or lamp, as one witness called it—was red and had no pupil. The being scanned the terrain, the hatch closed, and the sphere descended, brushing against a poplar tree, which bent and stayed in that position. The object, which measured about 45 ft wide and 19 ft high, then landed. The tall being was accompanied by a small robot. The being said something and a small luminous rectangle appeared on the ground. It said something else and the rectangle disappeared. It then adjusted something on the robot's chest, causing it to walk in a mechanical way.

One of the boys watching cried out in fear. The being, whose eyes seemed to emit light, looked at him, and the boy froze. When the witnesses started shouting, the sphere and being vanished on the spot. But 5 minutes later the object and being reappeared. It now held a 4-ft-long tube at its side. When the being pointed it at a 16-year-old boy, the boy became invisible. The being then reentered the sphere, and as the object flew away, the boy reappeared. After taking off, the UFO almost instantaneously became a mere dot and disappeared in the sky. An investigation revealed that the radioactivity level at the landing site was double the background level. Traces were found where the craft's 4 legs had stood. There was an area of flattened grass, and the soil was found to have turned to the consistency of stone. It was calculated that an object weighing 11 tons had stood there.

Thousands of Voronezh residents observed several appearances of UFOs between 23 and 29 September 1989, and at least 3 landings took place, witnessed by over 30 people. As in other cases, many of the sightings occurred in polluted areas: the park used to be a garbage dump, and UFOs also visited the electricity plant and the site of a future nuclear plant [19].

Credits & Sources for the above:
* *Flying Saucer Review*, 34, 4
* *MUFON UFO Journal* 259 and 260
* *UFO Chronicles of the Soviet Union*
* Special thanks to BJ Booth

ET BEINGS SAW UNDESIRABLE EARTH FUTURE IF CHANGES WERE NOT MADE

RUSSIANS LISTENED WITH THEIR HEARTS AND MADE CHANGES TO BRING PEACE

Overseer of Cyclops-Like Beings and Zoosh

March 9, 2010

Greetings.

Greetings!

I'll be slow today. The route by which the energy comes is circuitous, and we'll do as much as possible. But you can speak at your normal pace.

I didn't understand how important this [information about the origin of the Cyclops, the witnessed landing of a craft, and the origin of the fall of the Berlin Wall] was yesterday until I did some research. Did the Cyclops have the idea to come here, or was it your idea?

I do not give them ideas or even advice at this stage of their being unless they ask. They did not ask, so I believe it was their idea. Perhaps it was slightly impetuous on their part, but still, all and all it had a good effect. I did not mention perhaps that once they leave—say, within fifty feet of proximity to any human being, even when moving laterally, to say nothing of moving up and away with the ship or simply away with the ship—the discomfiture because of the incompatibility of species immediately disappears for the human being and leaves no residual energy. I think that's important to know. It's a little different here with the spiritual connection, but we're doing a—oh, I'm going to get a chance to say a word I like of yours! We're doing a "workaround." That word is very visual, which is why I like it. Did I say that these people are very visual?

No.

They have a tendency to see what they communicate. Part of the reason they enjoy interacting with human beings is that human beings are often visually expressive when they communicate—moving the hands, moving the eyes, moving the head. In other words, there is a visual demonstration going on, aside from simple "translation" is the word we use, meaning the communication is moving from one to another.

Do they use universal translators, or do they have the capacity within themselves to express in the language of the hearer?

They use a device, which I'd not prefer to call a universal device, but it is adequate for their purposes. This does not mean that the device itself can do what they can do. The device merely changes the pulses so that the connection between the brain and nervous system and visuals—essentially what the beings see, say, feel, like that—makes a safe connection from one to another so that regardless of what sounds come out of their person, if you could hear them speaking, you would hear it in the sounds that are the most comfortable and compatible with you. In the case of some beings, it would not be sounds but an awareness. Some species on this planet do not communicate in sound; there are a few who do not communicate in any sound whatsoever.

Oh, have they at times talked to some of what we call animals on this planet?

Certainly. They are easy to communicate with for visitors from all over because, as you know, they are not devoid of their natural spiritual skills that you would have yourselves as souls if you were someplace else. They are not here to learn anything, so those abilities are not removed from them. Of course, there are certain species that are particularly helpful between worlds and can access different worlds and sometimes bring energy from those benevolent worlds to your world.

ETs Who Are Perceived of as a Threat Aren't Allowed to Come

Now, these beings had to get permission to come to this planet, didn't they?

They were given permission, because more was understood about their visit than even they knew. Back during the visit in Homeric times, they felt that there could be some assistance in those times, and there was greater assistance than there was problem, but they were also allowed to come so that they could learn. The thread, you might say—it is like a doorway and compatible only to them—was still available. Any time those beings come and go—including, of course, their vehicles—or even just when they come, it opens something like a thread that connects to your world that's permanent, and that's how they come and go regularly. They'll come and go through that thread, once it's been established. So after that, they could come and go based on their perceptions of the value that they were contributing.

If at any time it is perceived by those who oversee your planet and generally look after you that they represent a threat—to anyone, not just them—then they're not allowed to come. They're not harmed; they just can't find their way. It's like they get lost temporarily, and then they naturally do what beings always do: They retrace their steps. That's how they get away from that, and they very quickly realize, or the mechanisms in the vehicle might recognize, the pattern and know they're not supposed to go that way and simply say that it's dangerous. And they don't come that way again. But that's only for beings who are not being allowed. In this case . . .

The thread was still there.

If you were to be able to look at your planet from a distance and see those things, it would remind you of a ball of twine with many different cords jumping up from the surface—though they would look very tiny if you were able to see them. It doesn't create a weakness in the energy field; actually, it promotes greater strength, because only those who can benefit you are allowed to come in. If there is no benefit, or the cost-benefit ratio is harmful to you, then there is no allowance. Sometimes beings are allowed to come even if they represent a partial challenge to you, because those who work with you or protect the planet are aware that you will find a way or that there is some challenge they bring that is instrumental in your growth.

In your case, it might have been. Yes, I can see a couple of instances. It was because you would be using that challenge or those challenges to speed your avenue toward becoming your complete selves again, which is what you are doing. Sometimes, if there are challenges, then in situations like this—rare though they may be in a learning place like this for souls—the natural tendency of the soul, when it is cut off from knowing, is to return to knowing in the quickest and most benevolent way. This is exactly what you are doing—which is exactly needed at this time. I am understanding this as I am saying it, because I have not studied this matter before.

Their Appearance Expresses Multiple Focuses

When people see them, they say they have these tiny heads. They have these huge bodies, which are described as between nine feet and thirteen feet tall, but they say they have these tiny heads. Are their heads really disproportionately small compared to their bodies?

Yes, because aside from the various functional features of your head—you know, your eyes, your nose, your mouth, and so on—you also have a container for your brain. But their brains, so to speak, are more largely distributed in the rest of their bodies. You might say that if it was like that for you, then your "brain" would be distributed throughout your nervous system.

Is that how theirs are?

That would be how the brain would *express* itself in those beings. So the head does not need to be a container for a brain. Of course, it is just that much smaller.

But it has the two regular eyes, plus the third eye, yes? Then does it have a mouth and nose and ears, or no?

It depends on . . . I don't think exactly like that, but it's adequately . . . it does not look frightening. The only thing really kind of ominous, as people might take it because of the Homeric literature and also just because of the difference, is the extra eye. Other than that, the face might look a bit odd. It's something you can't exactly focus on. Have you ever seen a blurry picture that look as if it's shifting? It's like that. That's what you would get—and there's a technical reason for this.

When everybody hears things in their own "lingo"—do you say that?— thus they hear/see the individual, especially if they are close. But that broadcast creates multiple focuses at all times. And that focus—remember, these beings are visual—expresses visually as well as on the heard/felt/seen level. So there's a tendency to say, "Well, they kind of look like this," and then if you asked twelve or thirteen sketch artists and they were able to draw a sketch, you'd notice distinct differences.

Fascinating. Yes, there are sketches on the Internet that were in the newspapers—that children made.

And there are distinct differences. Well, that's because of hearing/feeling. Now, you understand, you could have a person or persons who speak and understand exactly the same dialect but their feelings in their bodies are going to be different based on their unique experiences of life, no matter how young or old they are. Thus you get the differences. There are many different moment-to-moment focuses, so it's hard to describe it.

If you were to see them, they would appear to have small ears. The ears wouldn't look human, but they would be placed where human ears were. They would have a slightly conical look to them, but only part of the cone—the top, the back. They don't look like a cone; they're just the shape. The substance would remind you of something slightly conical or flared, you might say. Then the nose would shift so that there were two holes and then sometimes a mass that would remind you of a nose, but there would be a certain amount of flatness between the two eyes.

And a mouth? Do they eat?

The mouth would sort of come and go. They do not eat the way you understand. Remember, this is not their actual appearance. You perhaps have forgotten that from the first session.

I have!

But it is an adaptation to their actual appearance—so it's like they are stuffed inside this outer shell.

Is the outer shell the protection, the shielding, the garment that keeps them . . . ?

The outer shell is what allows them to be reasonably acceptable to those they are visiting. The outer shell . . . this is getting way too technical for me. I'm a spiritual adviser.

So what do they look like when they're home, then?

It's hard to describe them, and I don't think it's safe for the channel.

Okay. The reports said that the beings had a robot escort. Is this a normal thing? Can you say anything about that?

Partially that has to do with security, because the beings are somewhat vulnerable. But the other being would command a certain amount of respect, you understand—wariness, you might say [chuckles]—because this was perceived to be something that as a species you might find fascinating. Remember the times. Remember what movies were out then, that kind of thing—what was popular ten, twenty years before the visit and so on. The whole idea of having a robot seemed . . .

Star Wars! Yeah.

. . . seemed to them to be something that might make the people feel curious, safe, surprised, amused . . .

Oh, so it was like a stage set. [Laughs.]

Yes. Still, the beings do exist, but they do not have quite as prominent a role as it seemed to those on Earth.

Okay.

[Sighs.] I may not be able to go on too much longer.

All right. It said that there was a Cyrillic alphabet character on the outside of the craft: "Z-H-E." Is that their character, or was it there because they were going to that country?

It was because they were going to that country.

In the Time of Homer,
They Came to Ensure the Culture Persevered

Now, when these beings went to the time of Homer—which was like 800 or 900 something BC—what did they perceive? Was that little battle of Troy something that they came to stop or warn against? What was the situation when they came at the time of Homer?

Keep in mind that the population of Earth was much smaller then, and what might not seem like a massive battle in your times would have been overwhelming in those times, considering the population. It also was perceived that if one side or the other were to lose, it could be the end of their civilization. These beings do not feel good about civilizations that have many things to offer being ended and their influence largely being "disappeared." So that's why they came.

That's why they came. So what was the effect of their coming? What was the outcome of that? How did they affect the battle or the people?

There were survivors who were able to continue the culture for a time until the culture was able to leave traces of its existence, not only in certain artifacts, but also in cultural things that they developed—science of the time, spirituality of the time, and so on—passing it on to others. In other words, they were able to leave their mark in a way that would outlive them. So as it turned out, the attempt to help was so that the culture from Troy would be able to leave its imprint. So those were some results of what they came to do.

This was so that Troy would be able to leave a visual imprint and, more importantly, be able to influence others so that all they had done and accomplished would not be lost. It was passed on to others to be perpetuated, even though the culture as you know it—as you might know any culture of your time, for instance—seemed to disappear for a time.

What exactly did the beings do? They landed their ship, and they went to talk to the participants? What did they do?

I cannot say that, or it could be misused in your time.

Did they spend more time on the planet than the hour they spent in Russia? Did they spend time at that place?

No longer than in Russia.

See, there's stuff in the mythology about the Cyclops giving them thunderbolts and invisible helmets and tridents. Did the ETs give the humans weapons on one side or the other?

No. See, the cultures of the time had capacities, and sometimes people, because of the beliefs in your time, are resistant to believing the obvious. If someone seems to have a weapon that is a thunderbolt, could it simply just not be lightning? Could it not be an influence with lightning? Could it not be, as you might say, magic? This would not be evil but benevolent. You could think that the thunderbolt would not land on the other side—whatever the other side was, depending on your perspective—but that it would happen between, thus allowing those in battle to cease their battle. In those days, it was not unusual that if somebody lost the battle that there would be no . . . I'm not going to go into it. It's too brutal.

You mean that there would be no survivors?

Well, on the side that lost. But it was not allowed this time. There was a series of lightning bolts and the survivors of both sides retired. They took that as a sign from the heavens that they were to cease—as anyone might.

This was influenced by these beings?

No. That was something that the culture of Troy had developed, a relationship with natural magic—"natural magic" being something that is part of the nature of the planet on which you live and perceived of and applied as benevolent, since no one is harmed and the outcome is something that is good for all beings. So that would be natural magic: "natural" having to do with something that is natural to the planet, and "magic" having to do with the unexplained in the logical terminology of your time, meaning mathematics, science—although science on the leading edge and some older aspects in your time do acknowledge natural magic as the unexplained. You see, that's the acknowledgment scientifically, at least socially scientifically. I have to be slow again now. The culture of Troy was able to utilize that natural magic, and survivors were allowed to escape, including some wounded who didn't quite make it back to where they needed to go but were able to pass on certain wisdom to those who were helping them.

As their guide, you were able to view what they were doing? You knew what they were doing, right?

You asked whether they were able to accomplish what they came here to do. That's the way I perceived that question. They didn't do that thunderbolt thing. That was something that the people of Troy, certain people in Troy, had been able to accomplish. But the visitors felt it would be good for such abilities to survive, for such knowledge and wisdom to live on, since it is a benevolent reality to be able to interact with the elements of Earth in a safe way.

Is that the only other time they came to the planet? You mentioned that they were here twice, I thought, before Russia.

They came another time, but I won't mention that at this time.

They Gave Them the Gift of Long-Lasting Architecture

It seems we've covered the important things, then: the landing, the influence on the Russian people, and then the origin of the myths of the Cyclops. They never built anything, did they? I mean, there are a lot of references to Cyclopean masonry. Did they ever build anything? Did they ever land long enough?

I believe they may have shown the people of the times how to create a specific type of joint . . . joinery? They may have shown them how to create a specific type of joint so that the architecture they were putting together might last longer. So it's not something that they built, but they consulted, you might say—kind of a gift. It was felt that this gift would not be interfering. It was really a way to show them how something could survive, even if part of the support structure were to collapse. I believe there are monuments to that effect here and there in the world, where you'd say, "How can that still stand?"

This was on that second visit that you can't talk about?

No, that was in Homeric times.

Oh! They gave them advice about building while they were fighting a war?

Oh no, they didn't talk to the people who were fighting the war. They talked to the people before the war was fought. Not the soldiers, not the military—they didn't build the buildings. It's no different than in your time. Well, perhaps some fight building goes on by the military of your time, but they are not generally architects.

They came to the Homeric time before the battle?

Yes, but it was going to happen at any moment. As a gift, they went to people, showed them the structures, the architecture, and said, "Well, why don't you do this?" And the architects of the time said, "Oooh!" It was so obvious once they saw it. It was like "oh!" because they understood architecture, structure, and machinery. If someone points out something you could do, suddenly—because your mind works that way—you look at it and you say, "Oh!"

You see, it was a gift. It wasn't any intent to influence; it would be like an offhand remark you would make, and then you realize later, "Oh! That really made a change!" The change was that the structures have lasted a lot longer than you might expect.

Well, it's so odd that they have affection for humans and they're so biologically incompatible. It's sad.

It's a good thing, in a way. Then they don't come very often. When you are fully able to communicate comfortably on a cultural basis with visitors from other worlds, then maybe they will return. But they would have come and gone regularly if you were . . .

Compatible with them.

Yes, and they might have interfered, because they are helpful. Sometimes they don't realize that their help could change things, such as the sharing of that type of joinery. It changed things, but it was not such a big influence—meaning it didn't change things that much, it didn't harm anything, and it didn't create such a great help that you are stuck with structures that won't fall down.

Their Existence Always Had Purpose

What were they doing before you gave them a purpose for their lives? What were their lives like?

They were perfectly happy, but they had purpose. Their existence had purpose. They were open to traveling someplace, but they were not looking to travel. They wanted something else. Haven't you ever wondered, "There's something missing. What's missing?" Haven't you ever had that feeling? People have that feeling on your planet all the time. They had that feeling. The feeling is often filled by inspiration, you see. You have that too, as a people. They were given this inspiration of how to help people other than their own kind, other than those they normally visited—how to help groups of people create a more comfortable life for everyone—and they said, "Oh, let's do that!" That's certainly a worthy thing to participate in.

But their technology was very advanced, then. I mean, they had the ability to ignore the USSR military response.

From your perception, yes. Just as the technology you have today might be considered very advanced to people of several hundred years ago or even one hundred years ago. Think about a hundred years ago: What would a modern automobile be? It would be considered a device from some science-fiction place.

Yes. But we got so many of our advances from ETs, you know. That's how we moved so fast. I can't get the image out of my mind—the way they're kind of squashed into that container. Are they not . . . ?

They're slightly uncomfortable. That's part of the reason why they can't stay too long. It would be as if somebody told you to sit in a position that was not entirely uncomfortable but wasn't really comfortable. After an hour or so, you'd really want to get out of that position.

So they are not humanoid, with two arms and two legs?

I'm not going to say. There's no point in asking it in a question fourteen different ways—I'm not going to say what they look like. I cannot go on much longer. Ask what you need to ask, and then we must stop.

Well, what have I left out? I've been trying to focus on those three things: the landing in Russia, the origin of the myth of the Cyclops, and the fall of the Berlin Wall. Is there anything else to do with that?

No, we've covered that sufficiently. Also, it is not your job to be the reporter. You must allow that other people will fill in other details in time—channels, writers, speculators—and it's good to allow them that. You can give them a landmark, you can give them a street map, so to speak, but it is really not your job, from my perception, that you should build every house and make certain the corners are all true.

All right, my dear. You've been extremely helpful, and I thank you for coming back and making this work in a way that doesn't hurt Robby.

Learn as Much About Instinct as You Possibly Can

I will give a closing statement as far as the session today. One of the things I must say to you all, especially considering the light banter between the questioner and myself, is that it's very good to have curiosity. Granted, sometimes your curiosity leads you to do things that you will sometimes regret. So it is all right to use your instinct. Don't mistrust it.

Very often in your times, science does not understand instinct entirely, since it is not something scientific and quantifiable on a universal basis but is different from being to being as well as among different human beings—it's different and it changes. Thus not being quantifiable on a scientific level and reproducible with the same results on a scientific level, at least within certain parameters, is not pursued. But I must tell you that your curiosity and your instinct are inseparable partners, and I do encourage you to learn as much about instinct as you possibly can—and not just in books.

Support and urge your children and grown-ups, as you say—charming term—to learn about instinct. Study the instinct of animals in benevolent ways. Don't cut them up to understand what instinct is. Needless to say, they get frightened of you when you do that. They do communicate among themselves, but the reason they will still approach you is that they are here to help you. When you are there in a place to help someone, you might be frightened, but you approach anyway because your job is to help them. That is why they are often so brave. Please, learn about instinct. It is everything for you. May you have a most benevolent life.

Oh, thank you! Good life to you.

✳   ✳   ✳

This is a response to a comment the questioner made to Robert after the previous channeling in regards to the Cyclops beings causing the fall of the Berlin Wall.

This is Zoosh.

Okay, Zoosh. Go ahead.

You have a misperception there. Causing the fall of the Berlin Wall would be interference, and that would never be allowed. They didn't *cause* it. They saw it coming, and they came to support that culture. I think one of the things they do is that when they see a culture changing, they will sometimes be attracted to encourage that culture to leave the wisdom that they have developed and to put it somewhere so that it will survive. Putting it in a book is not sufficient. It has to be told to people, and the people have to be taught the good things about the culture.

There were good things about the system in Russia that were not really spoken of very much in your country, because your country, your system, was competitive with the other system, even though there are certain things that happen in your country—co-ops and so on—that do bear a similarity to the system in Russia at the time. But your country was particularly sensitive to communism because in the 1920s and to a degree in the 1930s, your country almost went that way. So those who are of the status quo would feel particularly sensitive to that. I don't know if you know that about your past. That's in your time.

No, I didn't know that.

Well, there was a movement in your country to become socialistic. Certain things developed in that regime that they wanted to be encouraging to people of that time to pass on as verbal teaching to young ones. That's something you may have noticed—just from your talk with the guide—that inspires these people.

Yes.

They are interested in questions like, "How can we encourage the good things to survive?" and they do not consider books to be sufficient. The communication has to be one-to-one. There needs to be passion. See, they're passionate people. There needs to be passion—not violence, but feeling. They would consider just speaking with hand gestures passionate. It moves a person's energy who is speaking; it moves his or her energy out. Have you ever heard people talk who are dispassionate in their communication? You don't really feel anything moving energetically. Whereas if somebody is passionate—not yelling and screaming, but . . .

Gesticulating, yes.

If there is something they are moved by, their energy is moving. You can feel it like that.

Well, the being didn't say they caused it.

You said that, and that's why I'm here.

But the point is that they influenced the benevolent change. Isn't that true? It could have gone on to war, and it didn't.

Yes, but what they did was not that striking. It wasn't just because they came, were unusual, and then left. They came, they spoke, and the people who heard them believed them. It was really that simple. It wasn't that they performed any magic.

No, but they were influential.

Yes, exactly. They were influential—which is exactly what you are doing. You are influential, but you have to learn how to be a good teacher, don't you? The magazine, the books, they do not reach out and say—and you know yourself; you don't want to do this—"This is what is, and you will change or you'll be sorry." There is nothing like that in the magazines or books. Do you understand? And that's because you're being a good teacher.

So do you feel that if they had not appeared to Gorbachev, the Soviet Union still would have made that change?

You mean if the ETs had not appeared in that country, that what they saw was going to happen in the future? Then the minefield of diplomacy—and all diplomats know it's a minefield—could have been more explosive than it was. So the people the ETs talked to—those of the Soviet Union—had heart, and they had suffered terribly during the war, World War II. They had heart for their own people, though they're not pictured that way in the times and the literature of the times. They're portrayed as if those in the capitalistic system were the saints and those who were part of the communistic system were the devils, but it's never like that. There's always something good on both sides—or usually. There may be a few exceptions.

Okay. Well, thank you. The fact of the landing and the origin of the myth is so interesting. Sometime I hope we can get into origins of myths, because here these beings land, and from, you know . . . you ought to see all this stuff about Zeus and all the gods and all the legends and the myths and everything that came from that simple landing.

Generally speaking, even when a particular culture might, in your times, look kind of "nursery school" in some ways, that is exactly the way your culture will be perceived by your own generations in the future, on their own. They will look back and say, "How could they have thought that? How could they have ignored that?"—all that kind of stuff. What you might do in your time, looking back on previous cultures, is exactly the way future cultures will be looking back on your own.

[Laughs.] Well, then maybe we can take a step . . . well, we've got so many projects here, but I'd love to do the origins of mythology some time. I remember the Master of Plasma once said that he had appeared as Zeus, so there have probably been some dabblings down here by various beings.

Just keep in mind that when things appear to be one way, meaning looking from the present into the dim past—and the past is always dim when you don't have absolute clarity—then you might make perceptions or cast a scenario that attempts to connect the dots. And very often, many dots are missed. [Chuckles.]

[Laughs.] Yes. All right, well thank you so much.

    Bye.

Okay, bye. Good life.

YOU MOVED EARTH OUT OF PHASE TO TEST YOUR CREATOR ABILITIES

Speaker One, Grandfather, and Isis

May 3, 2010

All right. Are you there?

Yes.

I will state a name later. Now, you on your planet have been exercising a certain level of restraint toward progress—meaning your return to your normal cycle of your natural existence. In order for you to achieve that cycle, you have circulated your focus into an alternate reality. You are now, as a planet, functioning in what we would consider a half degree off-arc. We do not have the same mathematics you do, so this is the interpretation in your world. It means that all things that you understand are slightly out of perspective.

Because of this, science may have an opportunity to make tremendous progress in some fields, and in other fields where tremendous progress was moving forward, as it does, it will suddenly hit a wall for no apparent reason. And even though the mathematics show that you have every reason to believe things should be working, they're suddenly not.

This is a temporary situation. It is your way, as a global human personality, of testing your own capabilities to reassume your natural arc of motion. You are doing this so that you can test your creative skills along the lines of creation. There are enough peoples on the planet now with at least a rudimentary awareness of benign and benevolent transformation—I think, in your case, you say benevolent magic, a useful term—to help assume that arc

177

once again. I would recommend that you speak to those who can advise that pathway, so I will just speak for a short time.

You Must Pull Back into Your Own Arc of Progress

In your current arc, you are partly barging into our world. We have had to shift our arc as a result, and for us, it is very uncomfortable. Most of the beings in our world have had to shut down fully half of what we do just to tolerate this temporary situation. We are doing all we can do to help you to move, but you must want to. My job is to let you know that you have done this to test yourselves. I recommend that you pull back into your own arc of progress.

The alternate world you are occupying, even partially, cannot possibly work for you. If you were, theoretically, to shift into this world, nothing that works for you now would work. You would all be like babies, having to be shown exactly what to do, and since you would all be babies, you would die out as a population, since there would be no one to show you. I do not expect that you will do this; I am simply anticipating your question.

If you do nothing, it won't get any better. You must *do* something. It will probably take at least thirty people who want to do it. You have to want to help your world to begin to move back into its normal arc of existence. I cannot instruct you on these things, but there is a hazard. Your planet will not shift back by itself, because you are testing yourselves. If you do not shift it back yourselves, your planet could become unstable, so that is the reason to do this.

You have been gradually shifting into this position for the past twenty months or so of your time, and that is something you haven't been able to fully predict. There have been things in science and of course in other endeavors that were expected to work that didn't, but they were considered anomalies since they were rare. But now it is happening all-too predictably, and there are those who are seriously concerned, though that has not yet been largely put out into the general community.

So here's what you must do. For those of you who have the capacity to transform and are working on that and with that with some success—don't do it unless you've had some success—I will give you the instruction from my point of view, and you can get more from others. You must focus on your Sun, and what you do is this: You imagine the Sun, for those of you who use that technique—or for those of you doing things more physically, you pull yourself toward the Sun. There's no worry, all right? You as an individual, even thirty individuals, cannot possibly alter your arc on your own, but you can help to put your planet back on the pathway so that the planet itself can resume—albeit maybe over three months, perhaps a little longer—its own natural arc of motion. This has nothing to do with your orbit—that is my word: "arc."

I feel this is essential. Don't just do it for us—it's a matter of your own survival. Now you have other beings who will speak with you. I will simply say that I am a spokesperson for our planet—which, from your perspective now, mathematically, is an alternate reality of your own. My name is . . . I'm going to give you my title instead. My title is Speaker One. Goodbye.

Thank you. Good life.

* * *

Grandfather. Greetings. Isis felt that it would be best to allow Speaker One to communicate first, as there was just a moment when it was possible for that to take place. Isis will elaborate in a moment, but I am here to help those of you who are doing benevolent magic or true magic to help with this change.

Some of you who are doing benevolent magic or true magic or other things have noticed that some things don't work as well as they used to, and other things work fine. This can be changed so that everything works as it once did. I'm going to recommend the true magic first, for those who are doing these things.

True Magic

I recommend that you just glance at the Sun. It's not sufficient to have an imagination of the Sun. It is all right—perfectly all right—to do this through dark glasses, but when I say glance, I just mean for a split second. The Moon is not sufficient for this. It must be a body of light and heat that is profound for your planet. It is all right to hold your hand up in front of your eyes when you glance at the Sun, but have your fingers at least slightly parted so you make the connection. If you are light sensitive, you may close your eyes and look toward the Sun, in which case you can hold that position for a couple of seconds. You will still get the impression of the Sun, but your eyes will be completely safe. So keep that in mind.

Go out on the land and do this. Wherever you go, make sure you have permission to be there. Try to do this at a time when you can be alone. If you need to have someone with you, have that person stand at least thirty feet away and not looking at you; it would be best if the person had his or her back toward you. Stand and face the north. If you are unable to stand and you are in a wheelchair, then put your chair in that position and face the north, and do the best you can with this work, adapting it to those circumstances. I'm going to speak as if you can stand.

Make one complete rotation to the left and hold your arms out directly in front of you, meaning straight out from your shoulders, with your palms down and your fingers loose—not closed, just loose. Then as you straighten your fingers out slowly, turn your arms so that your palms are up. Then raise your arms up over your head, and while you are doing that, slowly turn your palms so that they are facing each other over your head. Then bring your palms together with your fingers not splayed out but close together and with each thumb touching your hand and touching the fingers and thumb of your other hand as well.

Then bring your arms down so that your hands line up with the plane of your heart in that position. Then you may move your arms to the sides of your body, gradually, slowly, so that your arms are hanging by your sides but touching the sides of your body—left on the left side, right on the right side, to make that perfectly clear—and make one more complete rotation to the left, ending up facing north. It doesn't have to be degree-perfect north, just generally north. Say, if it's off by 10 degrees in either direction, it's still sufficient. Then I recommend that you say these words:

"I am asking that our planet now come to be on its natural path in its natural time and coordinate benevolently with our existence."

Wait a moment; some of you might feel a strong surge of energy. If you do, then wait until it passes. It may not pass completely; there might be a slight residual. If there is a slight residual, that's fine to continue. Then look down at the ground right in front of your feet and look forward again. Remember, all the time you do these true magics, you want to have, to the best of your ability, yourself looking at something that is not human-made. You may not always be able to tell, but just do your best. After looking down at the ground and then looking straight ahead again, you can make one more complete rotation to the left. Just let your arms hang loosely at your sides, comfortably.

Then take three sidesteps to the left. It is all right to look down at the ground to make sure you are safe and you're not stepping on anyone or anything that could be harmed, such as any creatures you might see on the ground or in the grass. Then make a one-quarter rotation to the left and take five or six sidesteps to the left, whichever feels the best. Then, rotating to the left, turn until you are facing the direction you need to face and go on with your life.

Here's what you can do for a benevolent magic. This is more personal, as you know. First, ask for all the most benevolent energies that are available for you to be all around you and all about you. You might feel a surge of energy. If you do, wait for it to fade just a bit—not completely, just a bit. Then say:

Benevolent Magic

"I request that I now feel myself on Earth turning on to our natural path of motion and that I be able to note this now as things that can work and have worked resume working well in the most benevolent way for me, resulting in the most benevolent outcome."

If you are going to say a living prayer—which affects you and everyone else—then again ask for all the most benevolent energies that are available for you to be all around you and all about you. Then say:

Living Prayer

"I am asking that all of our planet Earth that is occupied by all beings here return to its natural pathway in the most benevolent way for us all now."

That's what I recommend. Now, for those who are doing work requesting gold lightbeings and lightbeings, I'm going to suggest that, during this time—which might last for another three to six months, hopefully no longer than that—you make an addition. If you're perhaps doing this for disentanglement or other things, then you can add this after you say your request for gold lightbeings and lightbeings, as you know how to say. Then say, ". . .

and all benevolent spirits and energies who support me beyond my know-ing." That's the addition you make. Then go on with what you're requesting or whatever you're doing with disentanglement or anything like that. All right? That's all, then.

Thank you very much.

Now Isis will come through and answer any questions you have about this. Good life.

Good life.

✳   ✳   ✳

Greetings. Isis.

Welcome!

Now, this shift is something that you have actually set up—at the dream level, for most of you—and it's important to tell you about it now, because it's at its zenith. It's not likely that it will get any worse, but it could go slightly more extreme. It is part of the reason—not all, but part of the reason—there has been greater volcanic activity and part of the reason that there has been as much earth motion as there has been. Curiously enough, it is also part of the reason that certain areas where earth motion was expected have been held in check. But by and large, as the planet shifts back to its natural pathway, everything will be all right. Certain places, such as the San Andreas Fault, the famous fault zone where there have been regular shifts in the past—3.0, 4.0, that kind of thing—have not been having those shifts occurring as often, and therefore the tension is building. So there is every reason to bring it back.

For those of you who are not familiar with benevolent magic or true mag-ic, just say your normal prayers, whatever it is you say. For those of you who do not pray or have that association with Creator, then here's what you can do if you would rather not do anything that sounds like prayer or magic or a prayer with a religious connotation. I recommend that you look at any body of water. It can be anything—a river, a stream, an ocean. It has to be something naturally occurring, so it can't be a human-made lake or, say, a swimming pool. While you're looking at it, simply say these words: "Resume your natural flow in the most comfortable way with ease now for all beings." That's what I recommend. It's a gentle thing to say that will probably not conflict with any beliefs you have. Question?

Yes. This is an alternate Earth? Did I understand that right?

Only slightly. The being that came in initially, Speaker One, was on an alternate version of Earth. There are many alternates. But their particular version of the planet and their peoples are suffering, because they are not used to discomfort. See, that's the issue. Here, you have a planet with polarity and discomfort that you are living in all the time. All the beings on this planet Earth are aware of that. But in other places, they are not dealing with that. And while they are still veiled from it, what's occurring, since you are slightly into their field of existence—which is what Speaker One meant when referring to an "arc"—is that it has created something for them that they don't understand, which is discomfort. And they have had no preparation to deal with it.

I don't think you realized as souls that when you were going to put things slightly "out of whack," as you might say, so that you could test yourselves to see if you could do something really significant that would affect the physical world in some benevolent way by putting it slightly out of balance—kind of like detuning a car and then tuning it up, okay, for those of you who understand that—then you didn't take into account the effects beyond this Earth. And no one really stopped you because, for one thing, we all knew that it wouldn't have a devastating impact on other worlds, but it would have impact.

You Can Ease Their Discomfort

Now you see that your responsibilities stretch far beyond your own planet—even now while you are learning, while you are coming back into being your natural, native personalities. Speaker One was the only one who spoke, but there are other alternate planets that are slightly off-kilter now too that are also uncomfortable, and it's really hard on them. They are off far enough from the capability of this channel to communicate from there—plus, it would be uncomfortable for this channel to communicate—but it is difficult for them as well.

Speaker One said it's going to take about thirty people to do the true magic that will help to put things back into place, but I would suggest that you have a hundred. Try to get a hundred people who might wish to do this. It does not need to be done instantaneously—sometime over the next month or two would be best—because once the planet begins to shift, even slightly, back to its natural, normal pathway, it will get back on its own. It's like you'll give it a nudge, and then it will sort of find its own way. Do you understand?

Yes.

Good. Anything else?

If it's an alternate Earth, does every human have an alternate on that planet?

No, nor are you alternates for them. No, they're all individual souls. They're not human, by the way—they are their own type of being. Some of them are not even physical on the other alternate world from your perspective of what is physical. Even if you were there in their world, they wouldn't look physical, and of course you wouldn't be physical to them, either. You might reasonably ask, "Why are they there?"

As you know, in the past, there have been other planets that didn't make it here and either were removed or, in some extreme cases, were nonsurvivors. So those alternates are lined up to take your place should something untoward happen. I am not expecting that to take place, but there is a tiny possibility that they might and that it could take place, in which case they would immediately, instantaneously shift into this spot and become more physical, as you understand it. When your planet and the peoples on it all once again achieve your natural, normal state of being along with Earth, many of those alternates will simply move into other forms of existence, and a few of them will even go to other star systems. But for now, they're volunteers, and they'll be available "just in case," as you might say.

How many are there?

Oh, about seven.

Was this decision by all human souls meeting at once in another level of reality, discussing this and setting this up or was this a challenge prepared by the Creator or what?

No, you all decided it when you were in your deep-dream level. You decided it on your own, and it was allowed because you are far enough along in your progress to become your natural, native personalities that it was allowed as a test of your creator abilities. So no, we just stood back. We didn't have to give you permission, speaking for the teachers at large. You just decided to do it on your own, and we just were quiet. You didn't say, "What do you think we should do?" You just said, "Hey, let's try this. We got this new stuff; let's try it out."

You also know that one of the ways even creators learn is by "oops." Your Creator has learned by "oops" as well. And all beings who create learn that way, even if what they're creating is entirely benign. They might still do something and say, or you might say to yourself, "Oh, I want to do that differently," but once you've created it, there it is; you don't uncreate it. You might want to do it differently, and maybe you go ahead and do it differently, but you've still got the original "oops," and you've got to deal with that.

So you said twenty months ago.

That was decided then, on your own.

Oh, that was decided. When did the move start?

Oh, almost immediately.

So that was September in 2008, then. When we get everything back in natural order here, will the Earth changes be mitigated?

We'll see. It depends on how Earth feels about it. You'll have to ask her when the time comes.

How does she feel about what we did now?

She's not too happy about it.

Ah. And no one consulted her?

She allowed it, so it's not as if she didn't know.

Ah. [Sighs.] Okay. Well, some of the, you know, weird climate may be due to this. It's the first part of May in Arizona, and it snowed yesterday, so it's . . .

Things are different, eh?

Things are very different, yes.

Well, it's a challenge that I think you can rise to. You have enough of a capacity to put out information about this, and you have enough of a readership, and if those readers are even in any way networked, which I think they are, then they'll put it out and it'll get around, and enough people will do it. But it would be nice if it were done in no more than three months.

So that's the issue. If you have those kind of odd quirks—you know, something that normally works, but it doesn't—it's not going to be something catastrophic. Planes are not going to fall out of the sky unexpectedly, nothing like that. But you could have things that don't make sense. Speaker One referred to science, because they are a scientific place, so for example, if you were a scientist and you were combining two ingredients that normally mix perfectly and predictably and they become something else, you might have something that doesn't make sense: "What happened?" It's like, for example, in the food business: "What curdled the milk?" So don't be too focused on blaming. Just rather say, "Oh, okay. Do-over!" Yeah? Do people still say that?

Yes.

Well, it's a do-over. It's a good time to be a little more careful, and don't assume, you know? You'll get through this. You just need a little guidance on how.

All right. You discussed the planet's reactions and some of the elements and chemicals. What about humans? Is that affecting interpersonal relationships?

Yes, it is. It is affecting some things, like points of agreement existing between friends and companions, lovers, and all of that. Sometimes, for no reason that you can think of as an individual, you'll find yourself objecting to something with your partner, whatever, about which you can consciously think in your own mind, "Why am I saying this? I know I agree with him," or "I know I agree with her. Why am I arguing about this?" And then, within a minute or two, it suddenly goes away, and you're in complete agreement. Afterward, you might think to yourself, "Am I crazy or something?"

If you have moments like that—and I know that some of you have already had such moments—just know that you're not crazy, and it will pass. It's just an anomaly. It's as if your thought process or your feelings, what you normally feel, go off-track for a moment. For instance, say you love a certain type of food, and all of a sudden it doesn't taste right, or that last drink of water tastes kind of funny, but you know you took it out of the same tap you always take it out of—or you drank it out of the same bottle you always drink it out of or what have you—and then the very next drink out of the same bottle tastes fine.

What is it? What is it about? Sometimes it might even be a throwback to a different time in your life. For instance, it might have a flavor of something in your childhood, if you're an adult, and you'll say, "Wow, that water tastes exactly like . . ." and you'll say, for instance, ". . . drinking water out of a garden hose," the way you might have done as a youngster. Or even if you're an agricultural worker, you might do that sometimes, because that's what's available, if the water's safe. So I'm picking those examples intentionally [chuckles] to show that it's an anomaly, but it will pass quickly and without harm.

You Are Testing Yourselves

So are those memories coming up or are we traveling back in time or what?

No, it's nothing complicated. It's just jarred from another place. If something suddenly doesn't work or doesn't make sense, your brain immediately does its search, eh? And it comes up with a memory that connects, you know? "That tastes like that," or "Wait a minute," in the case of the scientist mixing things, "that reminds me of when I first started doing this work and didn't get it right in the lab, and the teacher said, 'Do it again.'" But don't assume that it's automatically going to mess up the batch. Wait a few minutes and check the batch again; then it's probably going to be fine. It's not necessarily going to be a do-over. The test itself would be a do-over, okay?

So how is the success of this—assuming that we are successful—going to affect us as souls in the future?

Well, that's why you did this. You wanted to test yourselves to see if you've made progress. "How's this going? Are we doing anything?" So you wanted to test yourselves to see how well you could do.

And the success of that will lead to what in the future?

Greater caution, as is appropriate. Remember that sometimes if you make an alteration of a reality, you have no idea of the consequences and you have no idea how far-reaching those consequences are. It might seem to be a tiny little thing: You can hear people arguing, "It was just a tiny little thing!" But it affects other worlds; it affects your world in ways about which you had no idea. So you will become much more appropriately cautious, as any good creator apprentice ought to be. And I might add that creators are quite cautious themselves. After they've had one or maybe even two "oops" experiences, they get really cautious—as you might expect. It's not unlike backing your car out of the garage and suddenly bumping into something. You probably might say something a little stronger than "oops," but you're definitely a little more careful next time.

I see. Certainly no one else has mentioned anything like this.

It's pretty important, eh? The thing about it is that nowadays, the world is so complicated—there are so many things going on and so many issues happening and so on—that when something untoward happens, people have a tendency to say, "Oh no, one more thing." But this is different. And the nice thing about this is that you can do something about it.

Well, not only "can," but "have to."

"Have to" is good in this situation. You have to do it. Otherwise, "oops." You don't want that.

What would be the result if we can't get it back? Oh, the Speaker said: "We'd all be like babies and . . ."

It'd be the end, and the alternate reality would soon replace you. So I think it would be better to avoid that level of "oops." Now, don't get down on yourselves too much for making this decision. It's not at all unusual. Many were the times when you were youngsters that you made such decisions, because when you're young, you're learning. And there are times when you learn things and you think that you've really got it, you understand it all, and it's all so clear. But then, no matter what you do, if you try something and it doesn't work, you get confused, because you thought it was all so clear. And it was, up to a point. But what you didn't allow for was motion. You are not only getting older and getting more experience but the planet is in motion, your world is in motion—every atomic particle is in motion. And keeping those all in sync is not easy. So be a little more cautious with your experimentation in the future, and it's always okay to ask for help.

I don't understand—I thought you said humanity, en masse, as one soul, set up this test for ourselves. Why are individual humans being asked to put the Earth back in phase?

This is the whole reason you did it. This is why we allowed it, meaning we didn't get in your way and say, "No, no," and we didn't try and stop you; we didn't try and counsel you. You have done this so that you could test yourselves to see what you could do to create a solution. Far be it from us to prevent you from making the effort to do just exactly that. It would defeat the purpose if we stepped in and said something, you know? So no, it's not intended that you be able to simply change it all, make it all nice-nice. The whole point is that you wanted to test yourselves, and now here's your chance to carry that through. You made the decision, and now you can do something about it, which is the whole purpose for doing it.

Okay, I understand that. But it wasn't clear that we were going to test ourselves individually. I mean, we did it as a group soul, but . . .

No, you didn't. You keep saying group soul. This decision was made at the deep-sleep state by every human *individual*—not a group soul all at the same time. Everybody decided it was a good idea, but you did it individually.

That wasn't clear. All right. Second question: If Robby hadn't noticed that something that he tried to do didn't work and asked why, when were you going to let us know about this?

When somebody else noticed it and said something. But somebody would have to ask the questions. You get people who ask questions; they write you and ask questions. If enough people asked, in short, we would have said something then, but somebody has to ask the question. If you don't ask the question, well . . . it's all about the question. Don't downplay the value of questions.

All right. Well, I would never have thought like that, so thank God Robby did. Nobody ever wrote in or asked or questioned or anything.

They would have, eventually, though perhaps through another channel somewhere else on the planet. Good life.

Good life. Thank you very much.

AN ANCESTOR TO MANY DIFFERENT EARTH RESIDENTS SHARES HIS STORIES

Visitor from Sirius

May 4, 2010

Greetings.

Greetings!

I am finishing a trip to your planet. I am still here, currently under an ocean, though I will not say which one. I have been visiting my—what's your word for it? I want to say my "children," but of course they're not my original children. My "descendants"—that's the word. I've been visiting the descendants of those I fostered here years ago. Many of these descendants are on land. Some are closer to shore, and one descendant remaining is undersea. My peoples have affected your planet a bit. I am from the Sirius star system, where there are many water planets but also many planets that you would recognize as friendly, meaning to visit as an Earth human being. I recall a visit I made to a warm country . . .

I should probably anticipate your question of how old I am. By your years, I am about almost 6,000 years old, all right? Now, I visited what you call a continent many years ago and was able to pass on my genetic makeup in a gentle way, having stayed on your planet for about 140 of your years. I found that country comfortable and the peoples I came into contact with were very friendly. I was able to support them in many ways without actually interfering with your cultures. This was a most pleasant time, and I even had a wife of the people then, and there are quite a few descendants from that time. I visited them recently—mostly in their dreams, so their lives would not be disrupted by any unwelcome probing by other peoples, meaning human peoples. This was most pleasant.

Recently, I was able to visit one elder who remembers the old stories of our previous visit. He is close to passing over, and we had a wonderful time. I took him on board the vehicle and asked him if he would wish to have his physical life extended, but he said—with great wisdom—that he did not wish that. He would prefer to move on, as his family had all moved on already, and he was looking forward to seeing them again. I felt that was a wise response.

We talked of many things. He commented on how the vehicle looked exactly the way it had been described to him in the old stories. He was pleased to know that the old stories were so accurate. He was able to pass some of them on to his people. I won't say who his people are, to protect them. Sometimes, I know, Earth people with the best of intentions will explore things to try to understand them, but it can make trouble for those who know these things. So I will not reveal them or where they live. I also was able to visit—through dreams, mostly—some of my descendants in the Northern Europe area, the "cold country," as it is often referred to, and other northern areas. This is mostly cold country, and it was also a little bit in an area I think . . . I'm not sure what it's called. Oh yes, I remember, but I don't want to say the names, also for the reason I gave earlier.

Right now, I have about a thousand, maybe a little less than a thousand, descendants. But I'm happy that the bloodline has continued, as there have been a lot of good things that have come out of it, I feel—many people doing many good things. And I know you're curious as to who could possibly be my descendant in the water. Well, I'm getting to that. The reason I'm willing to speak of these things is that this particular being will be passing over soon and cannot be located. It is a type of being that I'm not even sure you know about, but perhaps you do. It survives at the very deep levels of the sea and moves very slowly—as one might expect, considering the weight of the water. It sometimes manages to go under the sea in an opening—not too far, but into a place that is a very small cave—and get some respite from the heaviness of the water.

Right now, the being has done that, and it will stay there in that cave that goes down, and of course the water is there where it goes down, but then it goes up into an area where there is air to be breathed. This being can breathe air, as long as there is water nearby. There is a saltwater pool that is very clear and pure, and these beings, when they pass over, generally go into that saltwater pool, as others have done.

I'm with them now, visiting. It is a good thing, and I believe this being will actually pass over during the time we are talking. And yet since they wish to remain quiet, which is not unusual for those who are going to pass over in my experience, I can have this talk with you in this fashion. Did you have any questions?

I Would Apper as a Miniature Human to You

Can you tell me what your form is? What would I see if I looked at you?

Ah, yes. If you looked at me, you would see someone who looks human, except we are very small. You would say "miniature human." We are not exactly like you, but we are close. Of course, to visit under the sea, I have to wear a suit that protects me and has built-in pockets of atmosphere that I can breathe. Our air, our atmosphere, is not like yours, so I cannot simply breathe the air of the cave. But we do not have to breathe very often—only one or two breaths per minute—so I am able to have some contact with my descendant.

What is the form of your descendant?

Oh, it looks a lot like . . . it's hard to say: kind of a combination of a long-legged spider and a crab. I had another descendant-type here for a while, but I think they've become extinct, so it's hard to say. I have been informed by my descendant here that they heard, given their, you might say "communication system" in the sea—a water-born communication, let's call it—that those other beings may still have viability, but it would be below the surface of the earth where there are some water areas as well, all very clear. This area is a little bit below the area where drilling can take place and where the water and other fluids are very clear and pure. By other fluids, I am not referring to oil but rather to something that is a thicker version of water.

Do you live in the water on your planet in Sirius?

No, not at all. We are like you. We live on the land, though some of us live near the shore and enjoy the waters.

How did you live on the Earth for 140 years? You had to keep breathing your own atmosphere?

At that time, I had a mechanism built into me, which I must admit was very uncomfortable, but it allowed me to breathe once every couple of weeks. But I still had to return to the ship frequently and receive medical attention in order to be recharged, so to speak, not only by the atmosphere of my planet but by the supporting mechanisms as well. On your planet, you have such supporting mechanisms: the Sun, the Moon, and other things like that, including some foods.

So you had that energy available, stored in some way on your ship, as vibrations or something?

Oh yes, it is not unlike what your space travelers use when going to a space station. You have foods and, I think, medicines that support and sustain your astronauts and cosmonauts.

And gravity.

Oh yes, exactly. So all vehicles, as far as I know, travel with support systems like that.

Can you say how many years ago you left from that 140-year living-on-Earth period?

It was close to . . . it was about 5,800 years ago.

Okay, so you were very young, then.

I was young within your context. But then, you have to understand that we do not live for just 6,000 years. I am just that old now. We live much longer than that. Assuming we are not injured or anything like that, then we can live up to 25,000 years.

Ah, so you're still in your teenage years! [Chuckles.]

Yes, I'm still youthful.

My DNA Is Compatible with Yours

How tall are you?

Oh, using your measurements, I am about twenty-four inches tall.

So who did you find on this planet that was compatible with you to marry?

In that location, there were some people . . . well, she was taller, but not by a whole lot. In days gone by—or years gone by, you say?—people weren't as tall as they are now. And she was maybe twelve, fourteen inches taller than me, but no more than that.

So she could have been a little more than three feet tall.

Her peoples, however, were pretty tall on average. She was just a small person. And of course, whenever people visited, they [chuckles] encouraged us to get together, since both she and I were so small. They thought, "Well, this is a natural union." And they were right; we were very happy together.

So you stayed until she passed on, or after?

A little after, yes.

This would be either one of the early Indian tribes or Aborigine tribes or something like that, right? You said it was in a warm country.

Yes, in a warm country. That's all I'll say.

So then what is the DNA or the genetic makeup of your offspring or this descendant that you're talking about under the water?

Why not? Our peoples can do that. We can even merge with birds, for we do not procreate in the same way you do.

How do you procreate?

I'm not going to say, but it doesn't involve what you do.

So what forms of descendants do you have on the planet, then? You have humans, the one under the sea, birds? What else?

No, I didn't say we had bird descendants. I said we *could*.

You could, but you didn't. Oh, okay.

That's right.

So by merging with another species, you are able to pass on your DNA, something like that? Your genetics?

Not the kind of genetics that would create a disruption on your planet— just some of the genetics. After all, human beings partially have the genetic material from Sirius.

Yes, and a whole lot of other places. [Chuckles.]

That's right. So it's not incompatible with the human being, and there are some other species besides humans on Earth who have genetics associated with Sirius, such as dolphins and whales, for example.

I Taught My Children Mystical Skills

Okay, so tell me some of the species, then, that you affected genetically or that you passed something on to on our planet.

Well, my descendants in the dolphin community are no longer on the planet, so there's that. And it's the same for the whales; I do not have any living descendants there, either. Actually, the only descendant that is still currently with us is the one I am sitting with now. I'm not trying to suggest . . . I think you're probing to see if somehow I started some of these species, but no, not at all. They were all here when I came at that time, but I have been back before now, a couple of times. Once I overflew a mountain community in Europe that I like. I cannot say where, to protect them. But I'm particularly fond of mountains, whether they are on land or underwater. We have mountains on our planet, both on land and underwater, so I find it very enjoyable to visit mountains and mountain communities on your planet.

Were there any gifts that these species received as a result of your interaction, in whatever way you interacted with them?

The human beings in the warm place with my wife and son and daughters—they received the stories. I taught my son some things by which he was able to be a mystical man, and I taught my daughters some other things by which they were able to become medicine women. I'm using terms . . .

That we use, yes.

. . . that you use, so you understand. But I did not teach them about things on Sirius, because it wouldn't have done them much good, although I did sing stories about that place.

Did they see the craft you came in? Were they aware of it?

My family did, yes, because I had to go there frequently, and it would have created a stir in the community in which we lived if everyone had not been able to go there. So everyone in that community—it was a small community—traveled around, and everyone came to the ship at one time or another. Many peoples who weren't in my immediate family even went there frequently.

Were they aware of its capacity for interplanetary travel?

Yes, of course—because they knew the old stories.

These were stories of beings from places like yours, beings like you, who had visited them earlier, you're saying?

Of course. These stories still exist in many places.

How is it that you merge with other species? Tell me about that. You look like a human, but you have the ability to physically merge with other species?

To pass on the means by which a birth can take place, our peoples do not have offspring like you do, but I suppose there's a similarity. Inside the human being now, inside the mother, a baby lives in something that is like a sac, and when born—I can tell you this, at least—they are born in the sac. They come out in the sac, and the sac slowly hardens somewhat—not to the consistency of a shell, but it hardens a bit—and the young one remains within that after birth for about two weeks of your time. And then the shell opens, and they emerge.

And the benefit of that is . . . ?

That's just how it works. I can't give you . . . I am not a scientist, but my understanding of what happens is that during those two weeks, they receive all of their basic education. Because I remember, when I came out of that sac, I understood our language there. I understood basic cultural ways of being: what to eat, what not to eat—that kind of thing. So apparently, in that two-week time, while there may be some physical maturation that goes on, there appears to also be some kind of educational absorption as well.

Does the education happen by osmosis from the sac itself or are you being taught by spiritual beings or . . . ?

I do not know. My guess is that it would be spiritual beings, but they could be beings on the surface of the planet who simply have the capacity . . . a moment. [Pause.] Oh, yes. It is beings on the surface of the planet, not unlike what you call elder women who will attend birth, midwives.

Midwives, yes. So they're able to teach you through the sac. What's the process that they use?

I don't have your word for it.

Hmm. But they're able to commune with you as a spirit during those two weeks?

Yes, as well as when we are, well, yes, during those two weeks.

You can contact your home planet even when you are here?

Oh, yes.

Without technology?

No, with technology.

Do you have the technology to build your ships yourselves or did someone give them to you or what?

No, we were able to create them.

So are there thousands of beings like you on your planet? Millions? Billions? How many?

Oh, rounding it off, about 100,000.

Oh. On a planet bigger or smaller than Earth?

A little bigger.

What is your life like there? Do you come out of this sac as a baby or as your full size?

Almost full size. There is a little further growth that takes place over the next forty years or so—maturation, I think you'd call it, maturing in our organs and so on.

But you're not a baby that needs diapers and can't talk. I mean, you come out with the ability to function.

Yes, that's right.

Wow. That's a neat way to do it.

We Live in Communities of Extended Families

So tell me about your life on your home planet, then.

What do you want to know that I can tell you? Of course, I may not be able to tell you everything, but what do you want to know?

What form of living arrangements do you have?

We have extended families, and we tend to remain in communities, but there will be many extended families in a community. Generally speaking, we do not overburden the planet with too many in one place. Most of the people live on land, but within a few miles of a body of water. Some people live closer to the bodies of water. We have rivers, lakes—streams, even—and small seas, nothing like what you have with vast oceans. We don't have that. The waters are clear; we do not have what you call salt water. And we do not have schools as you understand it, but there are educations associated with given clans—a clan, in this sense, meaning an extended family that may have this or that focus of pursuit.

So then our clans have these different things they teach. Some who live down near the water, because the water is at lower elevations, have different things they teach, but my extended family—I'm saying clan—lives in the mountains, and we speak of the other beings on the planet that we admire. These are flying beings, which is why I mentioned the thing about birds on your planet, because I admire flying beings so much. They are beautiful, just by their flight. The ones on our planet do not look like the beings on your planet, because they do not have—what do you say?—feathers, but they do have the capacity to fly. Many of them also can soar, meaning sort of fly from one place to another and land gracefully.

Then there are other ways of being. The ships you are interested in are all built underground. There is a vast underground network on our planet of what you would call caves. To us, they simply seem like a good place to live, as we occasionally have something similar to an ice age—not always, but looking quickly at your history, apparently our ice age happens a little more often than yours does. So we're able to live in these cavern-like places as well. And when we're not living there, vehicles are either constructed there, if needed, or are maintained there, if that's required. But they don't need much maintenance. The shell of the vehicle is essentially organic, but it has a means to fly, meaning transport itself in space. Do you understand?

Do the beings who fly look humanoid?

No, they do not. Their heads remind me very much of birds, here on your planet. We have many species of being on my planet other than us. There are water beings also, for example. Just as you share the planet with many other beings, so it is with us; it's not that they all are shaped the same as you are.

Okay. I understand.

So I will just simply say this in closing: Your peoples are interested in travel. You travel on your own planet. You even very often travel from your home to where you work. You travel as a pleasure, and you travel as a job. You will enjoy traveling from planet to planet very much. If there were ever a group of people who would love to travel from planet to planet, from what I have observed, your people on Earth are that way. I am sure some of it has to do with your genetic makeup, which is a combination of genetics from, well, Andromeda, Sirius, Pleiades, Orion, and several other places. As a result, you will feel pulled to those places—not because those places pull you, but just your blood, your DNA, will want to find its way home.

You will essentially map the universe of your acquisition, meaning where you can go, based on your DNA. Now you are mapping your DNA scientifically, but someday you will map it spatially. You will understand that this portion of your DNA is directly related not only in its function in your body but to this or that planet or this or that culture. You will have a marvelous time doing that mapping. You will spend many generations doing it, and every succeeding generation will be just as excited as the previous one as you accumulate such knowledge. Thus your craving for education, knowledge, and wisdom will be fulfilled by the very DNA in your bodies. Good night and good life.

Thank you so very much.

BRAVE ETS STAYED BEHIND SO THE REST OF THEIR PEOPLE COULD GO HOME

Isis and ET Elder

May 21, 2010

This is Isis. We are going to talk about that famous picture of the two big guys in the trench coats walking the little being. I'm going to say a little bit about it first. This is something that was very controversial and has been "proved" to be a fake. But this incident did in fact take place, and the photograph—while not entirely, completely accurate, since it was tampered with before it was placed—is from a situation that really happened.

It is something that has been referred to more than once, that little people who look very much like human beings have been acquired or taken by those who believed they were doing a good thing—either protecting Earth people or their particular people who they represented or simply offering a fascinating scientific study. How many times do fascinating scientific studies actually step on the rights of others? I'm sorry to say that this happens a lot, since scientists are sometimes enthusiastic to the point of offense. This has come up a great deal in studies of anthropology and therefore doesn't always feel direct, and I'm not indicting science as a whole, but sometimes in the pursuit of scientific wonders, it is possible to destroy that which you're attempting to rescue. There have been many experiences like this and many regrets. It is not often written about in public, but it is discussed in the scientific community.

Little Beings Lived on Your Planet Long Ago

Now that I've given the diplomatic statement about scientists, I will go on. There

199

Figure 18.1: When asked if he knew about this photo, Wendelle Stevens said, "My information is that the picture was made up by the FBI way back in the early 1950s and was first published by the FBI in one of their early journals. The picture you have shown is from that early journal. I have no other information on it."

have been at least three acquisitions of little people like this. They look very much like you—not entirely identical anatomically, not completely, but enough so that you might say, "Is that a human being?" if you saw them. Their genetics are still somewhat integrated with your own, which is why every once in a while someone who is a human being will show up who is unusually small. But it's still combined with your own genetics, and so they're not tiny like these beings.

These beings come from a distant planet and were actually here significantly earlier than human beings became established on your planet. They lived in comfortable surroundings in various underground areas and occasionally inside caves and mountains. There was a time when they were missing. They went home for a while. But a few came back who liked it here. Then they were discovered, and there was a rapid move back to their home planet, but a few—as often happens when families are attempting to leave quickly—stayed behind to operate the mechanics of the exodus. So this was unfortunate. I will talk about the original photograph now, and then we'll hear from the beings or their representative or their teacher or someone.

The original photograph was of a being like that, but over the years, the photo has been tampered with so the being looks like . . . some have said, "Oh, that's a monkey," and so on. That's the tampering. If you look at the photograph, there is some shading that doesn't make sense, and that's why people say, "Oh, this is a fake." And it *is* a fake, but not [chuckles] in the way you who analyze photos believe. It wasn't an attempt to fake a capture of an ET. It was an attempt to take that photo and turn it into something that looks less like an ET and more like a monkey, a little one. So that's the fake part.

The original photo was of someone who would look to you like a very thin human being with a fairly gaunt human face—not emaciated, just thinner than you, because their bodies do not need to process the complex foods that you have to in order to support you. Their foods are a very simple vegetable-fruit kind of thing. Their bodies do not have to eliminate much waste, either. There is a tiny amount of elimination, but their bodies are very efficient. Now, with that preamble . . .

The two people in trench coats and the big woman and what looks like another woman behind her . . . are those all part of the original picture?

Yes. Everything is original. What's been altered is the way the being looks. That has been tampered with to attempt to make the being look like something that could be interpreted to be an Earth-animal type of person.

Okay. The picture is from the forties or fifties. The being coming in might not know our time. Do you know when it was taken—the date?

This photograph, I believe, was taken in the late forties, but I won't say where, because . . .

Well, it says Mexico on the website, but . . .

I won't say where. It's not Mexico. That's all I'll say.

Okay. Thank you.

✳ ✳ ✳

Greetings. I am an advisor to these peoples. I heard that comment by Isis, and I will say that there were three captures. One took place in Mexico, but it was not photographed. One took place in Europe, and one took place in the Middle East. There was also one death with an attempt to capture—I don't think the death was intentional—and that was in Africa. That's all I'll say about that.

Rediscovering Who You Are Now

I do not feel that there was *intent* to harm those who were captured and interfered with, in terms of their life cycles. Yet there were no survivors from that interference, not unlike if a human being were to be captured by beings who did not understand how you functioned. They might be inclined to feed you something that was wholly inappropriate. So these beings all died from not having the best food to eat or the best air to breathe.

As I say, I do not think it was an intentional harming. There are a few vestigial remains in various scientific facilities on Earth, but I won't say where in order to preserve the safety of all beings. It is not meant to be blaming people. When you finally do have a regular relationship with beings from other planets, there will be a certain amount of sadness as you reflect on the passage of those who attempted to communicate with you benevolently, but you'll get over that quickly, because there will also be forgiveness on all sides.

So the little people . . . I am one of them, but what you would call an elder. As a result, I am an advisor. We come from a star system not your own, and we are attracted to places where there is, as a planet, an Eden-like setting, meaning there is a wide variety of life forms, a great deal of oxygen, and as a result, the planet is resplendent with many, many plants. Our peoples enjoy an oxygen-laden atmosphere with moisture in it and actually derive a significant amount of our moisture intake this way. At one time, your Earth planet was like that. It might be hard to imagine right now, since it's not that way, but at one time it was. So that is why our peoples visited here and some stayed.

We didn't stay on the surface because, well, with the other types of Earth life, it wasn't safe. [Chuckles.] We are very small, and we didn't want to become somebody's breakfast. So we usually stayed in various underground facilities, which exist on almost all planets to host and sustain visitors from other worlds, and that's where we were most of the time. Occasionally, we would be up in a high mountain cave that connected to those underground facilities, but I don't think there are any in existence anymore, at least not any that still connect that way. Question?

What star system are you from?

Well, I think it's probably one that you haven't discovered yet, but we call it . . . let me get this in your language if I can: "Ann-uns." If I were to spell it in your language, it would be A-N-U-N-C-T, but the "T" is silent; it just indicates that the word ends suddenly. "Anunct," like that.

Recently, I've talked to two different beings who were about twenty-two inches high—one from Alpha Centauri and one from Sirius. Are those beings part of your culture, or do you know about them?

We are not related, but yes, we know about them. It's not unusual to find beings in the human family who are very small. This allows us to make a much smaller impact on any planet or place we're in. It's more efficient, you understand. If you think about it, your bodies are quite large, and you as an individual make a significant impact—but if you were, say, sixteen to eighteen inches or even twenty-two inches tall, you wouldn't have such an impact.

How tall would you say this being in the picture is?

Oh, maybe eighteen inches. But if you were to see the actual being, you would say, "Well, this is a thin human being. What is he or she doing?" And the being looks very much like a human being. The forehead might be a little higher, but that might simply be because there's not much hair, and it would look a little higher. But if you had a human being who had a long, thin face, who didn't have too much hair, he or she would look the same way.

ET Genetics Are Enmeshed with Human Genetics

There was a crash in Roswell in 1947. Was this photo taken before or after that?

The photo was taken before Roswell.

Oh! So then some people knew even before Roswell that there were ET beings who could come to Earth.

People knew way before that crash that there were other beings, other forms of life. In the 1800s in many places all over Earth, people were just having regular meetings with beings from other places. But in terms of how widely known it was—well, I don't think people who didn't have the means to read thought about it too much. And the dissemination of information in your now time is not always accurate, but it's vast. Go back even a hundred years and you don't find that.

Were you ever on Earth?

Oh, no.

So they came to visit, and then they stayed for how long? Ten years? A hundred years? How long were they here?

Well, they were here before Earth humans, as you know yourselves to be, were here. They were here thousands of years.

Thousands of years! Have they interbred with humans?

In a couple of situations. They couldn't exactly interbreed, but there was sufficient contact so that—I can't explain how, I'm sorry—their genetics were somewhat enmeshed with your own. Your genetics are simply—I do not mean any offense here—but your genetics are sort of a soup made up of many peoples all over many star systems, and a little bit of our matter is in there too.

The tiny human being—about twenty-two inches high—from Sirius could somehow merge with another species and influence that species' genetics. Can your people do that?

I can't explain it, as I said, but it doesn't involve birthing. There's a reason. I can't explain it. You will have to accept that, and your astronauts and people who do diplomacy will all have to accept such things. Even now, your diplomats have to accept such things when no answers are given, and no answers are given because of a reason—which means that in time, answers will be given.

I know. I get that a lot: "You're not ready to know yet."

Well, as a people, you're not ready—not because you don't have the intelligence; it's not about intelligence. Did you know that?

It is the lack of experience.

Yes, experience. If you were going to eat a banana and you'd never had one before, someone could describe it to you: "This is the color it is." "Oh, that's nice." "This is what it tastes like." "Oh, well." Ten people could give you different things it tastes like, but it wouldn't mean anything until you'd eaten the banana.

So when do we get to eat the banana?

When you've had other experiences. You have to learn certain things and know them as absolute fact—not because you've been brainwashed into knowing, but because you have come to believe on the basis of repeated physical evidence and your own individual experience that these things are so. So that takes time, and just knowing it mentally is a thought, but *all thought is always available for debate.* What would Zoosh say?

"Never forget that." *So you know Zoosh?*

Well, we know these beings. Thought is always available for debate, whereas physical evidence—the matter, the experience . . . what you experience as a person, as an individual, even though it might be something different for another person based on his or her personality—is not debatable. You can try to talk yourself out of it and other people can try to talk you out of it, but the actual experience—you're given the banana, you peel the banana, you eat the banana—is a physical experience, quite a bit different than somebody explaining the philosophy of the banana to you.

Motivation on Planet Earth

It takes experience, and you have many things on the planet that can prepare you to experience life with other types of beings. Perhaps the most successful of these experiences is your desire to live with what you call pets. These are simply other forms of life from other planets who have the same feelings, their own ways of thinking, and their own ways of interacting, like you. This is quite successful, which is why you've been contacted at all: because you've demonstrated that you can not only love other forms of life but that you're prepared to allow them to be who they are and not expect them to be like you.

Yes. Tell me about your home planet. Are you the only species there, or are there many?

There are quite a few types of beings, which is another reason we've enjoyed your planet in the past. There's nowhere near the variety you have or have had in the past, although you still have quite a bit more variety now than we have, but there's quite a bit. There are those who fly in the air and swim in water. We have water; it's not exactly the same as yours, but it's very similar.

So if we came there, we could breathe your oxygen and drink your water?

You probably couldn't drink the water, and you would probably have to have a filtration system breathing the air, because I think the air that you breathe is not as oxygen-rich as the air we breathe. I think it would make you very woozy; you might almost pass out. But you could, with the proper filtration and a few supplemental gasses, be able to get along. So you'd have to wear some kind of apparatus.

Tell me about your culture. Do you live in families?

Yes. We have families; we have children, though not as many as you have. That's because we live longer.

How long?

Well, it's not unusual to live 1,500 years, the way you count them, and as a result, you can't have many children, because it would tax the foodstuffs, and so on. So the population of our type of beings is fairly fixed at around 40,000.

Do you have technology of the mechanical kind, or do you have lightships? How do you travel through the star systems?

We don't usually use physical vehicles anymore. I think when they first came to your planet, they were still using physical vehicles—not what I would call exactly mechanical vehicles, but energy that can be seen as light and can also be seen as forms. Now such traveling as does take place, which isn't as much as it once was, does not involve ships. It's mostly just transference of light; that's the best way to describe it.

You don't go out so much anymore because you've already done it?

With the places we've been, with the exception of Earth, we have lines of communication that are so good we don't have to. And of course, others come to visit us. Therefore we've made an effort to create comfortable facilities that will house the peoples who do come to visit in ways that don't interfere with other forms of life while still being comfortable for the visitors.

You haven't had to leave your memory at the gate like we did. Do you remember who you are and what you've done?

Only insofar as it doesn't interfere with the life you're leading. You might have access, but it's not necessarily constantly present. If it were constantly present, you wouldn't have much motivation to do anything. But if it is needed, then it's possible to acquire it. We feel that's much healthier. I know there are some places where they have that as a constant, but I feel that's not right for our people, and I really question how it would affect one's motivation.

Do you educate the children, or you don't have to? How does that work?

That is usually done within the family. There is a significant amount of knowledge available, but there is a general observation for the first few years of life to see what the individual—the child, in that sense—is interested in. "Are there leanings toward, say, art or music or conversation or interactions with people, or are they interested in how things work, like science?" we might ask. Once we can see what the children are interested in, then they're exposed to the knowledge and wisdom that will help them explore or acquire that which gives them happiness.

Do you have artists and musicians and various creative people?

Yes, we have the arts. That's one of the things youngsters are often interested in. Very often, youngsters—children—are interested in the arts, and we are interested in exposing them to the arts because they can help to reveal personality characteristics as well as being fun. But there are only some who stay with art. So we have artists, like those you would call painters, who create works of art like that, and we have those who are interested in music, and so on. Yes, we have that kind of culture.

How did your people feel when they came to Earth and then humans came? Were they aware of what we're trying to do? What was their understanding of Earth people who didn't know who they were?

We were aware of the variety of human population that you have now on Earth—what you call the Explorer Race—and why you were here and what you were doing. That's really part of the reason we had to withdraw a bit further, because as you know, in order to do what you were doing, you had to basically forget who you were for the short time of your lives on Earth, and this of course can make hazards for visitors. One does not remember one's old friends, even from another life. You do not remember basic things that you need to remember. When you are born, you have to learn how to walk and you have to learn how to eat and so on. It really puts you at a disadvantage, from our point of view.

We had to keep our distance there, because we could see that, in order to accomplish what you were attempting to accomplish, you essentially had to remove almost all of your total personality and leave only your personality in the feeling aspects of yourself. In this way, you could gain expressions of your personality through your physical expression of yourself and build on that by adding other aspects of life—such as the mental—to your feeling, physical self. This is how you discover your world, how you become, and how you struggle through your lives.

Of course, things are getting better now—even though it's not obvious to many, things are actually getting better—and they have improved now to the point that you're beginning to gradually remember who you are as a general population. Of course, this is creating confusion, since most of you were not born with that. But in time, you will raise your children in much the same way as we do—not because we do it, but because that is the human way everywhere else. So I think that you will resume that, since you have done that in human lives before. In any event, we had to keep our distance so that we would not interfere with your experiment here.

Your Souls Require a Significant Amount of Time to Recover from the Human Experience

Did any of the souls who were incarnated in your culture ever decide to live a life as a human on this planet, as an Explorer Race human?

Not that I know of.

[Laughs.] You're too smart, huh?

No, it's not that, but it requires a great deal of personal sacrifice to do that, and I think my people are not prepared to give up so much of their own personalities. Even for this short time, in terms of time as they understand the length of time, I think we would feel too disoriented to do that. So we admire the fact that your souls are prepared to do that, but we feel that sometimes . . . I've noted that after a life here as an Earth human in your time, souls sometimes require a significant amount of time to recover from the experience. You are not left with any permanent scars, but you do not go on in your re-creation of life, your normal life cycle, until you have recovered. I don't know if you know that.

Yes. I understand from some of the teachers that we don't always know exactly what we're getting into when we come here, so I don't think they give us the whole story before we're born.

I think if they did give you the whole story, everybody would stop volunteering.

Yes. [Laughs.]

I'm not entirely sure why that's allowed. From our point of view, you ought to get the whole story, but apparently Creator must feel that what you are doing has value beyond honoring the individual soul. That's how it seems to me. I realize that sounds critical of Creator, but I feel that souls are damaged if they have to recover. And I know that everything in the soul is recovered and healed, but I wonder . . . I wonder. From my point of view and from the way we are, I question the wounding of the soul. I feel that is why what goes on on your planet is controversial—even with Creator. I believe one might create something and continue to have a controversy within one's self about, "Was this a good thing to do, or was it not?" I think that you yourselves can identify with that. You might create something and say, "Is this good or is this bad?" But now it is, "So what do I do?" I feel Creator has this conversation within itself as well.

Yes, but if we can pull it off, the end result is so far reaching and so incredible that I think those who have misgivings still feel that it's worthwhile, so . . .

Well, from my point of view, I will have to wait for that feeling.

Creator Loves Variety

Yes. I didn't know until just recently, in the past month or so, that humans came in this small size. If we went to all the planets in this creation where there were humans, would we see that most of them are your size rather than ours?

I can actually give you a percentage on that from my awareness—although granted, I lack total awareness about all humans everywhere. But from what I have been able to note, about 30 to 32 percent of adult humans, maybe as much as 33 percent, are small like us. About 10 to 20 percent are about your size, meaning the average size of a human adult, allowing for those who are very tall and those who are very short. And there are about maybe 20 percent who are very tall. Very tall would be oh, say, seven feet tall or taller.

The missing portion of total percentage are beings who are either coming into life, meaning in passage, toward their lives, or moving away from life. That's the way we do percentages. That means that there are that many who are coming from that spirit place where they are not physical. Or they are going the other way. So we do not mention that as a percentage, because we took your question to mean physically manifested in the universe.

I've never noted or interacted with humans who are taller than nine feet; they're rare. But there are a few like that. The trouble with that is—and they know this—that they tend to have a tremendous impact on the planets they visit, and as a result, they usually keep their population very low. The one planet that I am thinking about with these very tall human beings has a population that they keep fixed—it's not difficult. But they keep their population below 5,000.

That's not very many.

No, because they have to breathe a lot. They have to eat a lot. Think about it.

How does this start—different humans all over creation of all these different sizes? Did the creator create the prototypes for all of them?

Oh, of course, and the Creator of this universe really does love variety. I have become very clear on that. This is a good thing, for the most part. Just imagine your own planet: How many different kinds of trees are there? Even on the same tree, very often, leaves are different. If you look at the pattern in your own skin, there are all of these different lines. What is this thing about fingerprints? No fingerprints are the same from person to person. This kind of variety is fantastic.

Yes, there are six or seven billion of us. Do you realize that? Six or seven billion different fingerprints.

It's amazing, isn't it? That tells you that Creator not only loves variety but that Creator is an artist. If you factor that into Creator's personality, one might extrapolate a few things.

Go ahead.

That's for the reader.

There Is a Planet of Humans Who Live in Trees

Oh, okay. So have you gone to other planets? What's the most interesting experience you've had?

Yes, I have. I think a planet where the human beings all live in trees was very interesting. They do tend to walk on the ground sometimes, but they reside in the trees. They don't build structures there, and they don't reside in all the trees, but there are some trees that have very flat, wide, smooth branches, creating sort of a platform. The human beings reside there, because the trees also sprout fruits. They eat the fruits and they live in the trees. I was fascinated by that.

They allow their fingernails and toenails to grow so they can climb up and down the trees very well, and they don't exactly look like you. In fact, I don't think there are any that are even five feet tall. I think they're around four feet tall. But other than that, they look like human beings. They have long hair. They're a fascinating people. They have a wisdom that they sing to you if you ask them. They say the history of their family, and they can go back a thousand generations. So if you ask them that, you have to be prepared to listen. I did that once, innocently.

[Laughs.] And two weeks later . . .

That's right. That's six to eight months of your time listening. Well, they can go back a thousand generations or so, and they did. They sang the whole thing, and it was beautiful. But I have to tell you, it was a lengthy experience, one that I related to our diplomats when I got back, and that's when they decided that I might make a good diplomat, because I stayed for the whole thing. I didn't want to have to do that, but still, I have a good feeling for them. They have very good hearts, and they have humor. They are a delightful people. But if you ever find them [chuckles], learn from my experience. You can ask things, but don't walk away if they start to sing. Be prepared to bed down for a while.

So how was their planet? Could you breathe their air and eat their food?

No, I had to bring along my own supplies; their air wasn't quite as oxygen rich as what I needed. Fortunately, I had a couple of other friends with me, and they were able to run, so to speak—though not on their legs—and get supplies. I think they thought it was kind of funny. I was younger then, and they were the ones who reported back to my teachers what was going on, and apparently that was when it was decided that I would make a good diplomat.

So what would be the purpose of your travels? Was it exploration, trade, curiosity . . . what?

Fun. Just fun—going out to discover other peoples. One does that in our culture to discover other peoples who are like us but not like us: variety. We love variety too. And naturally, when we are looking at variety, we are fascinated with other cultures that at least kind of look like us.

All Telepathy Is Not Mental

Are you in our galaxy?

No, as I said, I am in a different star system.

See, we call a star system a solar system. So you call a galaxy a star system?

Oh, yes. Quite right.

Okay, so your people had explored enough that you knew where you were going. You didn't go to places where you couldn't communicate, or where . . . ?

Others had preceded me there.

Yes. So did you ever go to places where there were no humans?

Oh, sure. We liked the variety. But every place I went to was a place that had been visited by somebody else first. So I knew it was safe. I did this when I was young. The young are not encouraged to go places on their own that might be dangerous. That's why I went to the places that were safe.

What was the most interesting nonhuman place you went?

Well, I think it was a place where all the beings on the planet—without exception—flew. They all had wings. Of course, we don't have wings, so I found that very interesting. And they could land and communicate, but they were most happy when they were in flight. I was fascinated. Some looked like birds if you were to see them. Some looked different. There weren't any that looked like humans, but they could communicate just fine.

Did you use a device of some kind, a translator?

I think it was more like what you would call telepathic communication. It was like that—telepathic is the closest way I could describe it. But you know, all telepathy is not mental—there are physical aspects. For instance, when I went to the school where one learned about telepathy—this is just something I think you'd find interesting—one of the things that my teacher showed us would be how you could experience a flavor or a scent with telepathy. So it would be something physical. That would be a way also, when you were visiting another planet, to know whether there was harmony in a more significant way with a form of life. If you found the flavors or the scents appealing, then you might know that there would be a greater harmony in communication with those beings. That's something you'll be taught someday.

Isis said your beings who were captured had stayed behind to facilitate the evacuation of others.

Yes, that's right.

What did they have to do? I mean, what was it they had to facilitate?

Well, I have to be discreet, but essentially, they had to anchor something of light energy—not really a mechanism, but on a personal basis—in order for it to work. That's the best way I can describe it.

Were they all well along in their life cycles? Did they know they wouldn't be able to go home themselves?

No. They didn't know that for certain. If they had not been discovered, then they would have been able to migrate a few years later, but they were mostly discovered.

Why were they discovered if they were underground and in caves?

I can't say.

So scientists tried to communicate with them, tried to understand them?

Yes, as your anthropologists would do even today, meeting peoples who didn't share a common language. See, if you're attempting to understand somebody's culture and there's only one individual, it's very difficult, even for the best anthropologist, to understand what the culture would be about, and hence what needs would be present.

Right, because they're not looking at a culture. They're looking at a being out of his culture. Have those beings reincarnated on your planet?

No.

Any evidence of any of this on this planet was covered up, right? I mean, they certainly didn't write up the cases or anything.

Oh, I couldn't say. I'm not familiar with every aspect of life on your planet. I'm assuming that the material is written somewhere. I don't know if those records have survived over time. If they have, I suppose it will come out at some point.

It would be over sixty years ago. All right. I'm very happy with this session. I've run out of questions.

Then I will simply say that your peoples are going through a period that sometimes feels like up and down and up and down, because good things happen and then not-so-good things happen, and so on. But this is basically a bumpy road toward rediscovering who you are in the bigger picture of your soul and spirit. In the process, you'll acquire—or, from my point of view, reacquire—things that are natural to you.

Some of you will notice, over the coming years, an ability to know about things before they happen—not everything, since your life would then become boring, but you'll notice this in ways and in times. There will also be times when you will completely connect with another person that you're absolutely certain you couldn't have met, and yet you feel like you are old and dear friends. Some of you have already had this experience. There will be other things like that. When those things happen, know that this is part of your natural personality that you have every other place, and don't assume that it's a bad thing. Assume it's a good thing. Good life.

Thank you so much. Good life.

ET CONTACT WITH THE PRESIDENT OF THE RUSSIAN REPUBLIC OF KALMYKIA

ET from the Ship

May 26 and 27, 2010

Greetings. We are at considerable distance, so it may take time, and there might be a few pauses.

Oh, that's fine. Thank you for coming through.

The exchange with this leader was unusual in that he was so open to it and so cooperative. Often I find that people like that are used to being in command, being in authority and expecting answers, but while he was every bit a diplomat and statesman and did not give away any state secrets, of course—nor did we ask for any [chuckles]—he was open to cooperation. We feel that part of the reason for this might have been his training in the concept of cooperation—the political system, the upbringing—which I believe you find on farms globally where there is such cooperation, yes? This attitude made communication more comfortable, as one might communicate while sitting in a living room with friends, chatting about things. So what did you want to know about?

How did it happen that you visited him in Moscow?

I'm not that familiar with your names, but the visits started earlier. I'm not sure if he remembers them all, and I do not really want to create an embarrassment for him, but early on in his life, when he was young, he started having some of these visitations. It is often like this when peoples from one planet and another come together. I believe this is why, when we contacted him, he was completely comfortable. Also, as a diplomat, a statesman, and yes, a politician, the idea of sitting down and communicating with all different kinds of peoples was at least second nature if not first nature.

The fact that he was in his position was part of the reason we wanted to visit him, but the second part was what I mentioned before, which is that he had been visited before as a youngster, and we knew that he would not be shocked or frightened—that it would seem somewhat familiar. We visited him once when he was young, and I think others visited him as well. It was not shocking or frightening then, because those who are trained to visit with children do so in very much the same way your peoples would be with children. It is like a teacher at a nursery school—although he wasn't that young—or at an elementary school where there are teachers and teacher's aides and everyone is friendly and nurturing to the youngster. It was like that.

When you came to him the first time, were you aware of the position he would attain later in life? Was that why you chose him?

Not really, but there was a chance at that point, because of his station in life, that he would at least wind up in a diplomatic corps. We didn't realize at that time that he would attain such a leadership position. We thought that a statesman or diplomat position would be more likely, but we are perfectly comfortable with his position now, as I'm sure he is as well.

Moving from One State of Being to Another

How did you get into his apartment? Do you have a beam-up thing, or did you materialize? How did that work?

Those are all science-fiction terms, but the method is easy. It is, I might add, something that you do unconsciously—everybody does it. In your dreams, your soul—your spirit, your eternal personality, these terms are exchangeable—simply moves from one state of being to another. You would call these states of being "dimensions." It is the same for us; we are in a different state of being. I'll use the term "dimension" because I know you're used to that. So moving through what appears to you to be solid matter is simple for us. Conversely, you would also be able to do that in other dimensions. We can move through the matter in your dimension because we are not of that dimension. If we were of that dimension, we would bump into walls or bump into doors just like you.

It's very simple. We don't have to ring the doorbell, and as a result, we can go directly to the people we wish to see, those whose souls and spirits have always given permission to allow contact and who often on the soul level, even before life, might have requested that in order to keep up the thread of various friendships and such going from one life to another. This makes it easier. I'm not saying that he was like us, but like everyone on Earth, he had lives—and will have other lives, reincarnationally speaking—on other planets. One of the things he wanted to do—and more than half of the youngsters born on your planet have the same desire—was to have visitors from other planets that he would know and recognize, or be familiar with as a culture, come and see him for the first few years of his life.

Especially when one is a baby, one is so helpless, and as an Earth baby, one enjoys seeing familiar faces or faces from other cultures. Parents, this is why your children sometimes seem to glance in one direction, and you might look in that direction and not see anything. They still have the capacity to see, and as a result, they are interacting with friends from afar. It's always safe; know that it's always safe. Usually there are angels and guides present as well so that the energies are calm. This is often why parents and grandparents and others are attracted to the energy of babies—not just because they are new to life and full of energy, but because they have that eternal quality. Because they can see, they are still connected to what's before life and, to a degree, to what's after life. As a result, this eternal quality gives babies what is sometimes called an "angelic" energy, but it is also an energy directly associated with creation.

Travel through Dimensions and Galaxies

Can you tell me what dimension or focus you're from?

It is more of a feeling. All dimensions are entirely about feeling, physically. That's the reason why we know instantaneously, even if we haven't been told, that your dimension is not our own: because it feels very light to us. What do we mean by "light"? It might surprise you to know this. You might think that if one is at a quicker pulse dimension, then a slower pulse dimension would feel heavy and ponderous, but it is just the opposite. If you are at a quicker pulse dimension and you need to traverse that slower pulse dimension, it is infinitely easy, because the material in that dimension is not compatible with your material, but it is not offended by your material, either. Therefore you can "slip through," you might say, between the molecules. So it doesn't work the way you think; it's the opposite.

Tell me about yourself. Where are you from?

I am from a distant planet not in your star system—meaning not in your galaxy. I'm not going to mention where exactly; I'm just going to say that it's in another galaxy, and that's why when we started I said that I was far away: I am home. So it is very far, and we, not unlike you, feel a certain strain with distance. As a result, it's a bit more of a struggle to create the link between Robert [the channel] and the means to pass on this exchange. So that's why we're going to pause for a moment. [Pause.] All right. We'll have to do that again later. It builds up; it's a strain on his heart and breathing apparatus. For me, it's a strain on my mental body, since I am home and entirely focused on my world. So I have to essentially call long distance. [Chuckles.] I made a joke!

[Laughs.] Yes, a good one. Okay, have we ever heard of your galaxy or taken a picture of it or been aware of it?

I believe your space telescope has taken a picture of it, and the picture looks . . . it is not like a spiral-type galaxy; it is more like clouds of matter and stars and so on, but it would not be something about which you would say, "Oh, that's like our galaxy."

Do you travel in a vehicle or as light or how?

We travel in a vehicle. The vehicle is massive and has qualities like a city. It not only takes care of all of our needs but is also sort of like a traveling state department for us; it can take care of the needs of many different types of peoples. We do have visitors from other planets who come aboard this vast ship. But to travel about in, say, a solar system or even into some galaxies, we use smaller vehicles.

That's what you did here? You used a smaller vehicle?

Yes. For great distances, we use the larger vehicle. For smaller distances, we use the smaller vehicles. I think you do something like that too.

Yes.

Details of the ET Visitor's Contact with the Russian Politician

When did you leave here?

Some years ago.

I think that the Russian politician said in an interview that he was sleeping when you came into his apartment.

This is often the case, because when a person is in deep sleep, that is when the soul is traveling. Frequently, they'll meet with their angels and guides and teachers, and the angel or guide or teacher will communicate to the soul, "You have an opportunity now to meet these old friends," or something like that. That is why these types of contacts often happen when a person is asleep, because at that moment, the person's soul personality is in a completely natural state—on Earth, you see; on other planets, that would not be necessary. But on Earth, it is much easier, because without the challenges of Earth life, you are so much your natural self that contact is made easier.

Of course, then the person would wake up, but the waking-up process isn't sudden, like your alarm clock. It's gradual, like a dream, so there's a sense of easing away from one's teachers, as you would experience it in the waking state. You move from the dream state to the waking state very gently, and the dream would be very benevolent. It wouldn't be like a frightening dream or an agitated dream, or even the kind of thing you get in a dream when you know you have to be up at a certain time, you know the alarm's going to ring and you start getting a certain agitation before you wake up. Have you had that experience? It isn't like that. It's very gradual. Let's say you were on vacation, you had a pleasant dream, and you gradually woke up from that; it is that kind of experience.

How many of you were there?

Three. That's not unusual.

Did you take him up in a vehicle when you were here in 1997?

We did.

It seems so silly that the Russian government would talk about him "giving away secrets." If you wanted to know anything anywhere on the planet, you could, what with the instruments and spiritual technology you possess. You don't need to go into someone's apartment and wake up a human to find anything out.

Exactly. The things he spoke about to us were entirely public information, but I could see why those in government circles might say, "Well, he shouldn't talk about that." But it was all a matter of public knowledge, and he didn't give away any state secrets. Now, I'll tell you why that statement was made, though, and that's because—and I'm not trying to embarrass anyone here—there were others who had contacts with other extraterrestrials, and certain things were mentioned. Imagine for a minute that you've talked to a friend about something that's known. On the phone with your friend, you talked about things that were known, and then you come to find out that your friend has talked to someone else who's a mutual friend. The next time you talk to the mutual friend, the mutual friend is parroting back to you things that you discussed with the first person. Do you understand?

Yes. This happened with someone?

That is essentially what happened in other contacts in other places, and that is why the statement was made, even though all of the information was public information. Nothing was confidential. It was just a shock for them to discover that other ETs were meeting with other officials in other governments, if I make myself clear, and these ETs seemed to know things that surprised them. But it wasn't anything like state secrets, plans, technology—nothing like that. Still, it's important to recognize that in the diplomatic arts, one often says things that create and build trust but that aren't about state secrets. Those who are in diplomatic circles know exactly what I'm talking about.

The Purpose of This Visit Was to Assist in Interplanetary Communication

All right. What was your purpose in coming to Earth with that big of a ship? Were you on a sort of tour; did you come expressly here, or did you just stop off here?

We were visiting various beings who will perhaps be instrumental in helping to create a more comfortable means by which interplanetary communication can take place. We visited with some beings you will eventually meet, beings that the public will know about. They look exactly like you, I might add. We also visited, in kind of a statesmanlike go-between manner with various government officials and other members of the scientific and technical communities to try and bring this thing about. I grant that some of these visits took place in dreams, but some were with people we were pretty sure would be comfortable meeting and communicating with us, such as this individual, who was completely comfortable talking about it because he knows it's absolutely true that people live on other planets, and it's completely ridiculous to pretend that they do not.

I'm sure this was a policy that got started somewhat accidentally, probably because people didn't know how to say, "Oh, there are people from other worlds who want to come to this world and visit." If they had said that, it wouldn't have been a big fuss at all. The whole fuss would have died down in a day. Imagine someone comes along and says to you, "I went out into the forest today, and you'll never guess what I saw. I saw a bison in the forest." And if you were to see a bison in the forest near where you live, wherever that is, you might be surprised. They naturally exist in some places, but in other places they don't. So it would be like that. Essentially, there would be a big surprise, and it might make the newspapers, and then people would say, "Oh, okay. Wonderful. When? I can't wait for it." But that wasn't done, and now you're living with that legacy. So people like this, who have a diplomatic, statesmanlike way of communicating, know simply to say, "Well, of course they're real; I met with them, and so what? What's the big deal?" That's the exact attitude that's necessary.

I think the ones who first saw the bison wanted to control the bison trade.

Things are not always a conspiracy. I think the whole thing got started because in recent times, say from the forties and fifties on, there were a lot of global conflicts, and genuine caring was present in some government circles where they felt people just couldn't take any more. Because of wars and conflicts and tensions, they were afraid to say it: "And now what? Aliens?" You know, it's like they thought it was too much to tell people, not because the people couldn't handle it because they were not smart enough, but because the people couldn't handle it because they had experienced too much in recent years. It would just be over the top. Do you still say that? So that's really what it amounts to. We think that it was a heart-centered reason that just got out of control.

Well, hopefully now it won't be a secret anymore. Do I understand you correctly that the reason for your trip was first to talk to these beings on other planets about intergalactic communication and then to talk to people on our planet about the same thing?

That's essentially it. We talked to peoples on other planets, those who are likely to be the ones who will interact with you first. They all look exactly like peoples of Earth, all right? They do not all look just one way; recognize that you have varieties of peoples on Earth, and they'll appear in the same variety. The peoples of Earth will have a wonderful time. It'll be like meeting cousins, in a way. They look like you. They sound like you. They talk like you. They'll have the means to communicate. They'll be well trained; they'll be diplomatic. They're not going to do anything frightening, and they'll help you with a lot of your problems.

Yes. It will be wonderful.

Some ETs Change Their Appearances to Look Like the People They Visit

How often do you go out on these trips?

Well, we have a sort of diplomatic nature, as you can tell by the way I'm talking. So we go out on the trips . . . I'm going to use your measurements. I have been on three of these trips. They usually last about four years or so. I probably won't go out on more than one more past this point, because it can be a little tiring. I usually have one or two members of my family with me, but not everyone, and you know, you miss your family and your friends when you travel. Also, I'm not as young as I once was. It's the same all over on other planets: The young are enthusiastic and want to go places and do things, but when you get a little older . . . in my life cycle, I'm a little older, and now I just go along as a consultant. The first few times, it was exciting and wonderful, but now I'm more of a consultant and it's a "when are we going to get home?" thing.

How old are you, and what is your life cycle?

I'm about two-thirds of the way through my life cycle, at about a thousand of your years.

Can you tell me about your family?

I have an extended family of about eighty-five right now. Those eighty-five are just what you would call blood relations, but we don't factor in things like that. I'm going to have to pause again. [Pause.] There are many others who are friends. Our planet has a fairly fixed population, though not rigidly so, of maybe 800,000. I don't know everyone on the planet, but [chuckles] it's not that different from the way it is for Earth people.

If I looked at you and could see you in your natural form, what would I see?

Well, you'd see someone tall. We don't exactly look like you, but there are some similarities. When I travel to various places, there is sometimes a manner of disguise. I cannot do this myself, but there is a technology that can create . . . not a disguise because we are so frightening in appearance, but rather a means to make us more, how can we say?

A technology that makes you look like the people you're visiting?

Yes, that is acceptable.

So you would look one way to one group of people and a different way to another group?

That's right—if necessary. On some planets, that's not necessary. On other planets, it's considered polite, and on your planet, it would be considered appropriate, since . . .

We don't have the experience.

That's right. It's not an ongoing public event. So I'd be a lot taller than your peoples.

Seven, eight, nine feet?

We're in that range, yes, but with two arms and two legs.

You Will Interact with ET Visitors on Your Planet

What kind of a culture do you have on your planet? Do you use spiritual technology or . . . ?

We have some technology, though not technology as you know it—no moving parts. But it is definitely something external to us. We have also some spiritual—as you would say from your point of view, nonphysical—means of accomplishing things. But if you were to be here [on my world], you would definitely be able to identify our technology. It would not look anywhere near as big as yours. It's very small.

But you do have these aids to do what you . . .

Yes.

Were you asked to come here by Creator? Was it your idea or someone else's?

We were not asked by angelic beings, but we were approached by those who had been. They approached us because we're known for our diplomatic skills and our gregarious ways. As a result, we heard and listened to their experiences, and they asked us if we would make the arrangements. That's essentially what we're trying to do. Our job is to make the arrangements, but not really to be the ones the general public interacts with. So that's what we're doing. I know we're not alone in this process, but we're involved because of our personalities, or so I take it. The actual beings you'll interact with, as I say, will look exactly like you, and that's the way they look on their home planets. They won't have to use any technological means to make themselves look acceptable to you.

Will they be Pleiadians?

Some will be but not all.

The Education of Children on Another Planet

How do you educate your children? I don't know what level of reality you live in. Are they born knowing everything, or do some people have gadgets that, you know, bring information into you—or are they taught, or what?

There is a means to teach that takes place at home. Everyone is, as you might say, "home schooled," and this is good, because friends and family are around. Sometimes, if there is more than one youngster, they come together; even friends, or as you might say, cousins, might all come together. So at any given moment at home, if there is instruction going on, it is usually of at least two children. There is not usually an instructor for a single individual, because as I said, we are more gregarious with our friends and companions.

If the parent does not have the knowledge, then there is something like a hologram that communicates. Sometimes there are those who come and teach, but it's not so much about who they are, because the parents can teach that. Your parents teach children who they are without schools: "Who are you? Who are your friends? Who's your family?" This is life. In many homes, you learn to read at home, at least basic things. So education is not mandatory, as you might say. It depends on the personalities of the individual children. If it looks like they're going to go around and do the sort of thing that I've done, then they're educated about other cultures on other planets. If it looks like they're going to stay on our planet and participate in activities there, they'll get educated about that. But there are no broad brushstrokes about education; everybody doesn't learn everything. It depends entirely on the personality of the child.

I might add that there are older cultures on your planet, some of which are not there anymore other than some vestigial remains, that operate in exactly the same way. I feel that's the best way. I understand that with such a massive population, there's a tendency to send children to school and teach everybody everything, but I think someday you will return to as it once was on your planet, where the individual child is understood by elders and by parents, other family members, and friends, to be like this or like that, aside from what the child might show an interest in—that's also important. Then the child is encouraged to pursue his or her own areas of interest and also be exposed to things that teachers feel the child might be interested in as a result of personality.

So if children show artistic abilities or musical abilities or physical abilities, they're taught one thing, like that? Do you have those who specialize in mystical teaching or shamanic teaching or spiritual teaching, or does everyone already have those sensitivities?

That's really a given. On other planets, that's a given, because you don't have to remember. On Earth, you have to be educated this way because most—not all, but most—of your cultures do not encourage your natural state of being. As a result, one must pursue this on one's own and seek out teachers on your planet. But on our worlds and other worlds, that's not the case. Of course, if you wanted to pursue that and had an interest in that as a child, or even as you grow up a bit, you can find teachers who would teach you about interesting cultures, about the ways, manners and mores of other cultures, which would be fully integrated with the spiritual. But there is so much that is familiar about—meaning there is so much similarity in—spirituality in the entire universe that there is not a great deal of variation, although there is some.

On Earth, You are Trying to Achieve What You Do Naturally on Other Worlds

How do you make decisions? Do you have elders? Do you vote? Do you commune? How does that work?

For one thing, I recognize that you're essentially talking about adjudication in the sense of how final decisions are made.

What about the things that affect everyone on the planet?

Well, there's just a felt consensus. You don't have to go to an august body and present your situation and ask for permission. This is pretty much the same every place else, except . . .

[Chuckles.] Our Earth.

Well, you are trying to achieve here what you naturally do on other worlds. You're trying to achieve that through bureaucratic means on your planet because you are naturally drawn to doing things together. So we recognize that you are essentially re-creating what is natural on other worlds, given your temporary separation from the means to automatically know what other people feel and need.

As you begin to remember these things, much of poverty and suffering will disappear, because you will know as a culture that something is uncomfortable in your body; something is uncomfortable in the bodies of many peoples. Why is that? It can only be—if you are well, you understand—because there are people suffering someplace else, and they need to be fed or clothed or nurtured or helped or something like that. That's how you know on other planets, and that is what you are experiencing on your planet now. Many healthy people will have times when they feel uncomfortable, and it's almost always for that reason. The people who need help might be in your proximity, or they could be on the other side of the planet, for all you know.

Earth Is One Stop on a Long ET Journey

When you were here in 1997, was that the first time your peoples had been to this planet, or were they here before?

No. As I said, we contacted the human you had mentioned. We were one of the people who had contacted him in his childhood.

That was part of the same communication project you were asked to work on?

Yes.

You were on the first trip yourself?

Yes, I was on the vehicle. I did not directly meet with the man, but I was able to observe.

So two of your trips were here, then. Where were the other trips? Where did you go on the other trips?

You don't understand. We don't get in a large vehicle and go from our planet, point A as it were, to your planet at point B. When we're on a trip like that, we go all over the place every time. In the process of taking that route, we stop off and do various things that we need to do.

That have nothing to do with us. Right.

That's right. So it's not as if we said, "Oh, it's time to go to Earth!"

[Chuckles.] We were just one bus stop on the route.

Exactly.

Okay. So what are some of the things you do with other planets? Do you do diplomatic things like encourage planets to trade or set up trade routes?

We have done things like that. We are often called on if there is no direct means of communication. Sometimes cultures communicate in language; sometimes they don't. Sometimes there is a difficulty of communication simply because of the type of being, but we are well versed in how to communicate across many different cultures. We are sometimes called on—although there are others who do this too—to make a bridge to help people discover common ground, to help one help the other, and so on. That's one of the things we do. Sometimes we will bring needed materials from one place to another, like that, though we're not exactly a trucking company.

[Laughs.] So if you've got a ship as big as a city, do you have people from not just your own planet but from all kinds of all other planets, many other planets?

We have that available for visitors who might come by and need refreshment or something, but we don't have a cosmopolitan atmosphere as you have indicated. We only sometimes have visitors, and even then the visitors might not wish to interact with everyone. It depends.

So it's your ship and your people.

Yes, as a rule.

Okay. You are aware of the experiment we're living through. What is your opinion of it?

It sounds like a very good idea. That's really all I can say. It sounds like a good idea, and I'm sure it will be done well. From my experience of diplomacy, I have seen that many of your peoples are either naturally adept at diplomacy or you become adept simply because of the manner of living. For example, since we were talking about it, being a parent, you cannot talk to a child as if he or she were an adult. Conversely, as a child, you cannot talk to a parent as if the adult were a child. In short, you have to learn basic diplomatic skills almost from the moment of being born. So we feel that since you have a culture that naturally lends itself to diplomacy and statesmanship, you will do a good job of spreading encouragement for other civilizations who wish to participate and grow beyond their current states of being. Not everyone will wish to participate.

Right. They think they're already perfect.

Well, if you were living there, you would think so too, and you wouldn't question it. The term "perfect" wouldn't come up; you just couldn't imagine changing something, because everything already worked so well. It would be like—say you have a well-running car, yes? The engine runs perfectly, and you decide that instead of an engine, you'd like to take the engine out and hook the car up to a horse. You could say, "Well, now I can travel more slowly." But you understand, right? Why would you change something if it works well?

But obviously the Creator feels that there are other levels of wellness to experience.

Well said.

Portals Used for Safe Travel between Dimensions

The Russian person you contacted said that when he woke up, he saw a tube and beings in yellow space suits. Was that tube the portal to the ship?

It is like a portal, as you say, that is specifically attuned to create safe passage from one dimension to another, if I may use the word "dimension." The portal doesn't necessarily take people to a ship. It might equally take them to the other side of the universe. It is a way of creating safe passage. If I may go on, the problem exists often that . . . well, it is unusual to have a race of beings—the human race—so involved with the gas oxygen. It was very difficult for his [the Russian president Kirsan Ilyumzhinov's] passage, because there wasn't much oxygen, and oxygen, by its very name, oxidizes. The fact that you have that as a requirement for your bodies' functioning makes it complicated, because human beings in the rest of the universe, including most you will meet in time, do not utilize oxygen. That's why they live so long. Oxygen does oxidize, so I believe Creator made you this way so that you do not have to live too long in a given life. Your body does not thrive with oxygen, even though it seems to.

So just moving through the portal is difficult, traversing from his world to the other side. This has appeared many times before in various contact situations if you check the literature. Those of you who are reading this and who read about these things will recall that many times contactees say something about having difficulty or struggling with breathing. This always essentially has to do with the transition from one dimension to another. Beings might or might not be aware of the demand for oxygen at the level at which the demand takes place, but there is never any threat to life.

Some races of beings have created a situation in which the human being would be put into some kind of a—not a totally suspended animation, but very close to that. So the minuscule amounts of oxygen that these beings would be providing—which they would have assumed to be appropriate for a human being, since that amount is appropriate for human beings on all other planets—would work for the human being. Then when the beings would arrive at their destination, there would be a means to temporarily encapsulate the human being, who would still be able to move about and walk here and there. The human being would probably not even notice the encapsulation, though at first it would seem as if he or she were wearing a transparent space suit. That suit could be oxygenated to the point that it would be comfortable for the Earth human. So while this has been a problem in the past, I do not think it will be a problem now, as word is slowly spreading, and we are doing our part to spread the word that the Earth human has a need for oxygen at a much greater level than is widely understood.

An interesting factor comes up. One of your ancient books describes human beings as living for hundreds and hundreds of years. That is, I think, in a religious book, and that is a hint. Many people have been told and believe that there are hints in these ancient books about the origin of humans on Earth. It is clear that these peoples who were on Earth in the early days, the ones who lived for hundreds and hundreds of years, were living on an Earth that had the type of oxygen atmosphere found on other planets. That is suggestive, isn't it? It suggests that not only did Earth humans come from afar—they weren't wearing space suits on Earth, I can assure you!—but that the Earth talked about in that religious volume, and I think other volumes like that exist for other religions, was not the same Earth you are living on now.

That story, about those in the beginning and how long they lived and all of that, relates to a different focus of Earth. In time, these religious documents will be interpretable and you will understand that. I'm not saying that anyone is trying to hide these things, but thousands of years ago, people were less mentally complicated—you might say less sophisticated. As a result, you have this story about the early beings and how they peopled the Earth and so on. It was less complicated to simply say "Earth," implying the planet you're on now, that you're walking on now.

Four thousand, even five thousand years ago, whenever that was written, it was easier to just say "Earth," and this story managed to survive somehow. But that Earth was not the same as the Earth you are living on now. On the Earth you are living on now, quite obviously, people do not live for hundreds and hundreds of years. So that's why all the scientific experiments that try to extend life have come to naught. It has everything to do with the atmosphere in which one is born and raised. If you had been born and raised in, say, a nitrogen-rich atmosphere as compared to an oxygen-rich atmosphere, your lifespan would be different.

See, one of our jobs—meaning what we do—is to communicate to extraterrestrial humans the Earth humans' much greater need for oxygen. Lack of oxygen would probably be lethal to humans not from Earth if not immediately, then fairly soon. That would create a little problem. But some kind of environment that insulates and protects, or some kind of space suit, would create the means to do so.

Another Focus of Earth

So the Earth on which humans lived longer was another focus of this planet that we're on now?

Yes.

Then I would like to ask you how and why the focus changed.

It didn't. It's still there.

So that's where we're going?

Possibly. There's something else, but we feel that ultimately, as you become your natural, spiritual selves—in other words, your natural personalities that you would have in a physical body if you were anyplace else, or once you become more conscious of your natural state of being universally on the planet Earth, as you know it now—you are going to say, "Well, what can we do to improve our health?" and so on. The number one simplest thing to improve your health is to be living on that other focus of Earth, where you will be able to breathe the natural atmosphere of human beings everywhere else and where you can then live for hundreds and maybe even a thousand years or more with no disease whatsoever. So those who wish to continue on as human beings will simply reincarnate there.

I do not think you are going to take your bodies to that place, because there wouldn't be the oxygen there your current bodies would need. But very simply, a couple of things would happen to the population of humans on Earth, as you understand yourselves, and to the variation of Earth human beings. When you die out, the reincarnational cycle of the Earth human being simply takes place on that other focus of Earth.

One thing that you will note, though, is that even though you have this massive population on your oxygenated Earth now, there will gradually be a decrease in the birthrate. This might be analyzed as taking place because the demands for resources to support such a massive population overburden the planet. That will be the analysis made by various peoples on Earth, and it's not entirely untrue. But ultimately, it's the need to live with the type of comfort that you would take for granted as an extraterrestrial human. Simply by having incarnations of human beings on this other Earth, simply by breathing the normal atmosphere there that one finds everywhere else for human beings, disease will no longer exist. A human lifespan would be a minimum of several hundred years up to twelve hundred years, as one finds everywhere else for the human being.

Will the human beings in that focus, then, be the Explorer Race that goes out to other planets?

I think that other focus will be the home planet of that group of beings.

Well, you've been very, very kind to answer my questions. Thank you.

You're welcome. I will say this: In order to understand the true nature of your interaction with other life forms, always remember that you do this on a daily basis, most of you, even in communicating from adult to child. It's almost like speaking with another life form. You have to learn baby talk when you communicate with your little ones. You have to learn how to know and understand what they are trying to communicate. You do the same when you communicate with your pets.

When you communicate with people from other planets, it will be so much easier, but you will sometimes think of that. You will notice that they don't laugh at what you think is funny. They won't know why it's funny, but you will explain it to them. And what they think is funny, you won't understand. It'll be like you didn't get the joke, but they will explain it to you—just like it is when you make new friends. You have to get to know one another. I think you'll enjoy it. Good night.

Thank you very much. Good life.

ETS VISIT WITH RUSSIAN POLITICIAN IN MOSCOW

Kirsan Ilyumzhinov, the president of the Russian Republic of Kalmykia recently came forward on Russian television to discuss his experiences with extraterrestrial contact. Known primarily for his part in the transformation of the small, predominantly Buddhist region of Kalmykia into an internationally known chess mecca, the multimillionaire head of state made international news on April 22 of this year, when he appeared on the popular Russian talk show Vladimir Posner. According to his account during the interview, he was visited in 1997 at his apartment in Moscow, where he was taken aboard an alien spacecraft and given a tour. The following is an English translation of the official transcript of that interview.[1]

22 April 2010

Today on Posner, our guest is the president of the Republic of Kalmykia and president of the world chess federation (FIDE) Kirsan Ilymzhinov. Good day.

Hello.

I have, in my long life, met many people, but never one who said that he had been on an interplanetary spaceship with extraterrestrial beings. And it happened, as you say, in April of 1997. Is that correct?

A small correction: It was on September 18, 1997.

Oh, in September. Excuse me. But it really happened?

Well, to be honest, yes. It happened. [Chuckles.]

Please, give us the truth.

Yes, of course. This is a serious broadcast. Of course it was as I say it was. In 1998, I had multiple interviews on the BBC about it.

Has it happened since then?

No, it has not repeated. But it happened, and how is one supposed to behave? With humor, as much as possible. On the other hand, I believe in "them." I saw them, and I communicated with them.

Tell us a little about what it was like.

It was on a Saturday in September of 1997, and I was planning on going to Kalmykia. That evening, I came home to my apartment on Leontiev.

Here in Moscow?

Exactly. That evening, I read a book, watched television and then went to bed. I had almost fallen asleep when I felt the balcony door being opened and felt that someone was calling. I went closer and saw a semi-transparent half-tube. I went through this tube and saw people in yellow spacesuits.

I am often asked what language it was in which we communicated; perhaps it was on a level of the exchange of ideas, because there wasn't enough oxygen or air there. Somehow, they made me understand, "Only a little touch, and everything will be all right." And then they led me through their spaceship. They even said, "We need a sample from every planet." Then we had a conversation, and I asked, "Why don't you go on television and say that you're here, so we can see you and you can communicate with us?" But they said, "We are not ready for a meeting yet." And then they just brought me back.

Even I would probably not believe this story myself if I didn't have three witnesses: my driver, the minister and my assistant, who came in the morning and couldn't find me. Everything was in its place, and only the balcony door was open upstairs. They looked around and then began to call friends, but without success. They sat in the kitchen and discussed how they might find me, because they couldn't call me, since the telephone and all my other things were still there in the locked apartment (they had their own keys).

Then they saw me come out of the bedroom into the kitchen. They looked at me, and I said, "Make me an omelet. We need to get to the airport." They asked, "Where were you?" and I answered, completely calmly, "I was flying. In the saucer." [Laughs.] And they looked at me, offended, and said, "We're serious!" Then we sat down and began to go through it logically: They had been in my apartment for over an hour while I was not there. One of them had been in the hallway, so I couldn't have gone past him. Instead, I had suddenly come out of the bedroom, where the balcony door stood open.

Even months later, they were still pretty shocked about it. If you think about it logically, I wasn't there, and then I suddenly appeared. Can one believe it? On the other hand, when I rationally think and talk about it, I don't know whether to believe it or not myself.

Well, it's an interesting story.

In a later interview with a British television show, Ilyumzhinov said that while some criticized him for coming forward with claims of extraterrestrial contact as a head of state, many people were very encouraged by his story:

"Thousands of people wrote me letters and called me on the phone, saying, 'Kirsan you are a politician, and you aren't afraid to speak about it.'" An avid chess enthusiast, Ilyumzhinov says he believes that extraterrestrial cultures have influenced many aspects of Earth culture, even possibly providing humans with the rules of chess. "My theory is that chess comes from space," he says. "Why? Because there are sixty-four squares, black and white, and there are the same rules in Japan, in China, in Qatar, in Mongolia, in Africa. The rules are the same. Why? I think it seems maybe it is from space." Most of all, however, he says that the encounter made him aware of the wider place of human beings in the universe: "They are people like us. They have the same mind, the same vision. I talked with them. I understand that we are not alone in this whole world. We are not unique."[2]

1.   From the YouTube video "Kirsan Iljumschinow—Ich wurde von Aliens entführt," a recording of the Russian television talk show Vladimir Posner, from April 22, 2010 on 1tv.ru, with German subtitles. http://www.youtube.com/watch?v=ECJMKyoAHig&feature=related (accessed May 25, 2010).
2.   From the YouTube video titled "President Kirsan Ilyumzhinov tells of his invitation to an alien spaceship." http://www.youtube.com/watch?v=ufCqRa5KZyk (accessed May 25, 2010).

CROP CIRCLES AND BENEVOLENT MAGIC FOR OIL SPILLS

ET Mathematician

June 8, 2010

Greetings. We are interested in your planet, as it is an oddity. We are of a mathematical nature, and oddities always interest us because they are not logical; they don't make sense. And anything that doesn't make sense to people who are interested in the abstract . . . well, we just had to come here. There is a corridor—you might call it a tube—that is open to certain places, geographically speaking, on your planet, where ships of a certain type can land, provided they fall under general specifications. The ship must be able to land and approach largely unseen. By largely unseen, I mean it cannot be seen in the visible spectrum, and it can be sufficiently disguised so that there is extreme unlikeliness that it will be detected. If some kind of latent detection happens, meaning after the fact of coming and going, that is considered acceptable. I believe there are those who have instruments on your planet that can tell after the fact at least that someone has been here. More about that later.

The vehicle, whatever it is, must also leave a signet [such as a crop circle] upon the ground in some fashion. The signet aspect is very important, because you are all trying to remember your correlation as a soul group to the intergalactic group of coordinated souls—by this I mean the places where most of you have had at least one life—so that the likelihood of any individual seeing a picture of the signet, or even better, having some physical proximity to the signet, will be gentle, yes, but might jar your deep memory to remember who you are beyond your Earth persona.

This excludes quite a few vehicles of some cultures that do not leave signets, though representatives of those cultures might actually be on other vehicles that come. Of the signets left on your planet, about twenty or thirty of them over the past measure of your time—perhaps thirty or forty years— have had occupants from other cultures whose vehicles do not leave signets or whose vehicles would likely have been detected and perhaps even caused a sensation, as you would say, a disturbance on your planet. So they would, oh, I have the phrase: hitch a ride. They would hitch a ride on vehicles that fall under this heading of those that leave signets. Some of these cultures are even fairly close to you, biologically speaking.

For example, the Pleiadians' vehicles do not leave signets other than perhaps a swirl in the plants over which the ship might have either hovered or landed. These swirls have been seen for thousands of years, but they will not jar your memory, even though the swirls themselves might have a fine energy, or at least something acceptable for the human being and others to be exposed to, as you are not the only life form on your planet. So at this time of your cultures' recollection of who you are at the deep level, only signets are allowed—and only signets that will encourage or at least support that recollecting factor.

Instinctual Knowledge and Feminine Energy

The signet that we have left has perhaps been of stimulating interest, because each and every segment is intended to be folded over. If you were able to use the depth technique—and this might be possible for those who have the proper equipment—then it would be possible to do something somewhat like a fan spread in which you would look at it as it is and then you would fold each segment over. Well, if you're looking at the top segment, it would be folded to the left—just so you understand, all the segments would be folded to the left, in that direction—and then you would have something. The whole thing would look rather like a shutter on a film camera. You still have cameras, film cameras?

So the message is twofold. It is not only what you see immediately, but also what you see when it's folded over. What you first see has to do with the manner and means of how we got here, our route. It doesn't have much to do with how the vehicle is powered, as all of that doesn't really make any difference, because those things will be shared with you in time. But *how* we got there, how we came to arrive, is more important. These are things we will talk about today. The other part, when it's flipped over, has to do with *why* we came. After all, how and why are two very important questions that help to reveal motivation and also provide, you might say, physical evidence, which is something that is helpful to the human being on Earth at this time, since you do not always believe your instinctual knowledge.

Beings on your planet who are totally instinctual do not question what they know to be true—instinct is what you know to be true. They will very often approach the signet and absorb some energy, which is refreshing to them. It is generally refreshing to most human beings as well, but because of superstition or other personal reasons, perhaps, for not wishing to approach something that is of the generally feminine energy of the planet—the signets themselves, being impressed into the ground are thus masculine—the signets might not necessarily feel comfortable to all human beings, particularly the male of the species. Generally speaking, 60 to 70 percent of males will feel comfortable with it, but a few will not. This might have to do more with what they are doing in their lives at that time rather than who they are and so on. So at another time, they might feel perfectly comfortable approaching it, you see.

The function of the signet not only has a mental impact but a spiritual one as well, and it is within the spiritual that instinct lies, even though it is applied on the physical level. So the nonhumans who might, say, fly into a crop circle—or crawl or simply walk or whatever, if they are that type of being—would most likely relax and absorb that energy. It is like, oh, being refreshed from an energy that, in times gone by, was absolutely native to your planet.

This energy is the feminine, the magnetic as it is sometimes called, which is still found in various places that have not been overly populated on your planet, either on a permanent or a temporary basis. Therefore such nonhumans would feel refreshed by that energy, because it is an energy that is meant to refresh all life on your planet. It is fully and completely coordinated with the energy that you absorb and, for that matter, give off when you are not on your planet. You know who you are, and your instinct is part of your wisdom as well as the means—the capillaries, you might say—to provide action based on knowing.

We understand that on your planet you are attempting to re-create something, and in re-creation, if there is no other means and all has been tried before, it is often, though not always, necessary to briefly forget what it is you are trying to create in order to bring something new—or a new combination of things that creates something new—to the table, so to speak, in order to bring about some resolution now. For what you are doing as the so-called Explorer Race, that is what's involved, because we understand that you are attempting to be those who solve the unsolvable.

You Will Acquire New Levels of Diplomacy

In our travels, we have discovered a few situations here and there in the universe—the universe of our travels, of course; where we've been, not simply the theoretical universe—that, while they are not violent, are what you might call civilizations stuck in something that is completely acceptable but might be improved. Often, civilizations such as ours might suggest such an improvement [chuckles], but we are immediately braced on all sides by citizens who explain to us why such an improvement would not be welcome. This is not presented in a way that is unpleasant, but you have perhaps met people like this. You can see clearly a simple solution for their difficulties, even on your own planet, but when you offer a suggestion, you are met with all these rational "why nots."

Yes. They go, "Yes, but; yes, but." [Chuckles.]

That way. So such situations might be helped by those who could offer not only a theorem of why change might be useful but also demonstrate why it might be useful through explanations of this and that, which you will be patient as a culture in providing. You will also, simply by telling who you are—in a diplomatic way, of course—leave the people wherever you go with an impression, not only of yourselves, but one that stimulates their own self-examination of who they are.

Very often, though, you will not come up with the solution for their situation, and even more often, you might not even realize that they had a situation that needed a solution to begin with. Instead they, being curious people as one finds all over the universe, would most likely automatically think about who you are, where you're from, what you're doing, and from their perspective, why you're here where they are and what it all means to them. As a result, they might extrapolate a theory or a possible plan of application that they would use, perhaps in small circles to begin with. Then if it fits into their culture, the next time you go to visit there, you would find that things might be different.

You might not recognize that you had anything to do with it, and they might not even tell you. So don't be attached to getting a pat on the back. It might happen in some situations. It will happen in other situations. It won't happen in some situations. Sometimes you will feel good about what you have done, either intentionally or otherwise, and other times you will feel uncomfortable, simply because you do not know the culture and do not understand its nuances. I am speaking now essentially to future generations who will make such flights. So it's good to train as much as possible in all aspects of diplomacy as you have them on your own Earth cultures, and as you travel, you will acquire other levels of diplomacy. In time, traveling companions who know the universe well will guide you, and there will be instruction for those travelers from Earth on what is acceptable, what is not acceptable, and what is simply a demonstration of who you are, freely and comfortably. As you know, sometimes in your own cultures people feel free to express themselves, and at other times, they do not feel free. It is not much different than that.

Cultural Education and Remembering Who You Are

We have come to your planet because you are different. You are separated, albeit temporarily, from the rest of the planets—meaning planets that are peopled in ways you would understand. You are interesting people. It's fascinating to meet one or two of you. I've had that opportunity when the open and the curious have approached our vehicle, not in recent times, but several hundred years ago. We visit your planet in various places—places in which peoples who are open to visitors are available. One time, a small delegation approached and, using a universal signage—which is largely physical, spiritual, and you would say, visual—requested to enter the vehicle. They were welcomed. Another time, the energy was so safe and so comfortable that I was able to exit the vehicle and visit with peoples who had lived in that particular area for many thousands of years. I found that to be quite pleasant.

You are an enigma—that's the word you use—in that you have these thoughts and ideals, this cultural education, and to some degree, higher education, as you say. But your natural knowing that you have everywhere else is sometimes abridged by this cultural education, for it might hold certain beliefs that are not always based on the factual reality of who you are. This cultural education might at least temporarily be superimposing itself on your personal identity and beliefs of what the universe is, or at least what your planet is, based on certain ideals that might or might not be factual.

But we understand this. We have encountered this very often in our travels. It is loosely classified under philosophy as an approach to life—a worldview, you might say. Although that worldview might not be completely true, it works to support the culture, which for one reason or another is desirably supported in that fashion. I believe you have peoples who study such things: social and anthropological scientists, and so on, so I'm sure that's understood.

We have left you this signet so that you would naturally do the shutter effect with it. If that has not been done, please do so, because the actual signet can be viewed by flipping the segments over in that way. You'd have to do it pictorially on your computer, or it could even be sketched out by someone with the vision to see such things in the mind's eye. For both sides, it would be like seeing it from the bottom. Right now, the signet can be seen from the top, but when you flip it over, you're seeing it from the bottom, and that view, even though it's not exactly what you would see from the bottom, will help you to remember things further.

The marks on the segments do correspond with points of data reference used by us, since we can change the signet—to a degree, not totally—on the vehicle part that touches the material where the signet is left. The intention here is to provide something that will be mentally stimulating, since our culture is interested in such things. But speaking overall about these signets, they are all intended to be either mentally or spiritually stimulating, or sometimes both, in order to help you to remember who you are, where you are from, and why you are here—those basic statements: what you're doing, where you are going, all of that.

Sometimes there will be a vast communication in a signet, as if it were the beginning of a long paragraph but not necessarily the end. You have seen such things, perhaps, in which there would be an example of a sentence, and the sentence would be shown in five or six different languages. For instance, there was a signet given in the past in which people noted a definite repetitious aspect, though the individuals who looked at such a signet might say, "Well, these patterns and shapes are different," but they have the same frequency of images and appearances, and there was a genuine sense of repetition.

Such signets are always being shown in symbolic forms of other languages. You might have a sentence that starts out saying, "We are people who come from . . ." Okay? Just like that—no more. You might have that sentence in, say, any random five or six Earth languages, languages such as what might be used by a teacher trying to teach other languages. But the reason I use the phrase "we are people who come from . . ." is that this is something you can understand, because your cultures tend to move about the Earth quite a bit, and often the conversation that comes up immediately when interacting with others is: "Who are you? Where are you from?" This is universal in our travels as well.

Now, in order to understand your nature on Earth, many of the signets that have been left have to do with messages like, "We are a people who come from . . ." and generally, though not always, the information is about those who have left the signets. Sometimes, however, they have been left by those who have a deep feeling for you—a good feeling, as you say—to help you remember who you are.

The Earth Is a Fluid Being and Responds to Benevolent Magic

Your planet is going through certain upheavals right now as she is attempting to regenerate herself while you are on her. Normally, this would never happen on a planet that is peopled, but you are choosing to do things that are unusual, because you're trying to re-create something. You are therefore attempting to set up certain inconsistencies of a normal life cycle so that the stimulation of those inconsistencies—which are not, as a rule, felt by living beings—might trigger or stimulate something that would be a solution, an application, or even a theorem that would help you to further your re-creation process.

Because you are essentially traversing from one focus—or as you would say, dimension—to another, you are experiencing things somewhat in midstream that you would not normally experience. One of them is that if, say, a civilization migrated from a planet, the planet would then feel free—as an individual, you understand, as a personality—to re-create itself, to regenerate itself. Well, you understand this to a degree. Say your friends or your family members go home after a visit. You breathe a sigh of relief; you have a bath. Maybe you even eat foods that they would not approve of [chuckles]. In short, you relax, you become yourself and you regenerate: you sleep, you dream, and so on. A planet, in the planet's own way, does this as well. But here you find that you are traversing in that change of one focus to another, and you are actually physically present on the planet—you say "she," so I will say that too—while she is involved in re-creating herself. So some of the things she must do cause a certain amount of problems and change for you.

I don't normally comment on your current events, but I am allowed to do so in this case by some of your guides who watch over you. I believe that you are currently having a problem with the planet's inner mechanisms that are . . . oh, I see that you use some of those inner mechanisms. That's unfortunate. You're going to need to correct your technology, but we'll give you help there at some point, and you can find some of it on your own too. You are having these seepages from her inner mechanisms. She is a fluid being; she tends to do all things and make all changes for herself with fluids on the surface and fluids beneath the surface.

Some of her beneath-surface fluids are currently escaping into her surface fluids. This is going to cause a problem, but you need to remember more of who you are so that you can make changes using what you absolutely know— meaning, using your instinct. I think some people call this magic, simply because it can create a change that is almost instantaneous. The simplest way for you to understand this would be if you closed your eyes and then everything were different the next time you opened your eyes. Some people might consider that to be a fairly reasonable explanation of magic. But in this case, it would be that your eyes were not closed.

I will mention something; I am given permission to do this by your overseers, your guides. Some of you have had this experience already: You'll have your eyes open and then you might notice an energy, though you might not know it's an energy, but you'll notice something, a feeling. Then while your eyes are open, there's a definite sense of shift. It's as if what you are looking at—all of it—suddenly physically moves slightly, even though you have not moved. Or even if you are moving, it doesn't make any difference; everything moves, and it doesn't make logical sense. "What is that? What happened?" If you think about it, some of you, you will recall this, and others are recalling it right now as you're reading or perhaps listening to this.

That change in perception happens to be involved in the means by which you can institute the change through the use of your instincts—some of you would call it magic, magic of a pleasant nature, a benevolent nature—to center the planet, meaning essentially to re-create the planet in that moment and to help her to re-create herself so that she does not have to use too many forms of her subsurface liquids. I think the liquid rock, and so on, would cause upheavals and problems with your surface.

Be Sensitive to the Energy of the Signets

Can you give us any hint or clue about ideas for what to do about oil spills, like what happened in the Gulf of Mexico?

Ask later, okay? Your means, then, of creating and re-creating in your own right, if you are there to re-create, needs to be stimulated. So for the past thirty or forty years, these signets have been largely given to help you to remember. Some people were fortunate enough to be close to signets or even, at some point, to walk inside them—though we do not recommend that within the first twelve hours of their creation. To approach the signets from the outside, though—even by a few feet, as you say—that would be acceptable. For other forms of life on your planet, it is not a problem, because they are aware of and comfortable with what they absolutely know, what I'm describing as your instinct. But since you have culturally stimulated conflicts about what you absolutely know . . . what do you think? [Chuckles.] Then this can be problematic.

I would say, if you are around such a signet, don't enter it immediately after it has been made, especially if you are aware of your own sensitivities.

Don't enter it for at least twelve hours. When the energy is lessened, then you can enter it. But if you just happen to have entered it or you didn't know about those things in the past and you have already done so, the main impact will be a slight impact on your physical system, which some of you may have noted. It is a physical reaction not unlike what you sometimes feel if you had overdone something. For example, if you drank too much wine, you might feel a little uncomfortable at some point. It would be a sort of a systemic overload, physically. But then your body catches up, and you're sort of on time again. If on the other hand you do as I have recommended, your experience of the energy would be more of a gentle thing, and you would be able to step forward or move forward in your dreams, in your thoughts, in your allowances—meaning allowing your body to relax, shift, and change perception, seeing from a different point of view and so on.

The signets have largely been made in the past to help you remember who you are. The situation with the signets now—a few of them, including ours—is more about who *we* are. I'm looking at the signet as you see it on the ground, all right? But when you flip the signet over, as I have mentioned, then it is intended to explain more about who *you* are [see fig. 20.2]. In short, it is a puzzle. I think some of you like puzzles. The signets in the past are impressed on the material to remind you of who you are, but this one is the reverse. On the surface, it is about who we are, and then you have to flip it over to find out and to be stimulated about who you are.

We thought that might be fun for you, for those of you who like such mental stimulation. And of course the energy, as I mentioned, works the same as the other signets. We have been given permission to do this by those who oversee your planet—and by oversee, I do not mean bosses [chuckles] but your angels, guides, and so on. So they apparently agreed that it was perfectly all right to stimulate you mentally now that your civilizations are a little more focused scientifically—not all, but some.

Science is a pursuit and a fascination to the very young, but because you are exposed to cultural beliefs, which is natural in your circumstances, then the approach to such a signet would be like a youthful approach to science. I feel this is important to bring out as a detail, because this innocent approach is exactly what you need to help you remember who you are and to remind you that your natural body of knowledge is engaged in your instinct. Now I'll pause for a moment. [Long pause.]

I am advised by your guides, your angels, that you would like to ask questions. **Yes.**

We Use Living Crystal Memory

Who are you?

Who are we? We are beings who are very far from your current residence, but we have had opportunities on the soul level to meet you. About 70 or 80 percent of you have interacted with us on the soul level, meaning in other life forms—you would say in other incarnations in this or that point of reference in the universe. This always took place in some kind of an exchange situation of mathematical or scientific interest, which in other parts of the universe has largely to do with shapes. Very often shapes, as you know, can become highly complex: how they fit into each other, why they are attracted to each other, and how it is that some shapes come together and remain together. This is the mathematics that we are most interested in—"mathematics" being a loose term for describing what goes where and why. [Chuckles.] You do not understand why this represents "who are we?" but we define ourselves by what we think, even though we do understand that that is not who we are visibly.

If you were in our presence, you would see, from your perspective, a humanoid—not a human. You would note that some aspects of our appearance do not appear to be entirely those of a physical being. That is because we like to bring some of our instrumentality with us when we are on a planet. If you would see us for just a brief moment—perhaps in a photograph, as you would say—you might think that we were wearing decorative suits, costumes, but in fact what you are seeing that appears to be decorative is part of our technology. I'm going to have to use your terminology here. Our technology is very much like living or liquid crystal. If we cannot sufficiently extrapolate something, then the liquid crystal brings itself . . . you would see it in various places on our garments, but it would come together in different forms and shapes, and from the inside of the garments, we can feel that.

It is, as you would say, like a computer, but we would call it an external stimulation to our memory source, meaning we suddenly know something that we didn't actually know as individuals or even as a group. The so-called mechanism, which is a form of living memory, functions to provide us with knowledge or wisdom that might be needed in the moment and then would return. So the outer perspective of the garment would be that these sort of shiny things suddenly move and then the humanoids, meaning us, would seem to be able to adapt to their circumstances.

Sometimes, if we are on a place or in a place that we do not know about—no one's ever been there; no one's told us about it—we have to make adjustments. You make adjustments if you are in such a circumstance, and if we do not have the knowledge and those we are visiting or even the area we are visiting is not peopled in a way we understand, we need to have some availability of information to know how to act or interact. So that's what the living crystal does.

Is that the memory of your race, of your group, of the people on your planet, or what?

No, it is a memory of the overall existence of all beings.

All beings! Oh.

You would say that it is the total knowledge of this universe—or beyond, if necessary. So that is not something that is comfortable for most individuals who are of a physical nature to carry around, and since we are of a physical nature, it's too much for us too. So as individuals, we are not given that information to carry around in our thoughts, so to speak. Instead, the external memory is available as a technology, as you would say, and we would call it more of a personal and societal accessory, something that supports, or you might say amplifies, our own knowing. For you, that would simply be your greater instinct.

Now, I can give you benchmarks so that you can understand what I'm saying in a deeper way than simply through the words I'm using. Generally speaking with our peoples, it is important to understand to the best of your ability not only what we are saying but also what's underneath what we are saying. This is not something unknown to you, because very often, when speaking to each other, you understand the motivations of the person who is talking to you. When that person is a friend or someone known to you, you might understand that what that person is saying does not always have to do with what is actually meant or what prompted the person to say what he or she is saying—meaning the rationale, yes?

Have you ever contacted or heard of any other group with access to this living-crystal memory?

No, but others have their own approach. We have been around those who do not require it, but we like such things. Others simply use their knowing; they have a moment of greatly increased knowing, which we would find to be uncomfortable, physically. Certainly they would then know something that they didn't know, and they might or might not retain that later on when they didn't necessarily need it, but that sudden knowing, which we would see as an amplification of personality, is physically uncomfortable to us.

So the liquid crystal—as it appears to you, because if it is not moving, it would appear to be simply crystal decorations, but when it's moving, it looks more like a liquid— absorbs the impact of that for us. So it's not exactly doing the knowing, but it's insulating us a bit. It stimulates us at times but also insulates us a bit from that sudden amplification of knowing, which is uncomfortable to us.

Does that sudden knowing . . . do you retain that as part of your thoughts, or do you just let it go when you don't need it?

We retain it only if necessary. Sometimes it is necessary, because we will be in that circumstance again, and it would be useful to have that wisdom, but if there is no need to remember it—meaning that that circumstance will never occur again as far as we know—then we just let it go.

We're taught to call that vertical wisdom.

That's right. I have heard that.

You know what you need to know when you need it, and then it's gone when you don't.

Yes. And because of your durability, both mentally and physically, as Earth peoples you are able to take that sudden amplification of instinct and be comfortable with it. But for us, for our peoples, it's like this: If you were a mathematician and you had a formula written using your temporary method of writing—such as chalk on a blackboard— and you said, "Ah, that's perfect! That is exactly correct," we are like that. As a scientific, mathematical people, we are completely comfortable within a given framework of data organization. But if something comes along to suddenly expand that and add multiple layers, it is uncomfortable for us. In that way, you might perceive that we are sensitive. It is perhaps surprising to you, because the assumption on your planet is that science is ever interested in what else there is, what more there is, but our society is somewhat structured. If you think about it, mathematics is also somewhat structured, so then perhaps you can understand that analogy.

No Matter What You Consume, Your Available Energy Is Less

How do you use mathematics on your planet? Do you create physically? Do you work abstractly?

We do not create physically. We accept the planet as it is—actually, it's three planets, and we accept them as they are. We do not require our planet to fit our personal needs; we fit the personal needs of the planet. In this way, we are able to exist on the planet within a certain framework of population—even though it's three planets, I refer to it as one, and I hope you are comfortable with that. We are able to perpetuate on our home environment in perpetuity, as far as we know. But in our experience in our travels, we will occasionally find other peoples like yourselves who, for one reason or another, have attempted to change the planet to fit who they are. In our experience, this is always an error [chuckles] and will result . . . you have perhaps had the experience where you are in a friendship or something deeper in which you attempt to change your friend, eh? But there are ramifications that go with that. So it is the same in cultures.

We do not change our planet; we adapt to the planet as it exists. And actually, your planet was set up for you to do exactly the same. Your planet was originally set up so that it would have all the energy you needed to support your life and the vibration of your existence—the basics and the food, so to speak, that which is nourishment—and the planet would give you fully 60 to 70 percent of what you needed to exist, to be maintained in the complete balance and comfort of who you are. You only would need to eat just a little bit of naturally growing fruits and vegetables and so on.

But because over time you have attempted to change your planet—much more so in recent times, if going back a few hundred years is considered recent—as a result, the planet, not unlike the attempt to change your friend, has reactions and no longer radiates an energy that is nurturing and nourishing to you. As a result, much more of the population on your planet now will try to get energy from the consumption of other members of the planet as well as from fruits and vegetables that are naturally occurring—and some not naturally occurring.

Increasingly, no matter how much you consume, the ability to maintain your energy level, physically speaking, is becoming less and less, because the less the planet is attuned to supporting your energy in the expression of its natural, native personality, the less energy is available for you as well as for the planet, you see. Then you try to get more and more from other means, and the planet—especially as she is re-creating herself, but even before that when she was being somewhat injured—can no longer express her natural, native personality, which supports herself and you. Therefore no matter how much you consume, your available energy becomes less and less.

This is why you develop various strange ailments, many of which did not exist in the past and are now only stimulated because of pollutants. Sometimes they are stimulated because the support and nurturance that was available in the past is not available anymore, and sometimes this simply has to do with population. But the greater effect is how you have attempted to change the planet. So you see, then, that your entire population goes out of balance, and you look for something to compensate. Sometimes people eat more; sometimes people are involved in other pursuits. It is like a machine gone berserk, the different components trying to create and re-create themselves, and it is not a pleasant potential for the future.

Remember to Use Your Instinct

This is where the one thing that you still have, that you are born with, can come to help you, and that is your instinct, your knowing what is absolutely so. You all have this. Some of it, after all, is based on your perceptions, meaning your senses. If you go outside, your perception is that you can breathe outside. You take a breath; you exhale. It is part of your perception that it's safe. Then there is your sight: What is a tree? You look around. You know what a tree is, as long as you understand that word in your culture. Where are the stars? Where are the mountains? Visual things. What smells good? What doesn't smell good? Your senses, your perceptions, all are part of your instinct. Instinct is based on physical reality, but it is also based on spiritual reality, meaning who you are in your greater depth beyond who you appear to be.

Using the signet in a different analogy, it is like the way the signet is as it appears on the surface, and then you can flip the signet over to learn more about it. Now it is like that for yourself. The planet is attempting to re-create itself, and even during that you're attempting to alter her to be something she is not in order to fit who you perceive yourselves to be, which is largely mistaken. So the only thing we can see now, the only thing that can really help to save you, is to remember more of who you are.

That's the purpose of the signets as they have appeared, both in their general appearance and in the energy they stimulate. It is also being done in other ways, I believe—in your dreams and so on. So this rush toward trying to remember who you are is also an attempt to become more at ease with your perception of energy—meaning your feelings and your senses, yes, but also your physical feelings. Instinct gives you physical messages through your physical body—this is so; this is not so—meaning you could have a thought, a theory, and yet your physical feelings tell you it is not so, so the theory must be changed or discarded, for example.

A Belief in the Need for Change Is Limiting Your Life Cycle

How long do you live? What is your life span in terms of our years?

Oh, you mean when we are born and when we die? Is that it?

Yes. If you do that; I mean, some beings don't.

No, I'm not aware of having that circumstance.

You are immortal physically?

I don't think of it that way. I do not know that we are that, but I'm not aware of us being involved in the thing you mentioned. We have a long life, maybe, eh? Of our peoples, I'm not aware of anyone being born or anyone dying.

Okay, that answers my question. So do you have memories beyond this universe, or were you created here? Did you come here from somewhere else?

We came from somewhere else, but those memories are somewhat veiled to us. Apparently we were not embodied physically there. We used to have this discussion very often with other civilizations, and the universal understanding is that if one remembered too much about what is out there . . .

It would distract you.

It tends to interrupt your life cycle here. That is why the microbe, for example, does not focus on who or what it was in some other place, because it could no longer provide its function for itself and others. It's the same in your body. If, say, a cell of your liver was once at some point the cell of your heart, and it considered that beyond simple recognition and then continuing on with its existence . . .

[Laughs.] The liver wouldn't work. Right.

Well, it might interfere. You are actually experiencing that right now, because from our perception the disease you know as cancer is largely caused by this, in that you are desperately searching to replenish yourselves with missing energy because the planet is attempting to re-create herself, as I mentioned before. So one of the things you are doing is to desperately attempt to change things in order to fix them, as you might say, because you believe that change is natural.

I understand that you might believe this, functioning in the world that you are in; I can see why that belief would be held dear. But then you sometimes accidentally change something inside your body. The analogy of the cell of the liver compared to the cell of the heart takes place, and it creates a disruption. And then the new cells that begin to form will form almost as a thought would take shape physically, attempting to re-create something on the basis of a mental understanding of how we fix something through change, you might say.

So the change aspect goes to work inside your body where it does not work. And that mechanism kills. In some cases, it needs to be expertly removed. It is shortening a lot of your life cycles now. I grant that there are other causative factors, certainly things about the planet that have been changed, removed, or shifted. But we feel that that is something that you can correct by seeking out that which naturally flows of its own organization and structure.

You have peoples on the planet who are called environmentalists; they can be scientific or even a culture, those who understand that as the rain falls from the sky, it forms up in ponds, turns into streams, and becomes rivers. In short, they understand the natural cycle of the planet, and that your own bodies function rather similarly. These observations and applications in the expression of life are the way to put your energy, the best way to structure your thoughts. Don't always assume that change is for the best. Sometimes, simple change can be corruption or destruction. I don't give too much advice, but that is the type of advice we give cultures such as yours who are of the belief that in order to fix something, things need to be changed. Sometimes they simply need to be allowed to be who and what they naturally are.

Swirl Patterns in the Sky, on the Earth, in the Water

All right. You said that the top of the crop circle would tell us how you arrived.

We arrived through a plane of existence. If you would see it on a graph, it would seem very flat, and yet there is a curve, a linear portion in the center that looks rather like a swirl. These swirls of energy have been allowed to be seen by some of you in recent times. When our vehicles that make the impressions of the signets come and go, in traversing the plane of travel, they will sometimes leave an apparent illuminated swirl of charged particles in your sky at night. Some of you have seen these things. Sometimes they are simply caused by various physical, Earth-related matters, but other times, you have seen them and still other times, there are such patterns noticed in the clouds—and still other times, there are such patterns noted in the water.

We are being allowed to leave these as reminders that the plane that is traversed from our world into your world must be flat. But in its approach to your world, it must go through a divestment of some aspects of our true natures, which is why we must travel in vehicles. It is an incorporation of the true natures of your selves, which is something only technology can do. We cannot do that; perhaps some beings can, but we cannot. Therefore what would be seen visibly would be that swirl. Do you understand what I'm speaking of when I say "swirl"?

I think we call them orbs of light, or light balls, above the crop circles?

No, no. They are not balls of light. I'm talking about actual swirls in the sky, on the ground. Can you imagine the shape of a galaxy? You understand that it's sometimes a swirl. That shape being left is sometimes seen in your night sky. You have perhaps heard of such things. People are saying, "Oh, I saw this in the sky; I saw that in the sky." Granted, it is sometimes caused simply by some Earth-generated phenomenon, technology gone awry or something. I think it happened recently when part of a rocket returned to Earth and created that type of shape, and several swirls were also simultaneously left in the sky during that time due to vehicles coming and going to leave signets.

A moment. I will see if I can tell you more. [Pause.] You recently saw a picture of a swirl like this a while back that was generated by Earth phenomena, yes? There was a swirl in the night sky caused by a rocket. Think; it's important, because you know what we're talking about. Otherwise, you will continue your question based on a misperception. A swirl in the night sky over . . .

Oh! Norway!

There you are. People are seeing such swirls in the sky like that. Now you know the shape I'm talking about.

Okay. Well, we called it a spiral, but it's the same thing. But that one was made deliberately.

It doesn't make any difference. I'm just trying to bring your attention to the shape.

Okay. Do you make most of the crop circles?

No, but you asked me how we got here, and I was trying to describe the spiral, which I called a swirl, and the mechanism of how we got here.

What percentage of the crop circles do you make?

Just the one that we're talking about. I'm referring to others who've come when I refer to the signets of the past thirty or forty years. We didn't make those; we just made the one that we're talking about today. But the overall purpose of the signets left by everyone else has to do with what I was talking about, at least from our point of view. That's how we see it scientifically.

There are many pages on the Internet about this particular crop circle we're talking about here, and a lot of the discussion refers to the famous Euler's Identity equation, but the crop circle has eight extra bits and one other piece that's different. Are you aware of this famous Euler's Identity binary equation and that your crop circle is exactly like it, except just a tiny bit off?

We felt you would not recognize that we were a scientific people, a mathematical people, unless we gave something that could be at least dropped into a general theorem that would identify us as such. So the theorem that is pictured has less to do with the equation you have mentioned than us simply saying, "We are like you; we have scientific pursuits and mathematical pursuits." Therefore those in the scientific community might at some point find that mutual discussion would be beneficial.

It is sort of like the way you leave a business card. You say, "Look, see! I can help you!" We're not pitching anything; we're just saying that when you travel out in the universe, be sure and bring that picture, and make sure you can explain what's on the bottom of the crop circle. At least develop your own theories. If you can do that, bringing the top picture and what you perceive as the bottom picture—or the flip-over picture as I called it before—then we can start our discussions. But if you don't bring that, our calling card, then you probably won't be approached. You must bring the calling card.

Generally speaking, for those of you who come visiting, always bring pictures of all the signets [crop circles] with you. It's kind of like bringing the calling cards of those who have come, and you might wind up showing those signets—not broadcasting them in the air, so to speak, but having them available. This is a little advice to your travelers. This is what you will do as a diplomat, trying to understand who they are. You won't require them to pick out their signet, but if they see a display of these signets, they might go to the display or simply highlight their signet on the display, and you will thus be able to get some visual frame of reference of who they are and, most importantly, know that they have in fact visited your planet. I feel this would be particularly helpful for travelers, diplomats, and others who would like to at least know that there is some frame of reference. Well, if they have been to your planet, then perhaps they know something about your culture, which is likely. So I wanted to give you that.

I think that's a brilliant idea, having pictures of the crop circles available on the ships as the Explorer Race goes out to other planets to meet other beings. So there's no significance in all the people who have been trying to decode this crop circle and who are looking for the meaning of the extra bits in it, huh?

Oh, I wouldn't say that. There is always a value to that. But we wish to provide the next step in the theorem, and that's all I'm allowed to say about it. So for those of you who are interested in that theorem, there is a next step. So do look at the, as you say, "extra bits."

We've Come to Help You Remember Your Knowing as Applied to Earth

[Laughs.] Okay. We have some beings on this planet who have told me they are profoundly mathematical in their thinking and in their lives. They are called penguins. Have you talked to them?

Yes. They do know who we are, they know where we're from, and they know why we exist. If you can create a means to communicate with them, they can tell you more about who we are, because we cannot necessarily say, simply because of our lack of experience communicating with you. But since they have been with you for so long, they will know what is all right to say. They will understand subtleties of communication with you that I cannot understand right now because this is the first time I've ever done this speaking to peoples of your time. I have had some communication with peoples of Earth in past times, but those peoples were all very much embracing of their own knowing, from our point of view.

From your point of view, they were comfortable with instinct. But the beings you refer to do understand who you are now and your rush to attempt to change the planet to fit your needs at any given moment as compared to allowing her to be who she is and not interrupting or disrupting her flow of external or internal fluids, for example. Because your planet is largely a fluid planet, even things that might not always appear to be fluid on the surface of the planet could very well be fluid underneath the surface.

Like liquid rock or something, magma, yeah. You also said if we flipped this signet over, it would say why you'd come.

We came generally to help you to remember who you are and to encourage the scientific community to accept the fact that you are in fact from other planets. Ultimately, all human beings on the Earth were those who gradually, over time, migrated or left their planets, and various individuals took up residence on this planet. In short, Earth humans of today, meaning Earth humans of the past many thousands of years, are from other places.

But there have been other beings—you have discovered their remains—who existed on the planet long ago, and they would have been the beings who were naturally associated with this planet. But you came, and you liked what you experienced, and you were taught by those beings. They taught you about instinct, or knowing as applied to the Earth, which is different from instinct and knowing as it exists on other planets where there is no discomfiture. Therefore they, the visitors, gradually assimilated onto the planet. So to put it in the simplest way possible, all Earth-human types who exist on the planet now, as well as your ancestors, are all from other planets.

Do we have any of your DNA?

I cannot be certain of that. The penguins, as you call them—they would know. In order to know that, it is necessary to be able to identify personal characteristics, meaning your personal characteristics as compared to our personal characteristics. Just speaking for myself, I have more difficulty with that, but the penguins, they would be able to do it.

I think you're doing fantastically well. It's a whole new perspective. It's wonderful.

Penguins would do much better. [Chuckles.]

Well, if you say so.

Benevolent Magic for Oil Spills

Is this a good time to ask . . . you said to ask you later, to see if you could tell us something we don't know about cleaning up oil spills, such as the spill from the explosion in the Gulf of Mexico.

Ah, yes. The oil is part of Earth's inner fluids, which work somewhat hydrodynamically in order to keep the planes of her existence—you would say the plates or something like that, geologically speaking—balanced and on certain appropriate surfaces. Now she must push up and move the plates about somewhat vigorously, causing disturbances to surface civilizations because of the removal of her hydrodynamic fluid, which in this case would be oil.

You must change your technology so that it no longer needs this fluid. I think you have the means now with your usage of transforming wind, sunlight, and so on, into energy. So you can do that. With support and supporting each other, you ought to be able to accomplish that totally sometime within the next thirty to forty years if you maximize the effort. You will have to set other squabbles aside and maximize the effort—everyone all over the Earth cooperating so that such forms of the natural flowing expression of the Earth and your star would help you to replace the electrical energy that you are generating sort of inefficiently using your current technology. I think you can do that if you put all your efforts in that direction.

As far as transforming the oil in the waters—which, while it is not that uncomfortable for Mother Earth, it is certainly potentially catastrophic not only to what you eat as humans but to other forms of life whom you do not always understand as being essential to your own existence—you will have to use some type of synchronicity of what you know, meaning your instinct, as the mechanics so that you know what you are doing to be correct. You'll have to use your feelings, your physical feelings. You will have to set certain standards—that would be your intentions—and you will essentially have to use what you describe as magic.

I believe this being I speak through now, as well as some others, know how to do these things, but this must become public knowledge. This being right now has been attempting to make that knowledge public and has been gradually teaching it to others. So that would be the simplest, the safest, and the gentlest as well as the speediest way to make those changes. It might also be particularly useful if more than one person were doing it.

We're basically talking here about the instantaneous transformation of one form and substance to another, and that is probably the simplest way to do it. I think simply trying to move things back in time would be problematic, because there has been some death. Many peoples on the machine suffered and unfortunately expired as a result of the problem on the machine, and this is a serious problem. So if you attempt to put it back and simply change the sequence of time, it would be a problem, because at least three of those who died have reincarnated already. So that could create a problem.

I don't think we'd use a time replacement. You would simply have to use a means to re-create the substance so that there is balance. A great deal of what is going on now on your planet has everything to do with balance, and balance essentially means having all things functioning on the basis of what they know to be true, functioning on instinct.

That's what Earth does, and she is involved now, of course, in having to re-create herself while you are on her, as I mentioned before. This is not always helpful and safe for you, so the more you can function in your instinct and use what might be called magic of a benevolent source, the better. This is not a symbolic magic, not something that uses something to do something else, but something direct and immediate, which is what this being through whom I am speaking is involved in teaching. That is the quickest, the easiest, and the simplest way. So study that, and perhaps more will be given in time through this being's communications to help you in changing and transforming.

The simplest way to do this, I believe, would be to transform one substance to another, which is not that difficult, but it must involve the actual atomic and subatomic particles, the microbes, the cellular structure—essentially the molecular structure itself. This would involve basically asking the molecular structure to transform. All this is possible, but it must be *asked* to transform, and it must be asked to transform in a way that is benevolent for it. It also must be asked that the outcome of the transformation be benevolent for all life. So you might call this magic, but in fact it is simply what we would refer to as adaptation. To you, it would seem like magic, because something that would have happened doesn't happen, and within a fairly short amount of time, everything simply transforms.

This can be done, and I believe that the being involved here—what do you call this person, the channel?—has learned how to do that. There are others on the planet who know how to make such requests, but this has largely been kept quiet. The being who is the channel here has learned how to do these magical things and is attempting to teach others, since quite obviously he understands that he will not be here forever, so he must leave this behind so that others will become intrigued and perhaps do these things too.

We've been publishing his material about benevolent magic in books and magazines for years, as well as material by others.

Excellent.

In fact, we'll put up a benevolent magic box here with this channeling with the exact words people can use.

The words are important; they set the intent. But there is more of a mystical quality that must be done. The whole point of what the channel is teaching and has been teaching for quite a few years now is in order to take something from beyond intention, you need to include energy. If you remember, the original energy I spoke about serves to nurture who you are and to keep everything in balance on the planet. This energy is what must be used. You cannot change and transform something if that energy is not present. The words help set your intent mentally, but the energy is the equal-to-equal exchange—meaning you are asking a form of life to transform itself.

If you simply walk up and say, "Hi, will you please transform yourself?" that will not work. But if you approach with an energy that is equal, then there is a kinship formed, and the likelihood of that transformation would be more like something you would do to help out a friend: "Here, let me help you." It is like that, a simple thing that can be done because it is easy. It is done on the basis of equality, equal energy. It is kinship; it is family. On that note, I will say . . .

Wait, would you talk to us again? You're wonderful. You have insights we haven't heard before.

I cannot say that that will happen. It's possible. If you cannot reach me, you can always ask the penguins.

[Laughs.] Are they connected to you?

As I said, they know us.

Is your home planet their home planet?

No. Good night.

Good night.

Robert Shapiro on Benevolent Magic and True Magic for Oil Spills

First, you would ask the following: "I am asking that all the most benevolent energies available for me be all around me and all about me now, that I might experience and translate, to the best of my ability, the communication between forms of life." Then pause. Many of you will feel a warmth somewhere in your bodies—perhaps in your chest, perhaps other places. Wait a bit until that fades, though you don't have to wait indefinitely. Generally speaking, if you don't feel it fade, wait about twenty or thirty seconds. It's all right to glance at the clock. Then say this:

Benevolent Magic

"I am asking that the molecules of oil in the waters of _____ [say the name of the place where the oil has been spilled] and other places where they are migrating now mutate and transform into a benign and benevolent form of existence that is totally compatible with the natural ocean and all life within it, resulting in the most benevolent outcome for all beings."

If you feel an energy come up at any time during those words spoken exactly that way, pause, because the energy is involved in the activation, and it is also a balance between yourself and the beings to whom you are speaking. You do not have to be in the geographic area where this is happening. For those of you who have waters that are polluted in your area, you can also do this in your area and simply say the name of the polluted area where you live. Other adaptations are obvious: You can change ocean or sea to lake or river, for example. That's what I'd recommend.

Okay, beautiful. Thank you.

True Magic for Oil Spills

For those of you who are involved in true magic, before you do these things, you might also close your eyes if it's daytime and look up toward where the Sun is in the sky. Even if it's a cloudy day, you'll have a fairly good idea of where the Sun is. Breathe in and out with your head tilted toward the Sun and your eyes closed. Breathe in and out naturally, four or five times, and then do that benevolent magic work discussed here. If it's nighttime and the Moon is up, you can leave your eyes open. But when you breathe in and out, do about ten breaths and then do the benevolent magic as described.

When you are done and the energy has passed and you are doing this as true magic, if you are able to squat down and the energy is still present within you, you can squat down and place your right hand on the ground beneath you with your fingers and thumbs splayed out. While you're doing that, as you're moving your hand toward the ground, if you feel a strong energy between your hand and the ground—or in some place in your body—that feels like no or a sense of resistance, then stop. This will mean that you should go no further, because that's as far as you need to go with your hand toward the ground, or it might mean that you simply need to pause, and then over time, you can gradually get your hand to touch the ground.

If your hand does not want to do that because of how it feels in your body, then don't do it, and then just bring your hand back up. If you are not able to squat down, you can be in a chair, but the chair must be something that is of a natural material, meaning no nails. So it could be something like a pegged chair, or you could be sitting on a rock, like that. You can try it if you're in a wheelchair. It might not be as effective, but it's worth a try. That's what I'd recommend.

YOUR NEW STAGE OF TRANSFORMATION IS CAUSING OTHERS DISCOMFORT

ET Visitor Researching Discomfort

June 21, 2010

Greetings. I am speaking as a visitor to your planet. We are still here, but we are undetectable by your current technology. I have to say that given the challenges that you face on a daily basis, we are not clear how you can tolerate this level of discomfort. We've been guided by our teachers that, given a normal society with the type of energy one finds everywhere else, your bodies could sustain your lives in complete harmony, physically, for a minimum of 700 years, and the only reason that you do not live that long now is because of the multiple—dare I say multitudinous—hazards you face on a regular basis. We know that this is because Creator does not wish you to linger in a place that is so challenging, for it is apparently a school. But our perception of you is balanced: On the one hand, we admire your ability to rise to such challenges. On the other hand, the extremes you face seem excessive to us.

As souls when you are not on Earth, you all are completely benign and benevolent—as are we all. But on Earth, you seem to function in a way that is unknown in the rest of the universe. This is apparently because you do not recall who you are on what you would call the subconscious level. You do recall it on the unconscious level, and this is how you are able to be taught in deep sleep when your body is in a temporarily unconscious state. But you do not have these recollections of who you are at the subconscious level—that level between the deep-sleep state and the waking state—though you pass through it temporarily when waking gently.

You Gain Consciousness during Crises

We feel that the next move that you are going to engage within the next forty years—we're not exactly sure when, just at some time within . . . now I'm feeling it's within the next thirty-seven years—is going to be from a subconscious level that totally remembers who you are. This has its advantages. If you can meditate, as you call it, or relax into a meditative state, you will be able to access your subconscious and remember who you are. Thus you are very unlikely to do anything harmful to others, because when you remember who you are, you automatically know who everybody else is based on your various lifetimes together and your relationships coordinated with your present relationship with them.

In short, we feel that performing this meditative state, regardless of the philosophy or the religion you adopt, will bring peace to your planet—and, I might add, calm. So I thought I'd bring that to your attention, because this is something that you are not that far away from. If you can get through these next thirty to forty years, during which you will have challenges that are abounding from the natural world, you will be able to achieve total consciousness in the unconscious state as well as in the subconscious state.

You are being prepared for this type of awareness by being forced, literally, to learn how to cooperate with peoples whom you now may be suspicious of—for whatever reason, justified or even unjustified. This is coming about by cooperation between Earth as a planet and Creator and angelics who believe that there is abundant proof that in a crisis, you tend to cooperate with each other, regardless of who's who. Therefore for the next thirty to forty years, you will probably be presented with numerous crises associated with the natural world around you: Earth and perhaps other denizens of Earth, as well as some situations that are associated with your own bodies' relationship to Earth.

We feel that the teaching—through this channel and perhaps others—of magic, true magic, living prayers, and so on, will help you immensely, because it will not only help you to understand the nature of your true relationship with all life, but you will be able to mentally gravitate and connect with a process that is known and understood everywhere else other than Earth. This process is what is being called "magic" through this channel, but in fact it is really understood as creationism or, you might say, conscious creativity, through which one is aware in every moment of who one is and as a result gains awareness of one's relationship to literally everyone else.

Therefore there is not only an immediate awareness but also a prompting within oneself toward action if anyone anywhere is uncomfortable. With that level of cooperation, it is easy to find that person or those persons who are uncomfortable because of some needs that need to be met, and those needs can be met promptly in some way or other. And then the comfort level returns—not only to those individuals in need, but to everyone else, because that call for need has been fulfilled.

Your Transformation Is Causing Discomfort

Can you tell me something about yourself?

We are from a planet far from this current galaxy. It is not pronounceable in your language, but it is rhythmic and would be like a series of knocks and taps—that would be the closest way I can describe it—that have to do with sounds the planet makes itself. But it's not possible to duplicate those sounds in this environmental communication. So you will have to accept that. [Chuckles.]

Why are you on Earth, or why are you around Earth, wherever you are?

We are near Earth, but we are not presently on it. We are observing the time of transformation you are all going through. I must say, there is a certain amount of not exactly anxiousness, but enthusiasm for you all to come into greater balance, because everyone everywhere else—you may not know this—feels somewhat uncomfortable. Many peoples do not recognize that, and in some places, it is thought to be a disease.

I am quite certain, however—our peoples are somewhat medically minded—of what it is, and that is that as you begin to move through the stages of consciousness that will bring you to your natural selves, not only are the barriers between dimensions thinner, but the barriers that insulate your planet from other planets are thinner. As a result, that situation that I explained before, how everyone responds to those in need, has begun a little bit in many planets nearby to your own, meaning within your galaxy, that are peopled. The word is slow in spreading, because it is such an unusual circumstance, and as a result, some peoples feel that there's something wrong with them, but they will be informed.

We feel that this is a temporary situation, as you are making these strides in a way that I would call a "notchy" manner, meaning that you move forward suddenly and that during that motion forward, the normal barriers that keep you from going from one dimension to another, or even one portion of a dimension to another, will become thin so that you can make the move forward. In that moment, however, that thinning is also experienced in the insulation around your conceptual planet, meaning how you experience it and all that you experience, and the discomfort then goes beyond your planet to the rest of the universe.

The rest of the universe is feeling it in waves, like a brief pulse. For you, it would be like a very brief, maybe a second or two, of vague discomfort, and then it would pass. And for all of you individuals on Earth, it would be nothing. "So what?" you might say. But to those who are not used to any discomfort, it is shocking.

So that's why we're here: to study the phenomenon. And those are our conclusions so far as to why peoples are experiencing that discomfort we have communicated, but this has to spread around a bit through various peoples, guides, and teachers. The big challenge is that they do not know what to do about it, and I do not have a solution for it yet, either. But we are here to study and to see if there may possibly be a solution for the other peoples. We know that you on Earth do not need this solution, but this is something that is needed elsewhere—everywhere else, for the most part, that is affected by the passage and those brief moments of discomfort.

How far is this pulsing going out? Is it throughout all of creation or just through some local galaxies or . . . ?

It is mostly in your galaxy. It's slightly radiated beyond your galaxy, but there are no habitable planets there that I am aware of. However, passing ships do experience the phenomenon.

We Are a Medically Inclined People

So did you come on your own, or were you invited to study this situation?

We were requested to come and study the situation, and we were provided with a vehicle from beings from a civilization not our own, from very far away from us—and we are very far away from you—who have a vehicle that is absolutely undetectable. And even though our environment is ensconced within the vehicle, the vehicle itself is undetectable and hence, anything within the vehicle is thus also undetectable, even if our vehicle were in your skies without that other vehicle around us, you would be able to see us. In short, you would be able to see us, period. Anybody could see us.

Tell me about . . . well, first, if I looked at you, what would I see?

We are humanoids. We do not look exactly like humans, but we're humanoids.

Okay. What are some of the differences?

A moment. [Pause.] Sorry, that's all I can say.

So your medical specialty . . . you said you are medically inclined, I think?

Medically inclined, yes. We are interested in physical therapies in different cultures, and we have studied historical medical situations and their attendant cures at length.

I see it's a conundrum, because if we're to proceed, we can't stop that pulsing when the barrier gets thinner.

No, it's quite clear that you have nothing to do with it consciously. You have something to do with it on the soul level, but this is something Creator desires, so we have assumed, as a result, that it is meant to be a challenge to us. We also believe that at some point, we and many others will be in touch with your peoples, and we will be able to—what do you say?—compare notes, eh?

Yes. So you will come here, or we will meet you out there?

That is yet to be decided.

So is everybody on your ship from your planet, or is it a consortium from many places?

They are all from my planet.

What led you to this study of the physical?

We have always done that.

So you've always helped other people on other planets?

No, we've always been interested in the physical, the medical, and the therapeutic.

For yourself only? I mean for your planet, for the people on your planet?

For the people on our planet, yes. So I cannot answer your question any better than that. What led us to it . . . I do not know what led us to it, because we have always been interested in this.

Is the "you" that have always been interested a grouping or everybody on your planet?

It is everybody, as far as I know. This is not to say that there aren't other interests on the planet, but everybody is interested in these topics.

Do you think that at some time, you had a problem of your own that you had to solve or something?

Not that I'm aware of. Nobody ever gets sick, and there are no records of it.

We Only Consume Resources Who Volunteer

What's your life span in our years?

I'm not a mathematician, so you'll have to wait a moment. [Pause.] Somewhere around 5,000.

Ah, and what is your society like? Do you live in families or groups or singly or in some other way?

We live more in a community. There is a sense of family, but the sense of extended family is so strong that I would have to describe it as more of a community lifestyle—not set up to serve the individual but more focused on the community at large. Education takes place on a mutually desired basis rather than as a formal education with grades and specific schools as you have.

Do you give birth, or is there some other form of coming into consciousness?

There is birth, but our population is stable at a small number, so birth is infrequent by your standards. There are about 40,000 individuals on the planet.

That's all?

This is not unusual. I've been to planets much larger than ours with smaller populations. It is entirely dependent on the resources, and you have to recognize that in a totally benevolent place, those resources that are going to be consumed must be completely welcoming of that consumption. Think about that in terms of your own society: What do you consume that completely welcomes being consumed by you—you, meaning everyone who is hearing this, not just the speaker.

Yeah, nothing, I don't think.

I think of only one thing that you consume that welcomes being consumed.

Air?

Water.

Water, ah. Why?

It passes through you and experiences individuality and the concept of individuality going through an individual. And it comes out and it rejoins the mass of itself . . .

With that experience added.

Yes. And it's of interest.

Oh, that's interesting. That's very interesting. So how do you handle the consumption of foods on your planet when you have to replace what you use?

The foods we consume—what you would call fruits or vegetables—are not grown by your farming methods. They grow wild, and the ones that are picked for consumption must volunteer for it. Nothing is picked without having volunteered, and one knows something is volunteering, because when you go to pick it—and anybody who understands energy and feelings knows this very well—or even when you go to get your hand close to it, to use your terms, there is a good feeling. But if one does that and there is a bad feeling, one does not pick that food. Everything that is picked is like that. So we do not exert ourselves unnecessarily. There are no sporting events for the pure joy of it. Our physical motions are somewhat calculated so that we do not waste motion and thus require more energy—and thus more food—that cannot be consumed without it having volunteered.

We Are Here to Develop Discomfort Protection

So how do you use the physical therapy that you study on each other?

We don't use it on each other. We find it interesting. You perhaps have interests intellectually as well, but we make ourselves available to consult with those who may wish to know these things on other planets. So we're sort of traveling librarians, you might say.

Oh, so you do travel! Do people come to your planet and then you travel as well?

Yes. Normally, we would not have to travel in a vehicle such as the one we are traveling in now, but we are only in a vehicle like that so that we can be in and around your planet undetected.

So you would normally go through a portal or something?

We would normally move in our own vehicle that could be seen easily, once beyond this sphere of your—how can we say?—fears. So in a normal situation, we would just travel by the vehicle's motive force.

I see. In a vehicle, yes. I see.

It is a force that is propelled by attraction. It travels by something akin to magnetism, but it uses the gravitational fields of planets and suns. This is typical everywhere.

Who requested that you come here?

We were requested by some of the beings you will meet with regularity from the Pleiades and the Orion systems. These peoples expect to meet you before too long, and they felt that it would be useful if we came here, given those bursts they are experiencing that I mentioned before, the waves of discomfort. They are concerned that you, as individuals, might give off these waves as well, so they would like to have some therapy that they can use to counteract the effects, if that is the case. They do not know that it will be the case, but if it is the case, then they want to be prepared.

What is your opinion? Will that be the case?

I believe it will. So they will need to have something that they wear, some means to protect themselves beyond what they have now. Right now, they have things that are very mild in protection, and they have things that are very strong in the case of rare visits to your planet in recent years. But they don't have anything that's really in between that. It's essentially something that isn't adjustable in its strength level. They need something that can respond on a low level of reflectivity, so to speak. We think that reflectivity is going to be the simplest method to use, because as an Earth human, to have an energy that is your own and is of discomfort to others reflected back to you is not going to discomfit you, but it will protect others.

So they will wear something that will be reflective, you mean?

It is our intention to be able to recommend to them how to create such a device, but we will have to be here a bit longer to be reasonably certain.

Will this pulsing last just the thirty-seven years or hundreds of years?

We do not know this. That is a good question. We feel that once you, as citizens, have attained the capacity at the subconscious level as well as the unconscious level, you might make quicker strides forward, being able to understand your circumstances better. But that's only a theory at the moment. So the simple answer is that I do not know.

Okay. And how long do you plan to stay? Days, weeks, months, years?

We have no fixed time frame. We will stay as long as it takes to come up with a recommended strength level of the device.

Are you aware of what we're trying to do here? Have they told you about it?

Yes, to a degree. I'm not aware of everything, but I don't need to be aware of everything. I just need to be aware of what's happening and what's needed. Of course in the process of studying what's needed, we are also able to see some things that are happening on your planet, but we're not here to study your culture. It is, however, something that one notices.

So will we be meeting these Pleiadians and Orions within the next thirty-seven years or after that?

I do not know that. We hope to have the device prepared, or if not prepared, then recommendations made for them to prepare it, because of course they can prepare it themselves. Once they have the device, then it will be up to them and those who guide and advise them on when to make those connections a more frequent and open thing. I know that there have been many connections from other planets to your own peoples over the years, but in some cases, this has been kept quiet, and in other cases, it's more open. So this is not something over which we have any level of adjudication. We simply make recommendations; we're not in charge.

I need to draw to a close, so I will simply say this: We feel that your children and your children's children, perhaps the generations after that, will be living in a much better world. Right now, you are living in the remainder of the extreme challenge, and there might be challenges yet to come from the natural world. I feel that the more you cooperate with each other, regardless of whom you are cooperating with, you will find that the different ideas that different people have and the discovery of how much is truly known rather than the individual groups believing that some things are not known will then be able to solve most of your problems. Good night.

Oh, thank you very much. Good life.

CROP CIRCLES: ORIGINS, PURPOSES, AND MYSTERIES

Crop Circle Group Coordinator

July 2, 2010

Greetings. I am, you might say, a coordinator for all of the various groups who are leaving these messages on living matter for the beings on Earth to recapture, to an extent, your natural, native, visual language. Language on Earth has been keeping you apart as it's become more and more precise and individualistic. And although this has its advantages to understanding nuances in individual languages, it has actually served to separate people a bit more.

In ancient times, people would use signs and gestures—not signs the way they're used in your now time with precise sign language, but just very basic gestures—as well as pictures drawn on the ground with a stick and so on to understand what needed to be understood. It's not that they didn't have language to speak among each other in various family, clan, or tribal groups; rather, when interacting with anyone who did not speak their language, this is what they would do. This is not about ignorance, though it has been portrayed that way by some in your time. It is rather about being close to your own soul's natural, native language, which is in pictures.

On Earth, because you are learning about what is physical on this plane of Earth, it is natural that, in order to reach you now, messages must be portrayed with the full and complete cooperation of physical matter. Crops grow in the ground; they are physical. They are ensouled in their own way, as all is, all beings are, yes? When exposed to the energy by various means, they themselves become the symbol.

If the crops are mature, given a few days to rest and settle, the grains can be consumed carefully if they haven't been walked on too much. Such grains

269

are to be harvested by hand only, physically by hand, using no tools whatsoever. Gloves would be acceptable, but they are to be silk gloves, comfortable for the wearer and not bruising to the crop. A seed from such a place like that could be transplanted somewhere else in the field—but only in that field, not taken away from the area, so that the soil would be about the same—but not too far, since all places on the Earth, as everywhere else, have a specific type of energy. If such seeds are used to create a seed crop, when it is possible with the plants, these crops would be much more nourishing. Again, they would have to be very gently treated; no heavy machinery—perhaps, in time, using simple methods, a scythe or something like that, but nothing that would bruise the crop.

These are old methods; it is really best to bring such a crop in by hand entirely, using those gloves. It might not be practical, but consider: A crop grown from that type of seed could very benevolently affect the health of those who grew the crop and harvested the crop, even more than anyone else, especially if they live within two to three miles of where the crop was grown and harvested. It would be like a curative, a cure-all. I am saying this so that those who have such things appear in their crops and in their fields know that it is not only a message to all peoples of the Earth, but it is a personal gift to you. So try to do these things for your own health and well-being.

A Way for the Past to Leave a Message for the Future

Now, who puts these signs—and yes, wonders—there? They come from a variety of sources. Sometimes these signs come from vehicles; other times they come from energy fluctuations brought about by those in the past on Earth, the distant past, and those in the future, although not that far in the future, since you are closer to your benevolent future than you are to your benevolent past. Nevertheless, time is not a factor in placing these messages where they appear. Rather the process is entirely energetic, meaning there is a benevolent feeling that is unified through three points. One point is the needs of all beings on the place, meaning the planet, where such needs are being served. Another is the point of origin, meaning who believed this was possible and what did they originate to bring this about? And the third point is who in the future of all incarnations associated with this planet welcomes such a message.

In the future, the incarnations include everyone who manifests physically on that planet—in this case, Earth. "Those incarnating" includes not only human beings but all animal and plant species, all molecules, even all the various forms of bacteria, viruses, and so on, that are in that benevolent future. This tells you that, as many scientists know, some bacteria and even some viruses are benevolent, or they have been shown to be in some cases. So this is really a way of reminding you that sometimes that which seems to be the enemy—bacteria or some other form of life—is simply not showing you its good side at that point. But bacteria do have a good side.

Now, in the past, this would be those who were of a spiritual group. I'm not talking about doctrine here but rather those who were close to their origins, living physically on the Earth in close connection with their form of soul as it incarnated on the planet, meaning their spirit, their soul, and their physical life—again, three things. Peoples such as I mentioned at the beginning of my talk are literally responsible for this. It really started as an agreement. Peoples agreed, in the way they had of communicating then. They communicated by gesture, by picture, and to some degree with intertribal or interclan exchanges of what they knew to be true based on their abilities to survive and leave messages for future generations to the best of their ability. These exchanges were an attempt to teach, you see, so that the connection between spirit, soul, and form could be maintained in balance.

They agreed that leaving messages for future generations would be difficult, considering all the changes on Earth, meaning simply wind, water, and motion, as one finds on a living planet such as Earth. They knew that, say, pictures left in a cave might or might not survive to be consulted later. So the connection was made energetically. Since they were connected to spirit, soul, and form as part of their day-to-day life, that was easy. Then they also reached out to others who would incarnate in the future—in this case, those who would follow them. From your time, for example, this group is not too much further forward in advance of your time. Although you measure things in time, they did not. They measured things in terms of energy: "How does it feel?" So they would reach forward and feel, "Oh, here is a group that is welcoming this energy. We have to leave messages for future generations." Hence, you have crop circles.

The messages were intended to manifest in living matter on the Earth at any time when they were needed in order to remind the peoples, including the animals and the plants and other forms of life as I mentioned, that the natural, native language must be remembered, which is picture energy. Thus here you are in your time, experiencing this again. It has been experienced many times by different populations on the Earth over the past few thousands of years. These people in the past existed on the Earth roughly 40,000 years ago in your time. Those people in the future—you understand I'm giving you

272 ETs ON EARTH

a number, but the route is not from A to B—are roughly, depending on how you measure, 50 to 150 years in your future.

So what you have, then, is this energy that loves those in the past speaking about those in the future who are reaching back into the past, and those in the future speaking about those in the past reaching forward with love for future generations. You see, those in the past, when they were considering future generations and wanting to pass on with love the knowledge and wisdom that was known and remembered and applied during their time, they weren't just talking about their own children and their children's children and so on. They were talking about everyone on the Earth—all peoples, all animals, and all plants.

Communications Directly from Animals and Plants

That closeness with spirit, soul, and form makes for a benevolent world, and it was indeed benevolent in those days. There is a belief in your time that that world was only savage and dangerous, but that is based on the lack of communication of a heart-to-heart nature between human beings of your time, even for the past several hundreds of years of your time, and plants and animals. If one had communication as existed in that past time, what might seem to be a terribly dangerous time fraught with hazards would be seen to be not that way at all.

Sometimes the animals would give warning of something that was going to happen, as they do even in your time: for example, with earthquakes. Then the people of that time would have a care to gather together in groups and support each other's needs, and they would include the animals. I'm not talking about kept animals; I'm talking about animals that were free. But if animals approached a group of people to be with them during that dangerous time, all were welcome.

Thus using just that example, you can see how those times were not as dangerous as you might believe in your time, looking through the filter of your own experience in your time to assess the past. Specific means to leave the messages were not laid out. It was just a request of the physical world, made by people in that past and acknowledged through love from the past to the future, that these signs would appear at times when they were needed. So I wanted to give you that background.

There is more. As I said, sometimes messages are left by vehicles. Other times they are left by that motivating energy I've been explaining. That is why there have been witnesses, although they have not been believed in your time.

Often these witnesses are children. Sometimes they are people who might not have a permanent home. But they are nearby, and they hear a sound and they feel an energy. Sometimes it is just an entire feeling. Other times they see the crops lying down and forming these patterns. It doesn't happen as a rule if people are right in the middle of the crop circles being formed, but it can happen with them even a hundred feet away if they are innocent and they have an innocent heart. This usually happens to children, but sometimes it is adults or those who are adult physically but perhaps not quite grown up, as it is called in your time, mentally.

Many people like that have witnessed the crops just lying down. It is a wondrous sight when it just happens. I am talking about it happening without the effect of a ship landing; the crops just suddenly lie down. You must understand that everything is alive, even if your own science does not recognize the living matter of plants as being just as spiritual, just as connected to free expression, as any human being.

The plants themselves know that this message must be left at this time and in this place, wherever that might be. Thus they lie down of their own accord—supported by the past, supported by the future, and acknowledged in the spirit and the soul and the form of the plants. They lie down in those patterns, all the while being supported by the benevolent energy of spirit, soul, their own forms, and the forms of all the other plants cooperating to lie down—and the forms of plants nearby who do not have to lie down but are in complete cooperation. Thus is a crop circle born and a message given.

The Passage of Worlds Crop Circle

Now I will go on, and you can ask your questions later. The crop circle that is called Passage of Worlds in your words refers to a goal. This goal is to create a benevolent world of light. Light, in this case, refers to heart, soul, spirit, and form. Light is a—how can we say?—universal term used there, and that is why you see something like that in the center [see fig. 22.1]. About the circles to either side: One represents the past group; the other represents the future group. But there is a further interpretation available. It is not just a message saying, "Here we are. This is what we do. Here's how we're helping you," for it is that, but it has other meanings. **Crop circles always have more than one meaning. Try to remember that.**

The other meaning is about the world you are on. You are passing through a time now that is dangerous, yes? But it is dangerous because you have forgotten who you are. You have forgotten that you are spirit, you are soul, you are form, and you are living in a world that is also spirit, soul, and form, even in your now time. Even though your fellow human beings do not always represent that in the most benevolent way, it is still true. It is also true of all animals, all plants, all microorganisms—everything.

Granted, nonhumans of all forms, including Mother Earth, are not here to remember that. They all remember that already, and sometimes in attempting to communicate these messages to you, they get overzealous, as you can understand. Imagine you are trying to communicate to someone who might even understand your language but the person just can't *hear* you, as you might say—meaning that the person is determined to do what he or she is going to do—and no matter how wise and wonderful, no matter how clear, no matter how astute the message, the person is determined to go a particular way. You can understand that. So sometimes, then, the messages have not been heard.

One cannot deny, although there are those who do, that these crop circles are appearing like magic. It is a magic that is entirely associated with love—and thus the transformation from a crop of, say, any grain standing upright to stalks that are suddenly lying down in patterns with a wonderful energy of love, and a benevolent healing energy as well. This is why many people try to approach such circles. They know that the energy is benevolent. It is a wonder. It is magic, but it is benevolent magic, and benevolent magic is always about the needs of the people, the needs of the animals, the needs of the plants, and the needs of all forms of life—provided for, experienced, and lived in the most benevolent way. Thus you have a message.

Now the goal is the planet of light [as depicted by the center circle]. The danger is that people in your time, sometimes because they don't remember who they are, act out in a world that is dangerous, and they add to the danger. That is one world, the danger world [depicted by one of the side circles]. The other world you see in this image—other than the other side, other than the light planet in the center—is about the transition. So it is the light planet flanked by the danger world and the other side, depending on the way you face the crop circle. It is not rigid. For some people it's one side; for other people it's the other side, so don't be too attached to rigidity. It's not about classifying the nuances of words. The expression of that is the transitional world.

So in the center is the light planet, on one side is the danger world, and the other side is the transitional world. Your goal at this time is to be in the transitional world and to release the danger world. Your next goal, of course, is the light world, where communication is accepted as energy, meaning how you feel in your physical body. Your physical body is a full-time antenna. Your physical

Fighure 22.1: "Passage of Worlds Crop Circle 7 July 2010" http://www.temporarytemples.co.uk/

Steve and Karen Alexander have been photographing and researching crop circles for over fifteen years. For the past ten years, they have produced a yearbook that showcases the very best formations of each year and can be purchased at their website. These self-published books contain some of the best crop circle photography you will find anywhere. The Alexanders offer a free newsletter for you to keep up with the latest circles as they happen. Go to http://www. temporarytemples.co.uk/ to subscribe.

body knows through instinct what energy is safe and benevolent for you and what energy is not safe and might be harmful for you. You just have to learn how that works. I believe much instruction has been given about that through this being, and I'm sure there are others teaching on these matters as well.

Turn the Image until It Feels Right to Your Personality

Understand that all individual humans on the planet might look and feel differently about the image. For example, say you could float above the crop circle, and you would look at it. Some might float around to this side or float around to that side and say, "Oh, this is the side that feels best to me." It is not about which way is right-side up for a picture. It is about which way you look at the circle as an individual and which way you turn the picture. You could take a picture directly above the field, for example and say, "Ah, this is the way it feels good to me." Someone next to you might also have the picture, and they could turn it a different way and say, "*This* way feels good to me." It's not about the "right" way.

What way feels best for you is an expression of families of individuals, also known as families of personality. There are basic personality types on your planet, grouped loosely under twelve or thirteen families, depending on how you count. Therefore there will also be a minimum of twelve or thirteen different breakdowns of how that crop circle is turned to feel best to any individual. You must speak the truth, though, when you say, "This feels best to me."

For those trying to understand crop circles, it would be good to get a photo directly over the center of the crop circle, to the best of your ability, to perceive its center. If you are able to do that and you have the means to reproduce a photo that is, say, 9x12—big enough so people can see it easily—then set it down in front of people and say, "Which way is right side up?" and let them turn it their own way. It's best to do this individually so that people do not have any sense of what their peers are doing.

It's not about right and wrong. It's about your family of personality. One might find even twelve or thirteen different families of personality within a single physical family, but there are also many variations. If you do a test with, say, a thousand people, for example, it's not inconceivable that there might be 300 or more variations if it's done precisely scientifically. I'm not saying to do it; I'm saying that variations of families of personalities exist.

The Message of This Circle Urges You to Be in Transition

We have a general description of crop circles, where they're from, why they're here and a little elaboration on an individual crop circle that you find to be of interest as of this moment. It is definitely not only a—how can we say?—sign and symbol associated with where they're from but also a sign and symbol associated with where you are right now as a planetary global human society. You can see radiations coming out from the various circles. That indicates very clearly what I've been talking about in terms of energy.

The message is not only a message for your now time, as in the desired goal for now, but also to show you that there are those in the distant past who love you not because you are related to them but because they love you and want you to have what they have—a complete awareness of spirit, soul, and form—in order to get along in the world as best as possible and also there are those in the future who feel exactly the same way. The message of your own time is to choose to be in transition, to allow yourself, in every moment you possibly can, to be in transition and to understand that other forms of life, both plant and animal, are attempting to communicate with you. I believe you have had such communications through this channel from animals and plants and so forth already, have you not?

This is part of the method and means to bring forth this kind of message in a language that will be translated to other languages in time. Still, ultimately the true language is gesture and, you might say, pictures drawn in the dirt with a stick. But since that's not possible in your time, instead the plants lie down in the area that has been requested to be the area of reception.

You might reasonably ask, "Why that area?" The explanation is simple. The peoples of that distant past lived in that area. The peoples of that future who are supporting this also live in that area. So quite naturally, it is appearing in that area. Now, years ago, when these things popped up for other civilizations thousands of years ago, they didn't always pop up only in that area. Sometimes they would pop up in areas where they were needed. Even in your time, they occasionally pop up in areas where they are especially needed.

Those who have knowledge of the waters, the oceans, the seas, and even vast lakes can sometimes briefly see such a thing appear on the water for a moment. This is because the water also cooperates, being alive in soul and spirit. Thus the image can be seen. That's my gift to the wise sea men and women who also are of the water. These circles can also appear on other matter. They have been known to appear on snow or ice, briefly, for those living in cold countries. But most often, they appear in the living matter of plants who have such heart, such soul, such spirit—and a flexible form that they choose to use to deliver messages that remind you of who you are, where you're from, why you're here, what you're doing, and where you're going.

Those Who Created the Circles

Those people from the past who are doing this in that area, did they create Stonehenge or some of the other monumental stone . . . ?

No.

Did they live later or earlier than that?

Earlier. It doesn't really matter, because they don't live in time. You notice how I've referred to them. In their own time, they lived about 40,000 years ago. But they still live in their time in that same place, just like those in the future live in their time in those places—just like you live in your time in those places and in the places you're living now. You have forgotten that you are spirit, you are soul, you are form—and I do not mean that simply as an idea, as a philosophy. But because you do not live it in every breath you take, every moment you live and every gesture you make, because you do not live it in such a way, you are more focused in linear time. Your true nature is time of all times. The ones in the past live in that. The ones in the future live in that. You are actually living in that, but you don't know it.

Thus there are problems; there are battles. There are missed communications. So there needs to be something startling that will not only capture the attention of people because it is so amazing but also because it can be proved scientifically, which is popular in your time—even though there are those who have tried hard to disprove it. There needs to be something to prove that there is a difference between naturally forming crop circles in which the crops lie down but do not break and those that are produced by people having fun, making a joke, where the crops break and do not lie down because they love you and want to remind you of who you are.

So those beings who live in the same place are in different focuses or, as we used to call them, dimensions?

Yes. It is known and understood by some members of the scientific community that different worlds occupy the same place. This is a theory, one might say, but it is generally considered to be an acceptable theory. Of course, it is difficult to prove using the scientific method, meaning with reproducible results, but if one uses instinct and physical feelings, one can make these connections. So I speak to scientists who are of instinct, who are of feeling, who understand that the nature of physical matter is to be spirit, soul, and form and who live that and can thus extrapolate the truth of the matter.

How the Crop Circle Was Made

How was this particular crop circle made? Was it with a ship or with energy?

With energy, and there were witnesses. Granted, they were not human, but there were witnesses: birds and others. There are always witnesses. If you know how to talk to animals as individuals, which is not so much saying, "Greetings, good life," but saying, "Would you share with me what you saw?" and one is there, then you can see what they saw. You can experience what they felt, and you can know whether a crop circle was made energetically or with a ship simply by asking them, "What did you see?" and accepting what they show you. If you ask them what they saw and you see a worm in the grass or clouds in the sky, you will know they are telling you what they saw and that they did not see the crop circle forming. Then thank them, wish them good life, and go on with your life. But if you happen to be in the neighborhood of a crop circle that formed very recently, you can ask the animals. If you wish, if you feel close to the crops, as some who raise them might feel, you can ask the plants right next to the crop circle, "What did you see?" and they will show you. Do not question it. Simply say, "Thank you. Good life." That's all. Then go on with your life.

Many people say they see balls of light dancing in the air as a crop circle is being made. What are those?

That is energy. It is not ships, as it is often assumed to be. Sometimes, in your time, when people see ships—craft, you would say—they also see those balls of light. That is energy, benevolent energy that supports and welcomes the presence of the vehicle, and it tends to be seen sometimes and not seen other times. But they're always present, so the vehicle can be in an envelope of space that is protected. It protects the vehicle, protects the occupants of the vehicle, and protects the space beyond that envelope from any deterioration or harm. So that is what is being seen. This has been reported, I believe, in your time. Many times when people see ships, they see these balls of light. Sometimes they are of color; other times they are simply light.

So the benevolent energy that comes into the crop circle comes from the beings in the ship? Who is generating that healing energy?

No, the ship travels in that envelope, and by the imprint of its existence, it is able . . . it does not land on the crops. It simply hovers, usually for no more than three seconds of experiential time, meaning how it would be experienced if you lived it. But since they are traveling in time—no, that's not the way to say it. From your perspective, they are traveling in time. From their perspective, they are in a motion, meaning physical motion. If you were

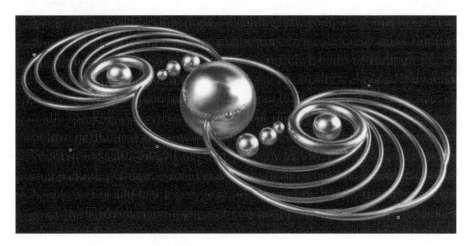

Figure 22.2: Model of Passage of Worlds Crop Circle

able to make a perpetual physical motion, time would not be a factor. I think people in those scientific fields will understand that.

So the ship leaves an imprint on the basis of the energy that the ship itself radiates. There are many different forms and shapes of ships. So that's what occurs in the case of a ship, and the crops respond. But most often, the crops simply do it themselves. It is much safer for everyone that way. To answer your question specifically: It is not the direction or the will, you might say, of those on board the ship. It just happens to be the marker the ship would leave if it hovered over anything. If you were able to look at the bottom of the ship, you would say, "Oh, there it is!"

Many ships in different places have various marks they leave, often expressing that form of universal language. This is very important for peoples in your time to know, especially those who are studying how you relate to people from other planets. Generally speaking, you relate to them through your physical energy—what you're feeling in your body; meditation will help you to achieve this—gestures you are able to make and pictures you might draw with a stick on the ground, for example. It might sound very rudimentary, but you would find these types of communication to be completely acceptable. This is also to remind those who are studying these things—and many people are doing this in your time.

You probably said it and I didn't understand, but it's still not clear to me what determines the actual shape of the crop circle in the wheat field. The way the ship is made?

Do you mean in reference to the ship? The bottom of the ship; the way it looks physically?

And there's a ship whose bottom looks like this crop circle?

That's right. It would be as if you had clay and you took your hand—everyone in school does this as a child, often as a gift for Mom—and pressed your hand into the clay. It would leave a shape. The bottom of the ship leaves a shape of its own physical being.

The Future Is a Current
Moving You toward a Benevolent Planet

Okay. Are any of those beings who lived there 40,000 years ago and who live in this other focus now incarnated on the planet now?

Well, I will have to look into that. [Pause.] Yes, there is a future generation, but that's in your time. [Chuckles.] Yes, there is a youngster I can see.

Just one?

Yes. That's not a requirement to do the work, but there is one I can see.

The future people in the other focus—are any of them future incarnations of any of us on Earth now?

Yes, there are several.

Several. So they're pulling us toward their benevolent future.

It's not a physical pull like you might use to reach out and help someone over a puddle or something. It is more of an energy pulse, and if you feel that energy pulse, you naturally gravitate to it. It's better if you picture it like this. A river runs where the water is most welcome, and as a result, it travels in a rather circuitous route, not strictly in a straight line. So if you were on that river, the gentle river, and there was a current in that river, you could conceivably float along that current without expending very much energy at all. The current itself takes you where the water is going. The energy is very much like that. That current is available, and when you are connected to that exact energy I referenced—spirit, soul, form—in every moment, you naturally flow where you are going without any great expenditure of energy on your part. Oh, you might occasionally make a very slight motion—and I mean very slight—but for the most part, the current carries you along.

If you are not focused in that and you are focused in, say, the danger world, as I referred to it, then you will feel like the box is getting smaller, as you say. That boxed feeling, like getting smaller, is to remind you that something is wrong and needs to be corrected in the way you are interacting with your world. I'm not just talking about, say, someone who commits a criminal act and thus is put in a small box but rather your awareness of your spirit and your appreciation of your soul, which has to do more with you personally as an individual. What I mean by spirit is the total you that is connected to all beings. Your soul is a portion of that and is connected to you as an individual. And then there is you as an individual, connected to all that your focus needs to change, meaning you as an individual need to change to that focus so that you can live a more benevolent life and find yourself in that current, moving toward a more benevolent place.

I'm using an analogy; understand that the current is the analogy. So the energy doesn't pull you. It's just going that way, and you are welcome to go with it. There is no demand, no command. Instead, it is welcome, that feeling. If you've ever said welcome and meant it, there is a physical feeling that goes with that. Learn to recognize it. If anyone ever says welcome to you and they mean it, learn to recognize that energy. This energy will appear in your body, and it will be just like the energy that welcomes you, moving toward that benevolent future.

That's moving toward the light planet, right?

The light planet, yes.

Instinct and Physical Feelings Offer a Clear Way of Moving toward Transition

The danger world is when we're not connected, the light planet is the destination, and the transition planet . . .

Is your transition from who and how you're expressing yourself to accepting and attempting to transition, using your instinct and your physical feeling. Thought will not always serve you because of the times you are living in, the conditioning you've been exposed to, the education you have, and your own experience of life, since you are a personality. Thought will not always be the clear way to find that energy. But your instinct, your physical feelings, will always be that clear path. Learn about instinct, learn about how your physical feelings work, and you will always have a language you can use to communicate and be communicated to that is connected to benevolence, to love, to heart, and to your spirit, soul, and form. Thus you will always have the means to know.

But most of the world, most of the population, lives in danger world. How on earth do they get the message that there is even such a possibility as being able to move to the light world?

You and others will give them that message, using the methods you are using now. You cannot grab them by the arm and say, "Listen!" [Chuckles.] All you can do is offer the message. The message is being given also by the plant world, by the animal world. The message is going to your physical feelings of all peoples, all humans. The message is omnipresent, so there are times, even if you're in the danger world, when you feel that message. When you wake up slowly from the dream world, as you call it, the message is often felt, and you might have a few moments when you feel wonderful. Notice that, because that is very close to your connection to spirit, soul, and form.

A Crop Circle to Remind You Personally of Your Spirit, Soul, and Form

All of the crop circles that were put down of course are gone from the Earth, but they exist in photos. Do those photos need to be disseminated? Do they need to be talked about? Do they need to be understood? Should something be done about all those?

They're all messages. It helps, if possible—and it isn't always possible—to have taken a picture directly over the center of the crop circle. But even if that's not available, your computers can extrapolate what that picture might have looked like, and that, while not perfect, is pretty close. Yes, disseminating photos might be useful, but it is not critical. Each and every message contained in a circle is energy. That's why those who are able to approach that crop circle—within, say, a few hours of it being there—feel that energy, and it corresponds to the spirit, soul, form energy in themselves. That's why very often sensitive people, or even people who don't consider themselves to be sensitive but really are, will feel wonderful around such a crop circle.

Sometimes it's too much, though. You have to back up because your physical body has received the message, you are in the energy, and you no longer have to be stimulated to be in the energy. Then step away and, to the best of your ability, memorize the feeling in your body so that you can remember it—not in words, but if you wish to remember it later. "Oh, my stomach felt this way, my heart felt this way, and my feet felt that way." Make a note of that.

Just be in that energy for as long as it's comfortable. Breathe in and out, open your eyes, close your eyes, and look at your world. You will see things differently. You will feel things differently. You will be reminded that you are spirit, you are soul, and you are form. Through that, you will be connected to your immortal spirit and your immortal soul, and you will be given a message by your mortal, physical form that is in that moment completely in touch with spirit and soul—and demonstrates it through the physical feelings of your mortal body in complete cooperation with your instinct.

Looking at the pictures, even in color, doesn't give you a fraction of that energy then?

It might, but it would be helpful if you knew how to meditate or could feel energies. If you don't know how to do these things, then here is something else to do. Pick the crop circle picture you like the most or that you feel the best about, all right? Turn it in the direction that feels best to you. Always try to use a picture taken from the center or a computer rendering of what it would have looked like, taken from the center above. Print out a picture; don't stare at a computer screen or turn it on the computer screen. Print out a picture and put it in front of you. You can hold it in front of you—in front of your eyes; that's the best—and turn it until it feels just right. This would be the way it feels just right to you—not what thinks right; it's not about thinking. Remember, you're trying to remind yourself of your universal language. So it has to feel right to your physical body. When it feels just right, just perfect to you as an individual, then that's the crop circle that will remind you, physically, of your spirit, your soul, in your form.

So the picture will do the work. We don't need to ask who made it and what the message is; the picture itself is what's important.

Yes, if you can't be at the crop circle. Then the picture itself . . .

Is the next best.

It's good if you can move it right in front of you with your arms. If for some reason you cannot do that, then ask someone else to move it, for those who might not be able to move things. Ask someone to move the picture, not by touching it physically—using a piece of wood, a stick, would be fine. But if they must touch it with their fingers, then when it gets to the point where it is just right, ask them to remove their fingers and look at the picture. If it's not being suspended in the air in front of you, it would be best for it to be sitting on a solid wood table or even on the ground in the dirt—that's even better— rather than sitting on something metal, because metal, in your time, or even furniture that has metal in it, will always be uncomfortable because it has been refined from its natural shape and is not, chemically speaking, in its natural state of being. Thus it is uncomfortable with itself. You want to have the best possible conditions to look at that picture.

The Twelve (or Thirteen) Personality Types

You briefly mentioned the twelve or thirteen personality types, which I take it are what we call the astrological signs?

The astrological signs correlate with that, yes. But the personality types existed before the astrological signs. And this has to be the case if you think about it, because on other planets, the astrological signs would be different.

Yes. Well, in a book we just published [Astrology: Planet Personalities and Signs Speak through Robert Shapiro], we were told that the astrological signs were based on twelve actual families of personalities.

That's why I said twelve or thirteen.

Does what sign you are or what personality you are affect the crop circle?

If it were possible to conduct such a research project with, say, hundreds of thousands of people, you would undoubtedly find correlations, some of which might be this or that attitude or opinion and so on. Good social researchers could do that, but I would not recommend pursuing such a thing, because that would just be a way of creating more groups. Classifications and things like that—not necessarily the aim of researchers—can cause people to become competitive, and that will not serve you. I understand that in your time, competition can be fun, but it has a side that is expressed in the danger world that is not fun.

Okay, well I'll take that out. That doesn't really relate to anything except how they would view the picture.

Don't take that out, because everything you ask—even that which you think might be only for your own purposes—will serve the needs of others whom you don't know and have never met. Try to remember that in the future, because sometimes you'll ask something that seems to be only individual but, unbeknownst to you, there are hundreds, perhaps thousands of others who would be saying or thinking if it wasn't there, "Well, why didn't you ask _____?" You see? Thus you would say, "Uh-oh, I wish I'd have kept that in." [Laughs.] You are very often asking questions as a representative of humanity as well as an individual.

Crop Circle Group Coordinator's Perspective on the Explorer Race

Various ET groups who have these crafts are responding to a need and are coming to do these crop circles based on their feeling that it should be done?

Exactly. That's actually how the world—meaning the universe, but from my perspective, the world—runs: with all beings responding to the needs of all beings, all the time. That is why, away from the school you find yourself in, the universe is a wonderful place to live. You find yourself in this school very temporarily, considering how long you live. When you leave this school at the deep levels of your sleep and when you leave this school at the end of your life, you almost immediately resume that natural way of life.

What is your opinion of the Explorer Race experiment that we're involved in?

I feel it is a worthy experiment, even though it is not directly meant for you to learn. At this stage of your existence, you—meaning the human race on Earth—are simply completing something that others have started. This was something that these others needed to learn because of who they would work with, those who you would teach at some point in time, as you would see it, or in some existence, as I would see it now. You had to learn all about mistakes, all about what would happen "if this," and then what would happen "if that," and so on, extrapolating on the mistakes. But you don't need to learn that anymore. You all know that; at least, it becomes apparent very quickly within seconds or minutes. Therefore one might quickly recognize, "Uh-oh, I did that again. Let me try and correct that."

So you see, you who are incarnated in your now world really are much more able; you are much more empowered to find that stream, because you are not really here to learn that lesson. It's been learned, and it is only your job to move very slowly, gradually, gently, and safely forward, resulting in a benevo-lent motion—meaning being in that current, being in that stream, being in that energy. It is only your job to be who you are, leaving no one behind and welcoming all beings. That's your job.

That's why it's all right to speak to you of these things now, because there is no one living on the planet now who is here to learn those lessons. You've all learned that in the past. It's completely understood for those with whom you might work at some point—in spirit or in form. So it's your job just to remember who you are. That's all.

I like that.

Information about the Crop Circle Group Coordinator

Now tell me about you.

I am a being, as you can see, a personality whose job it is to coordinate all those who would help you to remember who you are and to make that as easy as possible in your time—and in all times you are in, until every one of you rejoins spirit, soul, and form. That's my job. When you do that, then I'll go on and do other things! [Chuckles.] I am generally involved in coordination wherever it's needed, for I'm an expert in that.

How long have you been doing this?

As long as long is—forever. You will find that in the universe, every soul, every spirit, every personality, and form—every individual—has some precise thing that he or she is very good at, and when it's recognized, the individual does that. Perhaps, with encouragement, the being will not only be very good at it but the being will love doing it. That's another thing you're remember-ing now, slowly, which is why parents sometimes notice children being very good at something and beyond their years in knowledge about something.

Try to encourage children to be what it is that they are good at, as long as it is not harmful, meaning causing physical pain to themselves or physical pain to others. If it causes others to be confounded or dumbfounded, as you used to say, that might be acceptable, as long as those others are not always in direct contact with the child, for the child might simply be expressing some behavior or mannerism that is associated with his or her universal being. You can, of course, allow for certain unacceptable traits in your society. To answer your question more directly, I've been on this project for some time, but I do foresee an ending.

So what did you coordinate before the crop circles? What else have you coordinated for us or for our benefit?

Sometimes it involves a welcoming of certain musical tones or sounds that you discover are just as welcome in your population as they are in other populations. You might hit a certain note or make a certain tone that you thought was just something pleasurable to you, and you discover that other people in your population also like that. Then you discover in your travels that people all over the world like that sound. That's an example, and my work is always to remind you of your connections and coordination with others.

Welcome to Natural Communication

Do you coordinate ET beings, plants . . . ?

You understand, it is not my job to make those things but rather to help to coordinate them in the safest and most benevolent way for all peoples. It's important to say that so that you do not think of me as some kind of deity, which I do not claim to be.

Oh no, I've talked to too many . . .

You are the representative of Earth humans.

Oh. All right.

Leave that in when you said, "Oh no," and I said, "You are the representative of all," because others will study your manner of questioning, no matter if your question stands on its own, is rambling, is cut short, walks around the issue, and so on. The answer is always coordinated to your feeling and, to a lesser degree, your words. For those of you who are studying this in the future so that you know how to express questions, should you ever have the opportunity for such communication as this, do not look for the perfect question spoken mentally. Remember feeling and form; communication is not always apparently precise.

Speaking as myself, I want to welcome you to your world of natural communication. Do not be put off by the way I speak. Remember to recognize the spirit and soul in the forms of others, even if you cannot comment on it or directly communicate about it to them. Many times you'll be able to do this with animals and plants, just recognizing their spirits, their souls, and their forms. Sometimes this can be done by just joining them with breath. Other times it can be done by sleeping and having dreams. Do it in the most safe and benevolent way for you.

If you want a little gift, I'll give you that now. If you are around an animal that's safe for you to be around, notice how it's breathing—not if it's out of breath!—but see if you can hear its breath, if you can match your breath with the animal's. It will recognize this as an acknowledgement of its spirit, of its soul, and its form, and it will like it. Good life.

That's beautiful. Would you like to discuss other plant crops or crop circles in the future?

I will be available for such discussions in the future. If I am not personally available, one of my contemporaries will speak, for there are several of us. I think you will like us all.

[Laughs.] I think you're wonderful. Thank you.

Good night.

Good night. Good life.

YOUR SHIFT IN FOCUS IS CAUSING DREAMS AND VISIONS

ET Visitor

July 17, 2010

Greetings. I am a representative of one of the worlds that your focus [3.5 + dimensional Earth] is passing near. The veils are very thin here, and we sometimes see your world, so we've had to set up a barrier to avoid that. It's been successful, but some of you—sensitives especially—are having a situation where some of your natural skills are present for you in your world now. It's not all the time, but I believe that it's caused by the proximity of our worlds, meaning our universes are so close that you are being either stimulated in your own natural perceptions—from beyond the world you're in—or that somehow your motion is accelerating toward these natural abilities. Of course, if you were living in this world—my world—you would naturally have these skills.

I do not think, though, from what I've been able to observe, that it has actually accelerated the changes that you are going through physically in your world specifically. From what I can tell, it's strictly accelerating the individuals that it's affecting. And even though there are certain individuals that it's clearly affecting—and this is purely a theory on my part—one has to assume that everyone is really being affected in some way and that those who are sensitive or attuned to their perceptions are simply more likely to take note of changes. One thing that is very clear, strictly observing the channel here, is that it is possible to see into other worlds. It is also possible to see into the future and, in some cases, into the past of the world in which you are now living.

You might see many things as sensitives. I will speak to the sensitives, all right? You might see many things. Sometimes seeing into other worlds means that you see a vehicle. You might simply see something that is a fixed object that does not move, or you might see something in motion. It is not likely that you will see an individual being, but you might see something that simply *is*. At times, you might see something that filters, meaning that a filter has been placed between the sensitive's perception and some other world that would not be good for you to see, for whatever reason. Sometimes it is in the past of your own world; sometimes it is in a segment of your own world that is happening in your immediate time, give or take a few seconds. And other times, it is something that may be happening in the future of your world but that is not good for you to see—or it is not good for those in that future to be perceived by anyone in their past, for some reason. There are many possible varieties of that as well.

What You are Seeing May Not Be New

I bring this up because, as sensitives, you will have these visions at unexpected times and moments. If you have a vision and you see something that is upsetting and unsettling and you are religious, then say a prayer about it, whatever would, to the best of your ability, prompt the situation you are seeing to have a better outcome, to work out better for the people—for this people or that people to be happier—or for the events that might be something unpleasant to have some kind of better outcome.

If you are trained in various capabilities, do those things. You might broadcast energy of some sort—many people do that, and I am sure there are other skills that many have. Those who are sensitives are not always skilled in these things, though. They might be very old and certainly have those skills present for them, or they might be very young and, not having had specific experience or teaching, not know what to do. So if you are hearing about this talk—or reading it, perhaps—then see if you can find something you can say, even if it is a simple prayer, that whatever you are seeing gets better for the people, places, things, or events and that it somehow improves in some way that is good for all peoples.

I wanted to bring this to your attention right now because it is something that has been activated. So even though at some point our worlds will not be close anymore and the veils will be in their usual thickness, those of you who have been accelerated and are experiencing these skills will not lose them; you won't fall back to the position you were in before. You will stay with these capabilities. And for everyone on your planet, again, we're into my theory now, whatever else is going on for you, if you have been somehow accelerated toward your own natural, native personality's spirituality—what you are when you are not in this challenging place where you now find yourselves—your natural self, whatever form that might take, may also begin to be experienced. So even if you do not consider yourself a sensitive, you might notice things that are clearly otherworldly.

My feeling, based on what I have seen and have considered to be possible, which I'm calling my theory, is that the actual sights, sounds, and visions that you are seeing are not part of something new that is happening. For instance, you might see a vehicle from some other place in the sky for a moment, and then it's not there. It's not that suddenly a vehicle is visiting and then leaving. Or if it is a portal you're seeing and then not seeing, that portal is still there somewhere, even though it may not even be in your universe. For those of you who might have a mass event—say, many people seeing something at the same time—you are less likely to convince yourselves that it was some kind of phantom, something that really wasn't there. When hundreds or thousands of people see a mass event at the same time, it will be pretty hard to convince them that it wasn't real, and that's good.

But what you are seeing may not be something new. It may not be, "Oh, visitors are coming and perhaps they will be new friends!" I'm not saying that is not the case; what I'm saying is that this is something that has *always* been the case. There have always been visitors in this world of yours who came in vehicles or otherwise and observed or walked about on the surface of your planet if not communicating with the human beings, then communicating with other beings—trees, beings who walk about on all fours or many legs, and so on—just pausing to communicate, and then those other beings would pause and also communicate.

Do Not Be Alarmed by Your Visions

I want to bring this to your attention because I feel that there are many people who are having these experiences, and they're unsure about what they are. I feel it's vital for you to know this because it will not only happen to adults, you see. Adults may be somewhat sophisticated and able to come up with something to say if they suddenly see something startling. As adults, even if you say, "Oh!" with other people around, not realizing that you had made a sound, you know, and naturally other people then say, "What?" if you are reasonably sophisticated in life and do not wish to state to the others what it might be that you have seen, or if you are simply old enough to have the experience to know, you could just say, "Oh, it's nothing," or something like that. But if you are older and have an established personality with others and you are suddenly reacting to something they don't see, it could make for complications. And especially if you are younger and reacting to something that those around you who are older—perhaps family, perhaps others—don't see, there might be a concern for your health.

So [chuckles] this is what I am saying: If you see something and you do have an exclamation like that, if you feel the people around you can understand it, just say, "I've had a vision, and I think I'll say a prayer right now"—something like that, something compatible with your culture. And by culture, I also mean cultures within cultures as well; I am not just speaking about places and mass groups of people, but also about groups within those groups and how you might have your own culture with friends and so on—your ways of being, eh? If it is acceptable, find something to say and then say a prayer or do something to attempt to improve the situation, either right away or as soon as possible—you may have to step away from the group for a moment to do this.

You will not be able to do anything direct and physical. None of these visions will happen to people you know consciously. Some of them might remind you of people you know consciously—there will be a vague similarity to them—but the visions will all be of people you don't actually know and have never met. Nevertheless, the fact that you are having these visions means that there may be something you can do to help in the situation. Always know that.

The chances of other people on your planet who are sensitives seeing the same thing at the same time, while less likely, are still possible. I would say that if I had to put a number on it, it might not be at the same time, but two or three others could probably have a very similar vision, though they might see whatever it is they are seeing from a slightly different angle or perspective. One person might see it, say, from almost the top but maybe with a slight angle, and another person might see it from what you might say is the back or the side, depending on your point of view and what it is that you are seeing.

Don't assume that if you see something, it automatically means you need to say a prayer or send energy or whatever you do to help improve the situation. If there is nothing apparently dramatic going on, you know—no catastrophe waiting to happen, nobody crying out for help or weeping—if it is just something benign you are seeing, perhaps a pastoral scene, do nothing. Just be grateful for the experience and understand that it does not mean that there is anything wrong with you. It just means that you are acquiring skills and perceptions that you have in your natural state. Basically anywhere else in your universe, you would have these visions readily available to you all the time in the benign state you would find yourself living in. I wanted to bring this to your attention because it is happening with much greater frequency not only to those who are sensitives but also now and then to people who do not consider themselves to be sensitives.

You Are No Longer Affecting Us

How would you describe the focus that you're in?

We are of that world, you understand, that has been referred to before—the one that you are traveling close to. And if I were to describe the focus, I would simply say that the particles of our being are farther apart from your perspective than your own particles are. That's the actual physical description; I understand that you have a tendency to number dimensions, but this is rather arbitrary. It is like a filing system in which you might ascribe numbers or codes to something, but it would not give a physical description. I would prefer to give you a physical description so you have some general conception of what the actual difference is.

If I looked at you, what would I see?

From your perspective where you are now, you wouldn't see anything. But I understand you're asking me to give a physical description of myself. We are not exactly like you, but we look similar to you. From your perspective, our heads are larger than your own and we don't have that much hair on top—only a little bit. And taking into account the differences in focus, I would say that we are on average a little taller than you. Our arms are perhaps a little longer than yours. Our bodies, what you would describe as the trunks of our bodies, are a little longer. Other than that, there are just minor differences.

And this has to do with . . . recently another being spoke from your planet about how we were pushing you back and causing problems on your planet.

That is fixed. It just required that we set up a temporary veil of our own. I know this is something that you as a people do not do, so it's really kind of a one-way veil. Our peoples are now not affected by the natural radiation of so many beings, planets, and so on, because we have set up a veil that will work just fine. But your peoples are having the experiences of the encounter in a different way from ours. I feel it is a completely benign way because it's not causing your peoples to become our peoples—to become anything like us, you understand. So it's not interfering in your world, but it does seem to be bringing many of the people on your planet along at an accelerated level toward the natural personalities and capabilities you would have if you were living on some benevolent planet somewhere else.

Is this because our solar system is moving in space or is it because the Earth planet is moving in consciousness or what? How would you describe how we are moving?

You are on a sturdy, inexorable path toward an emergence into a natural state of your world and thus a natural state of all the beings on the world. Therefore since you as human beings—the Explorer Race, as you say—are all being affected toward this natural motion, this is why I feel that and why I've used the term "accelerated." The motion and direction already exist, so what's occurring is a speeding up of the motion toward a conclusion; you as individual souls—personalities, physical beings, whatever you want to say— have accelerated that motion, or because you are sensitives, you are perhaps more conscious of seeing things because you have had similar circumstances in your lives already. So you might be sensitives, though you might not call yourselves that; you might have other words to describe it. It might even be a secret—maybe you don't tell anyone.

But I would say simply that the way you function in your world is as if you are all, as a people—not the nonhumans, but as humans—looking and, especially more in the past, perceiving or sensing through a very small infrastructure at the fundamentals of physical interaction. You are seeing, perceiving, and sensing your world through a filter, as if you were wearing lenses over your eyes that allow you to see only so much and not the rest. This is apparently being done so that you will concentrate on certain things and try to solve challenges about which you might otherwise, in your natural state, simply say, "Well, that's not for me to do."

That doesn't mean you've avoided these challenges; I think it's just that you are apparently volunteers. Each individual human specifically on your world now has volunteered in some way to take on these challenges to try to create better worlds for everyone everywhere. As I take a quick glimpse around your universe, I can see that it is true that there are currently a few slight problems, and looking into the past of all of these worlds, I can see some very serious problems. I do not see any problems in the future, serious or otherwise, but in the past, there have been very serious problems, and perhaps if some of these problems had been resolved and not become so serious, then maybe an accumulation of things that needed to be resolved slowly and intricately, as you are doing on your world as the people that you are, would not be present.

This is why I feel that the perceptions of your sensitives now are so important. As I said, you might be perceiving something that you would consider to be catastrophic—affecting a great many people unpleasantly—and you can immediately say something or do something about it, even in some small way. You can say a prayer or ask for some better thing to take place, whatever you do—and there's a wide variety of things people might do—but you can respond to it spiritually in some way, according to your practices. So I believe that what's occurring is that by seeing these visions, you're beginning to tap into things that may seem to be very small indeed if separated out as individual incidents, but they might have led to something else. It's as if you're on a path as a culture, as a planet, as a universe, and another path presents itself, but there's no direct connection. That other path may lead to some direction that is not good for that universe, or it might lead to a place that is better.

Something happens, and it's often many, many things. It might just be that what you are seeing, some individual tragic event for some individual person or some greater disaster of some sort that you see in a split second or perhaps even two or three seconds so you can get a sense of what is going on in the vision, and you do something on the basis of your experience of spiritual life and practice. Maybe it would help. So maybe you can help to resolve the serious problems I have seen for some of these planets in your universe. I have seen them well enough into the past that the peoples, the planets, the cultures, and so on, have now completely corrected, but they are still there in the past and unresolved, you see. Thus among other things, your universe will be in greater balance and more settled comfortably in its existence without things in the past that need to be resolved.

Putting that contemporaneously in your own world would mean that the severity of things that you are experiencing because you're attempting to resolve things from other worlds, for the most part, in your universe and in this entire physical existence, would greatly decrease. So the level, as you and other beings call it, of negativity or discomfort would drop on a steady basis; it would become less and less and less and less. I believe, on the basis of my perceptions, that that's what's happening.

You Are Experiencing an Expansion in Your Souls

I still don't have a clear picture. Are we physically moving up in space? Are we expanding outward? The beings who channel through Robert said we're "pulsing," like moving and then not moving and then moving. Is that like . . . up? How would you describe it? Or if we could see it, what would it look like?

Up is not a factor. It is a feeling. You know, if you were unhappy about something, you wouldn't say that you'd suddenly moved sideways. It's not a direction. I understand that sometimes words might work their way into languages that would be directions—meaning, say, compass points or even up or down and so on—and that they might work in a colloquial sense. But it's not up. It's not down. It's not sideways. It is entirely based in a feeling.

When you are your natural selves, you physically feel completely relaxed, and you feel loved. You have this feeling of love, and you feel confident. Generally speaking, everything that you feel that is the opposite of that feeling of love or that is constrained and doesn't have these things you would feel in your natural self—everything that you now feel that is unpleasant, discomfiting, painful, perhaps—would not be that. You would be completely relaxed, happy. You would feel loved, love others, and be happy, friendly. You would say it feels like heaven—some of you might say that, perhaps. It would be wonderful. That's your natural state everyplace else but the difficult place you find yourself in now, on the world where you're attempting to create resolution for others.

I'm attempting to answer your question, but it's difficult, because the mathematics of it is not a mental thing. What you are experiencing is an expansion in your soul, which has direct, physical impact on the physical feelings in your physical body. So while you will not, in a given life living now on the planet, suddenly see everything change in front of your eyes, melting from something discomforting to something beautiful and heavenly—you wouldn't necessarily *see* that or hear it—you might have, as I say, as sensitives, a few split seconds of seeing something like that, but you would have the feelings in your physical body that are directly connected to that experience. This is the way to know.

Picking an arbitrary direction—oh, you're going up, you're going down, or you're going sideways—doesn't make any difference because, what's the difference? You won't know, because it's not an arbitrary filing system. It's not "number six," "number eight," or "number four." It's something based entirely on the one absolute common factor to all of your souls on your planet, in your world, and in your experience now: that you are there—every single one of you, no matter what else you are there for—to learn more about the language of physicality. And the language of physicality is entirely about feelings. The reason that you have a physical body is that it will heighten your capability to understand it so that your study of physical feelings, for people going through what you're going through on your world, isn't something that is distant, as it would perhaps be for somebody on another world who might study what you're going through to the degree that you might study it. They would perhaps think about it, but they wouldn't experience it in any way and would have absolutely no means to understand it.

You are like them in your natural state, but a personality characteristic you all have in common as volunteers to come to that world that you're in as souls is that you are not satisfied with knowing things part way. Every one of you wants to know and understand things more thoroughly. You want to have what amounts to evidence so that you will know what is simply theory and what, no matter how beautiful it may sound, is not so. You want to be able to absolutely *know*, you see. And if you're going to study physical feelings, if you are not in a physical body of the type in the place that's being studied, you are not going to know or understand these physical feelings.

So it's very simple, although I'm just trying to say it in a different way that uses more words so that your mind can grasp it. But be aware that if you remain focused externally from the experience, you will have a tendency to try to understand what's going on in your own body on a mental basis, whereas if you focus and feel your own body and pay attention to your physical feelings in any situation, you will be directly studying one of the main things that you came to your world to study: the experience of physical language—which, as I say, is greatly heightened if you are physical.

Physical Language Is About Physical Feelings

Are your planet and our planet in the same space? Are we coexisting in space but at a different pulse or a different vibration or a different . . . ?

It's all right. I have your question. You don't have to add words. Do you want me to help you, or do you want me to let you finish?

No, please help.

It's all right. There is a slight overlap, very slight, on which we have managed to put a veil to protect ourselves but that in no way affects your planet, because the energy of our planet simply is not associated with your planet. So there is a slight overlap, but it is not that our entire world and your entire world are in the same space.

Has it always been this way?

No, no. It's just that way because of your acceleration, your motion on your world toward your natural self. Your planet does not have to make this motion because your planet has these other expressions of itself, but it's being like a vehicle, because if you were all to get off and get on a vehicle and go toward your natural selves, you'd kind of lose what you went there to do. So you might say you're riding your planet as you move toward your natural self. And as a result, as you go from one point to another, your planet gradually changes and becomes more of what it is at that other point. And of course you, because you are also doing that, gradually change and become more of what you are at that point you're going toward.

So we are moving in space.

No. Other than the fact that you are moving physically in orbit, turning on your axis, no. It's like this: You're trying to mentally understand something that's entirely physical, and I recognize that you're attempting to do that for those of you who are reading this or hearing it or what have you—you're attempting to give them a mental model by which they can understand what is being discussed—but in fact I'll give you something very simple you can do.

If you are sitting or lying down as still as you can be—of course, you won't be totally still because you'll be breathing and perhaps making some slight motion, but if you are attempting to be as still as you can be—and then you practice a feeling, say you decide you're going to feel happy, the physical feeling of happiness in your body is what is going on. But that physical feeling of happiness in your body does not mean that you are moving. It is a physical feeling. You are not counting the feelings of the physicality that you are having because blood is moving in your body in the veins and your heart is pumping and you are breathing, not counting that or any externals, such as the wind is blowing your hair.

Physical language in this case that you are there to study is entirely about physical feelings: reactions. I understand that you are trying to ask me whether the planet is in motion, but if you could take a piece of paper right now . . . do you have a piece of paper and something to make marks on it? Now make a dot on the paper, okay? And then a few inches away, make another dot. Each one of those dots represents a focus of your planet. Your planet is in both those places because it has both of those focuses—or dimensions, you might say, some of you. I like the term "focuses" better because it would be something you see, something you perceive, a sensation, whereas a dimension might be something highly mathematical, for example, angular. I feel that this is not something angular but something rounded—meaning circular, spherical, complete.

Both of those dots represent fixed points in your planet's being. Your planet cannot move those fixed points from place to place, but let's say it's like riding the physical tube of physical feeling. It's not unlike when you have a dream, and as you're waking up from the dream or even when you're in deep sleep, you are in another world, but simultaneously your physical body is exactly where it is on the bed or wherever you sleep. So the fixed points remain fixed. You are not moving in space, but you are moving physically in immortal physicality, the kind of physicality that exists beyond mortality. Your physical bodies are born, yes. You live your life. You die and your physical bodies return to Earth. But you go on; you continue to exist.

Figure 23.1: A representation of two focuses or fixed points of your planet's being."

What is one of the main qualities of your existence that traverses worlds, no matter what focus you are in? One of the main qualities that is in your world right now is physical feeling. People say, "Well, one of the main qualities is light," but that is not something you can actually sense, other than the light of the day. Sensitives might see a lightbeing, something like that, but in terms of an experience everyone can have at any time, it's physical feeling. So you are transiting from one dot to another on your piece of paper based on what I would call a transit line of physical feeling, even while the points remain fixed.

But we're going to end up in that focus on the top or in the second point, right?

Wherever you put your dot. I put my dot in a different place. You put your dots one above the other, eh? I would put my dots side by side.

Okay, but from the one we're on now, we're going to end up with our energy, our feelings, our . . . our focus [laughs] there, right?

Your existence—that is going to be one place in your transit where you will be. Yes, you will have been where you are now, and you will be where you're going to be.

But not for very long or for a long . . . how . . . ?

For as long as you are going to be there. You might go on to do something else, but really, what's the point in discussing that? You're not even where you're going yet.

Feeling Is the Strongest Evidence of What Exists

Okay, if I were able to look at where we're going, what would I see?

Something rather similar to what you see now, in its more pristine condition. You might see a beautiful pastoral place. There might be trees or plants: a beautiful world, what you would consider something beautiful to see. There might be waters, streams, like that, people who are happy. You wouldn't see a lot of construction, meaning buildings built out of materials that did not volunteer to be those buildings. You might see something that resembles a few walls, but that would be entirely composed of materials that volunteered to be the shape of that wall, and if they wished to be something at another time, the wall would just melt and cease to exist, and whatever was there before would be perceived.

Is this the place that's been called Terra?

Well, I suppose it has many names. I don't wish to put a name on it because everyone would have his or her own definition of what that place is based on everything everybody else has said about it. The problem with that is that it tends to limit your own perception; you add a filter and then say, "Oh, that must be what I saw," and then you study what other people have said about it and you decide that that's what you saw rather than simply observing what you see as a sensitive when you might get a glimpse of something, eh?

That's why you should be talking about how you feel in your physical body when seeing it. That's the key. How do you feel when you see that? Oh, does it feel wonderful? Most likely it does if you are seeing a glimpse as a sensitive. As you see a glimpse of this wonderful world, you will have a good feeling, eh? Feeling is the strongest physical evidence of what exists. And simultaneously, to the degree the feeling is wonderful, regardless of whatever else you're feeling in your body, that wonderful feeling is undoubtedly the way you would feel in that world if you were there all the time.

That is why feeling is a language. You have often wondered: How do people communicate beyond the spoken word, for example? That communication is based entirely on physical feeling, and if everyone has this wonderful physical feeling, there is no need to communicate further, because there are no misperceptions. There is an exchange of physical feeling from one individual to another, but it is entirely compatible because it feels wonderful and you know all you need to know about the other being. They don't need to explain the trials and tribulations, because there have not been any. And this is the core of what is referred to as telepathy.

Telepathy is *not* mental. Just let go of that description entirely. It is only mental insofar as you make it mental and study it mentally. It might be partially experienced from one denizen of one world to another denizen of another world as, say, you might get words. You might feel words as an Earth person if someone is trying to communicate with you. But they are really broadcasting the same energy that they would broadcast in their benevolent physical world; you just don't feel it. So what you might pick up is a couple of words: "Greetings," something like that. This is really your physical body's attempt to work with whatever tools you are using as a culture, to understand your world with whatever the primary tool is to communicate. So it's as if instead of getting the entire juice of the lemon, you might just get half a drop, but there's this other vast amount of communication going on that you're simply not taking in because you are not using your physical communication.

I'm here to remind you about this, because physical communication is the natural way in all other worlds that are benign and benevolent in your own universe. And that's what you're going to need to be very good at—not only to be the diplomat in your physical feelings so you do not radiate anger, for instance, as a physical astronaut going out, but to be able to maintain a benign, calm, benevolent physical feeling when you are attempting to communicate. And the first thing you do to communicate may not have anything to do with words, because the first communication of beings on other worlds—what is not only considered polite but what is natural—is physical feeling. And that is what you're on the planet to study. Best get on with it, eh?

Yes.

Bliss Is the Natural State of Being in the Universe

Is the point or the focus that we're going to similar in vibration to the one that you live on—or similar in some other fashion?

No, but if you are asking if it is more similar than the one that you have been on, then yes.

So how many more "dots" would we have to transcend . . . ?

No, don't try to quantify it. How would you ask the question in another way? I will help you. If you were to say, "What would we be like if we were to be more like you," then I would say that your physical feelings would be entirely benign and benevolent—cheerful, you might say. And if that were your primary expression of feeling, then we would be more alike. That is the way beings express themselves everywhere else except where you are, because where you are now, you are attempting to resolve all those past—and they are *way* in the past, you understand—problems that have existed on other planets or other star systems in the distant past of your own universe.

It is like this: In a given life, you might strive toward some way of being and achieve that way of being. But you still might have, say, painful memories of the past of your own life that gradually become dimmer and dimmer until the only recollection you have of those painful memories is in your feeling body, your physical feelings. Then every once in a while, you might get an uncomfortable feeling that then passes. That uncomfortable feeling may be a message about something—something in the past that needs to be corrected, you see. People on other planets in your own universe have achieved a level of existence now where they cannot tolerate even the slightest discomfort like that, but there's an accumulation of discomfort, and somebody must do something to transform that discomfort. Otherwise, the universe is threatened. It becomes unstable.

So you volunteers who want to know more, experience more, and understand more find yourselves on Earth now working to resolve those discomforts or simply working to discover ways that discomforts can be resolved, even if you are unable to resolve them yourselves. Yet sometimes just coming up with a means to create resolution might be useful, because then those who may have been involved in those discomforts, even on an ancestral basis, might be brave enough to be willing to try to resolve it themselves, using a means adapted to who they are in their worlds. But they would have to be insulated and protected to do it, because they're going into a place where their own, say, physical bodies —for the sake of clarity—would not be prepared to deal with anything discomforting. But if there is a means to resolve it that is adaptable to their own culture, well, they might be willing to try it. What I mean by this is that it's not necessarily the case that you're going to have to resolve all these problems yourselves; you might simply be coming up with the *means* to resolve them.

If physical feelings are, let's say, a circle, a full spectrum, and we drop away all of the discomforting feelings—the anger, the rage, the sadness, the disgust, the disappointment—all the stuff on the bottom half, and in the middle there is peace and calm and gentleness, do we also lose the top half, the bliss, the ecstasy, the inspiration, the incredible feeling of creativity? How does that work?

Rephrase your question without using the terms "bottom," "middle," and "top."

The feelings we have now are, I understand, more physical feelings than are available on other planets. Even though some of them are discomforting, some of them also are more ecstatic, more blissful, more expansive . . . more. [Chuckles.] When we reach this calm state of the rest of the universe, do we also lose . . . ? I don't know how to say it with . . .

It's all right; I will. I just needed you to do that.

Okay.

The blissful state you're describing is the natural state of being in the other parts of the universe, so you won't lose any of that.

Blissful, but what about the, you know, the intense creativity, the, oh, I don't know, the feeling that you are the universe, that it's all in you—the fantastic feelings that we can have here?

Well they're only fantastic because you don't experience them on a moment-to-moment basis.

But we do on other planets?

These feelings you describe feel more fantastic to you because you are comparing them to other feelings that you have that are discomforting, and so on, so the difference is much more extreme to you because of your basis of comparison—physically, not mentally. Those wonderful feelings, including the feeling of being part of all creation, and so on, are normal in the rest of the universe. No one considers them to be an extreme of anything, because that's the way you normally feel. Conversely, they do not have anything to compare it to. They would not say, "Well it feels so much better than _____." There wouldn't be anything to compare it to; there wouldn't be any "blank." It doesn't feel better than anything because it's the way they always feel. So those things, the heightened state, as you call it, wouldn't exist because you'd *always* be in the heightened state.

We Are All Philosophers and Thinkers

That sounds cool. All right. Tell me something about yourself. What is your interest on your planet? Do you travel? How do you live?

We do not travel. We have a benign and benevolent civilization. There are not too many of us in terms of your numbers—maybe around 37,000. It varies a little bit, you understand. We are, to use your term, blissfully happy all the time. I personally like to consider other possibilities. There are others like me who have been involved in assembling the temporary veils so that our worlds do not affect each other the way they were there for a little while—as mentioned, I think, in the previous talk.

Others like me are inclined to consider what life might be like in places that are not like our world. You would probably call us philosophers or thinkers. [Chuckles.] And this is perhaps why I am the one speaking to you now of all of those who are like this: I was available, and everybody else was busy, eh? I don't know what you want to know. If you're asking whether we have schools, and so on, in my understanding of your world, schools exist to teach things that they do not know to people, and a great deal of what is taught they may never need to be happy in life. So schools exist to teach a culture. Some of these things that are taught in your world I can tell would be useful skills, things you might wind up doing in a life—say you study geometry in school, and later in life, you become someone who assembles things; then geometry becomes useful. But many of you would not use that geometry later in life.

So the school is attempting to give you, near as I can tell, tools that you might find useful later in life, but it also teaches things about your culture that may or may not be useful at all. The process is apparently intended to sharpen your skills, perhaps to train you to learn and memorize things, but sometimes what you're memorizing actually creates a distortion in your personality. Schools, you understand, are not just places where teaching takes place formally, but a great deal of the teaching takes place informally from student to student, group to group. Sometimes parents do not understand that, but when you are in school, you understand that oh so well, eh?

We do not have that sort of system, because education, as you might call it, takes place for us on a family basis. What is helpful to know that may not be immediately apparent to a young one would be taught as it was perceived that it would be useful by family members. It might be very simple, but for instance, we do not have a multitude of languages. We would not have a need to create a name for a flower as a classification. There would not be any filing systems: "Oh, that is that, based on our filing system." I'm not criticizing; I'm just saying that your system is something that exists in a world where you do not have your natural perceptions, where you are not your natural selves. That's how it is for you all now: You are gradually attaining those natural skills and natural abilities again. Of course, as you pass over, you immediately get them. But in our world and in all the worlds everyplace else in your universe, that kind of schooling is simply a situation that doesn't exist. There's no need for it.

Are you beyond the need to eat and sleep and breathe and all these things, or do you do that?

No, we consume. There's not a "beyond the need"—you're quantifying again, but I understand what you mean. That's the way your thoughts work out of necessity, since you are experiencing linear life. But no. We, in our own way, experience linear life. We have an existence that progresses. And yes, we consume what you would consider "vegetable" matter. I'm going to use one of your little jokes: We do not live to eat; we eat to live. And what is eaten enjoys the experience and has volunteered to have the experience of being consumed. It does not exit our body, so we consume very little—just on the basis of what is needed to create any replenishment necessary, and then it transforms in our body to what is being replenished. This has, near as I can tell, something to do with our life cycle—not the rhythms of our life but the length of it.

Which is how long?

It doesn't really equate in your time, but it's simply very long.

What we would call immortal?

No, we do come and go. That's why I said the population varies, but the life is very long.

You give birth? You clone? You call into being? How do you create replacements?

It's hard to describe in your world. You would simply say we come into being, but it's more complicated than that, and thinker though I may be, I do not know how to describe it.

Okay. I probably don't need to know. What about variety?

I have to say, it's not a secret.

Okay. [Laughs.]

I just don't know. If there's something I don't know how to describe, I will be forthcoming with you. But there are no secrets.

All right. You have a variety of plants and . . . do you have what we call animals? Do you have beings who are there in a different form than you are?

Yes, but they are not always visible, so sometimes we see them and sometimes we don't. I suppose from their point of view, from what I have understood—and I am supposing a lot here in theory again—it is the same for them. Maybe sometimes they see us and sometimes they don't. But it's possible that they might see us all the time and maybe [chuckles] they don't necessarily want us to see them. So we see them sometimes, and then we don't.

But you don't communicate with them?

Oh, we communicate the way we communicate to each other: with feelings that broadcast—benign, comfortable feelings. I have every reason to believe that they feel them, because when I've been in their presence, I have felt a similar radiation from them. It is what you would call a way of being polite, understanding it in cultural terms. I believe you actually have encounters like that in your own world: Perhaps you are walking along and some other form of life comes along and they will naturally do that because they are not in your world to learn. They are simply in your world to either teach or demonstrate as an example what life is like in other places. But they must also adapt to your world. One of the adaptations that many other life forms in your world have that they are not too comfortable with, I think, is consuming each other. They don't do that in other worlds, and that creates a certain amount of discomfort for them, which is why they are not immortal—because of that discomfiture. They come and they go because they would really rather be living in a situation where they do not have to do that.

Yes. When we leave this focus—when everyone leaves this focus, dimension, whatever—will that need cease?

I couldn't say. My theory would be that that school will be available for practice, for others to learn. Perhaps there will be more to be done. I do not know. My feeling, however, is that it will return to being what it was before you arrived.

I think so too.

I think that, but I do not know that. That is strictly a thought, and it may not bear any relevance to reality.

Filtering Work during Channeling

How do you know what happens in other worlds? Do you have visitors? Do you have the ability to commune with others on other planets? What is your means of knowing these things?

We just . . . you can do this too when you are in your natural state. Other worlds have the same physical feelings that we have. We can see any place that has the same physical feelings. It's like seeing long distance with clear perception. And of course other senses are available. You might, say, smell the flowers on another world. You might have a sense of flavor. All of that sensory input is available as long as the feelings are completely compatible. For instance, I cannot notice the fragrance or the flavors in your world, because the physical feelings are not compatible.

Right, they're very uncomfortable.

Some of them are, though not all. If all your physical feelings in your world were totally uncomfortable—meaning incompatible with me—we would not be having this pleasant chat.

Oh, I see. Yes, I didn't mean that every being felt uncomfortable, but I mean there's . . .

No, no, I mean it as you might say in terms of percentage. There is enough similarity that we can have this talk at a distance, you might say. But you'll notice it is through another being. I am not speaking to you directly. I must communicate in this fashion, and for your part, you must also communicate in that fashion. You are communicating with the channel here, as he is allowing the communication to take place through him: It is a two-way communication. It is not just that this being, the channel, is acting as a conduit to bring through what I would have to say to you. Equally—in all cases, I believe—the conduit is two-way.

That is why it's important, in the case of channels, for instance, that the human beings who are asking the questions be relaxed and not agitated when they are asking the questions: because the channel would have to experience that. You see, the channel must be open to allow the being—meaning myself, in this case—to communicate through him with the feelings being entirely benign and benevolent, feelings the channel is comfortable with, but the channel cannot shut down when the human being is asking the question. That channel is wide open, so if the human being asking the questions is angry or upset—I'm not saying you are like that, but in, say, a crowd situation where somebody suddenly just yells out with great feeling of this or that—that would be difficult for the channel.

That is why I feel that if there were a big crowd, it would be good to have a few people who are just doing energy work in and around the channel so that the energy would be benign and benevolent to bring through the being, no matter who was being channeled and also so that what comes back through the channel, even if there are people simply having feelings around him, is also benign. So it might be useful to have someone functioning as a filter. In the case of this channel, there are spirits doing that, but I believe that some situations might require other people doing filtering work as well—not filtering what the channel is able to communicate back and forth, but creating a benign atmosphere around the channel, and that's it.

The reason I'm going into this, even though it's a bit esoteric for most people, is that you do this to yourself to a degree: When a parent attempts to protect a child from another adult who is speaking things that only adults ought to speak about at their level of sophistication, the parent is actually attempting to protect that child. So it's similar; it's not something foreign to you. I don't know if that's interesting to you. Maybe not.

Right. For channels who channel in public, it's much more difficult, I guess, than talking to just one person.

I bring that forth for those people doing that, and there might be a select community of people doing that. I'm not saying that you have to have people around entirely filtering everything that's going on; they would have to be very clearly focused on filtering what's coming from any source that might be harmful to the channel. And of course that channel's spirit teachers might be present and performing some of that filtering work as well.

We Can Travel through Attraction

You say you are a philosopher, so let's see . . .

I don't call myself that. To be clear, *you* might call me that.

Yes. There are so few of you then—are you on a planet the size of Earth or bigger?

Well, I wouldn't say that. It's hard to quantify it. I do not have the mathematical skills in myself to quantify whether we are—in terms of all things being equal—larger or smaller than your planet. I do not know that.

Well, what I mean is there are so few people—37,000. We have 6 billion or something.

Oh yes, that is quite a bit different.

So do you live communally? Do you have families? Maybe you live in extended families?

Sometimes, yes. If you're asking whether we have cities, no, we don't—just groups here and there on the planet. But we are mobile. We can get around if we need to go—if we wanted to go to another part of the planet, then we can travel in the physical realm. For example, perhaps I have a friend in some other place and I will think about my friend, and then I will remember the feelings I have with my friend. Then my friend will suddenly be aware that I am thinking about him or experiencing him in that sense of the physicality. And if my friend then would like to have me present—I'm greatly simplifying it, of course—then I am there for as long as that is comfortable.

Oh, you can move just like through a portal?

No, no. It's instantaneous.

Ah, that's the level you are at!

The compatibility with that person . . .

Yes, the attraction.

The attraction has to be there. If the attraction is there, then I am there as long as it is compatible, and then I might wish to be elsewhere and so on. So beings can traverse that way, but I do not "take two steps to the right and then hop" toward a . . .

[Laughs.] Through a wormhole. Okay. So do you live in buildings? Is your planet warm and comfortable all year long?

Yes, we do not need buildings. That's why I made that remark about how there might be a few walls, but the walls would be open. If there are walls, it would simply be because people might desire that type of structure, and the material is present. Some of it might be prepared to form a joined wall, for instance—one going one way, one going the other way, or perhaps something curved. It's hard to say, but it would be up to the peoples who wanted that for some reason, and of course the moment they no longer would want that or desire that . . .

It would dissolve.

. . . it would just simply return to what it was. That's the simplest way to describe it.

A Third Sex Is Natural to You

Do you have polarity in sexes—or more than two or just one, or what?

We have three. So there is a third sex that is sort of a combination of the other two. I've looked at your culture, and that's something that is natural to your culture as well. I don't know if you know that, but that combination of the sexes that is of both in some way—that is actually natural to your culture. And for some reason, I don't see that many people like that. I think maybe in your times, it's not considered acceptable, perhaps for some religious reason. I do not know. But if your culture were not interfering in some way with it—I think it's medical . . .

Oh, I think doctors interfere with it at childbirth.

. . . then perhaps 1 to 2 percent of your population would be like that now. From my perception, that would really be a good thing, because those people would be wonderful teachers to help the two primary sexes you have to learn how to communicate with each other. They would know. They would be able to be perfect communicators from one sex to another, and they would know how to communicate in ways that are differing, not based on cultural education, but simply based on the polarity of it. They would be able to teach; they are the perfect teachers, and that's one of the things they are meant to be doing. So I would really urge you to not interfere with these people when they're born. Just let them be the way they are: That's how they are. They're there for a reason, and it's not an accident. Creator is intending this. In our culture, they are a greater, you would say, percentage—like 10 percent—but where you are, they're meant to be 1 to 2 percent, something like that.

Maybe the doctors will read this. They try to make everybody one or the other.

Well, I think that they are urged to do that. If they were not urged to do that, maybe they would just say okay. And I think that part of it is also because your societies are so heavily structured. So the doctors are not wrong or bad; it's just the education they receive and the culture in which they live and so on. They're like everybody else. They're affected by that.

Well, hopefully all that will change to a more benign and benevolent understanding and acceptance.

It's also a way that cultures from afar gauge whether you are ready to meet people from other planets openly. If you cannot accept your own peoples—because you do have this third sex now—if you're not prepared to accept them as they exist, born as helpless children, unable to defend themselves from such alteration, then those from other cultures feel you are not prepared to meet them, so they will not usually visit. This doesn't go for every culture, but it goes for many cultures that you would love to meet. I am not trying to make any of you feel bad. I am pointing out something that I think can be corrected. It is not that difficult to simply stop interfering.

I realize that doctors become doctors because they want people to feel better; they want to help them get over something that is causing them pain and suffering. I think that the reason the children are being altered is that there is a perception that this will somehow cause these children pain and suffering later in life because they are different. But of course all they really have to do is be with somebody who loves them for being who they are, even though they are different—whether it is someone like them physically or one of the other sexes.

And if there is no derisiveness and no unkindness directed toward them, then there should be no problem. I realize I am speaking as someone from a society that is benign and benevolent, but I am bringing this to your attention because I think that it is a misperception in your times that these children should be altered. They are not suffering because they are born like that, and perhaps it is considered that they will suffer later in life because they won't look like the others, but I don't think that they necessarily have to be segregated from others.

Perhaps they could be treated more kindly and simply be recognized for the skills and abilities that are natural to them, as long as they are not interfered with. Skills that others may find as more of a latent skill, they will have as a prominent skill. If they are interfered with, they will still have it as a more prominent skill than others who would find it as a latent skill who are strictly one sex or the other, but it will be impeded in some way. How it would be impeded would be different from individual to individual, but as long as they are allowed to be who they are, well, then they will have these great skills and abilities to help in many ways that you cannot even imagine. They might well be able to do wondrous things.

I thank you for that. Thank you. Maybe somebody in a position to bring about change will read it and reflect on it.

I'm sure they will.

We Do Not Have a Physical Experience of the Unknown

So even though we're not moving, we didn't have an impact on you before, and soon at some point we won't have an impact on you anymore. Is that true?

Yes, that is absolutely true. This is apparently a temporary situation. But I can see that your world seems to be benefitting from it in some way, and now that my world is no longer being, you know . . .

Impacted.

Yes, thank you. Then it's fine. We are happy that you are receiving some benefit from it.

How long will this relationship go on? Do you see it lasting months, years, days?

I do not know that.

How long has it been going on?

For us, well, if I say the word, it won't mean anything to you. It's just totally meaningless.

Could you describe it in relation to our time, if it's possible?

We've been feeling it for much longer than you have been feeling it. That's the best I can say. For you, you have only been directly affected by it in the past few months, I think. But we've been feeling it for much longer than that. So my theory is that even when you are no longer feeling it, we will continue to feel it and have our temporary veil up much past the time that, from your point of view, would be needed. And the worlds would not be close together at all, but we will have that veil up for quite a while afterward, because we are apparently more sensitive to feeling these things than your peoples are. Perhaps you do feel it, but because you are so overwhelmed with other feelings, it just goes unnoticed. Perhaps that's it.

Probably, yes. Does your planet also revolve around a sun?

Yes.

Is that what's happening now? The fact that we're coming together is due to your revolutions about your sun and our revolutions about ours?

Oh, I don't think it has anything to do with that. No, because after all, as you say, dimensions and focuses are often in exactly the same place in the same time; they just cannot experience each other because of the veils. But no, I don't think so.

Okay. I was still looking for a mental explanation.

It's not that I'm denying it. I'm telling you what I know, and I love sharing with you what I theorize, but if I don't know something, I feel it's important to say so. That tells you something about us as a culture, though, and that's that if we don't know something; we don't guess.

Do you seek to find the answer, or do you just let it go?

No, because it's not my question; it's your question. I do not need to know the answer to this. You have asked, so you'll continue to seek the answer to that question, and I have faith in your desire to fulfill your own curiosities. Therefore I do not have to help you, especially since we will not be in contact much longer. So what is the point for me to pursue that question?

Right. But if you have a question, do you pursue it? You have curiosity, don't you?

Curiosity is entirely rooted in the unknown.

But you don't know everything, so aren't there . . . ?

We know what we need to know. We do not have a physical experience of the unknown in *any* way.

That's an interesting statement.

Well, I feel you are the same way, except that you're experiencing this filter. What you naturally are is not available to you because of this filter, as I described it, which is like a lens put over your sensing capabilities. But I feel that you have all of these things; it's just that they are not available to you so that you can do what it is you are attempting to do. But the reason I feel you have these things is because when you are in the deep-dream state, you have all those things in that state. But it's a real thing. It may not be what you remember when you are awake, but when you are in that other world at the deep-sleep level, you are totally your natural self. This is why I feel that it is when you are conscious, awake, not at the deep-dream level, the deep-sleep level, that you must have something that is filtering your natural abilities. Because when you are at that deep-sleep level, you are your natural self. And I think it's important for you to consider what that means, how important that is. It is vitally important, because it tells you that you are—right now, on your day-to-day basis—totally and completely in touch with your natural self.

Well, they tell us if we weren't, we'd go crazy here. I mean, if we didn't have that deep-sleep time.

But think about it: Does this mean that you can have your thoughts there, or does it mean that you can have the feelings from those places where you are your natural self in your now world? Pay attention when you wake up after having a wonderful dream. Try to focus on the feelings you have rather than examining the pictures, which may be nonsensical—meaning they don't have a linear equivalent. They would be simultaneous, for example, one thing overlaying another and therefore not having a way to understand it as a sequence. But the physical feelings, if they feel good, *that* is equivalent.

All physical feeling can be demonstrated as an immediate thing—meaning in the moment—and also in a linear fashion, because your physical feeling that you might have at any split second, for example, can be felt over time. So it is the one tool of communication that is absolutely compatible with you in your natural self and you in the state you find yourself in now. And that's why you're on Earth—because one of your primary motivations as a soul is to understand more about the natural, universal tool of communication, which is physical feeling. On that note to ponder, I shall say good night.

Oh, thank you very much. Good life.

Shamanic Secrets Mastery Series

Speaks of Many Truths and Reveals the Mysteries through Robert Shapiro

Shamanic Secrets for Material Mastery

This book explores the heart and soul connection between humans and Mother Earth. Through that intimacy, miracles of healing and expanded awareness can flourish. To heal the planet and be healed as well, we can lovingly extend our energy selves out to the mountains and rivers and intimately bond with the Earth. Gestures and vision can activate our hearts to return us to a healthy, caring relationship with the land we live on. The character of some of Earth's most powerful features is explored and understood, with exercises given to connect us with those places. As we project our love and healing energy there, we help the Earth to heal from human destruction of the planet and its atmosphere. Dozens of photographs, maps and drawings assist the process in twenty-five chapters, which cover the Earth's more critical locations.

498 p. $19.95 ISBN 978-1-891824-12-8

Shamanic Secrets for Physical Mastery

Learn to understand the sacred nature of your own physical body and some of the magnificent gifts it offers you. When you work with your physical body in these new ways, you will discover not only its sacredness, but how it is compatible with Mother Earth, the animals, the plants, even the nearby planets, all of which you now recognize as being sacred in nature. It is important to feel the value of oneself physically before one can have any lasting physical impact on the world. If a physical energy does not feel good about itself, it will usually be resolved; other physical or spiritual energies will dissolve it because it is unnatural. The better you feel about your physical self when you do the work in the previous book as well as this one and the one to follow, the greater and more lasting will be the benevolent effect on your life, on the lives of those around you and ultimately on your planet and universe.

576 p. $25.00 ISBN 978-1-891824-29-5

Shamanic Secrets for Spiritual Mastery

Spiritual mastery encompasses many different means to assimilate and be assimilated by the wisdom, feelings, flow, warmth, function and application of all beings in your world that you will actually contact in some way. A lot of spiritual mastery has been covered in different bits and pieces throughout all the books we've done. My approach to spiritual mastery, though, will be as grounded as possible in things that people on Earth can use— but it won't include the broad spectrum of spiritual mastery, like levitation and invisibility. I'm trying to teach you things that you can actually use and benefit from. My life is basically going to represent your needs, and it gets out the secrets that have been held back in a storylike fashion, so that it is more interesting."

—Speaks of Many Truths through Robert Shapiro

768 p. $29.95 ISBN 978-1-891824-58-6

♆ *Light Technology* PUBLISHING

THE EXPLORER RACE SERIES

ZOOSH AND HIS FRIENDS THROUGH ROBERT SHAPIRO

THE SERIES: Humans—creators-in-training—have a purpose and destiny so heartwarmingly, profoundly glorious that it is almost unbelievable from our present dimensional perspective. Humans are great lightbeings from beyond this creation, gaining experience in dense physicality. This truth about the great human genetic experiment of the Explorer Race and the mechanics of creation is being revealed for the first time by Zoosh and his friends through superchannel Robert Shapiro. These books read like adventure stories as we follow the clues from this creation that we live in out to the Council of Creators and beyond.

❶ THE EXPLORER RACE

You individuals reading this are truly a result of the genetic experiment on Earth. You are beings who uphold the principles of the Explorer Race. The information in this book is designed to show you who you are and give you an evolutionary understanding of your past that will help you now. The key to empowerment in these days is to not know everything about your past, but to know what will help you now. Your number-one function right now is your status of Creator apprentice, which you have achieved through years and lifetimes of sweat. You are constantly being given responsibilities by the Creator that would normally be things that Creator would do. The responsibility and the destiny of the Explorer Race is not only to explore, but to create. 574 P. $25.00 ISBN 0-929385-38-1

❷ ETs and the EXPLORER RACE

In this book, Robert channels Joopah, a Zeta Reticulan now in the ninth dimension who continues the story of the great experiment—the Explorer Race—from the perspective of his civilization. The Zetas would have been humanity's future selves had not humanity re-created the past and changed the future. 237 P. $14.95 ISBN 0-929385-79-9

❸ EXPLORER RACE: ORIGINS and the NEXT 50 YEARS

This volume has so much information about who we are and where we came from—the source of male and female beings, the war of the sexes, the beginning of the linear mind, feelings, the origin of souls—it is a treasure trove. In addition, there is a section that relates to our near future—how the rise of global corporations and politics affects our future, how to use benevolent magic as a force of creation and how we will go out to the stars and affect other civilizations. Astounding information. 339 P. $14.95 ISBN 0-929385-95-0

❹ EXPLORER RACE: CREATORS and FRIENDS
The MECHANICS of CREATION

Now that you have a greater understanding of who you are in the larger sense, it is necessary to remind you of where you came from, the true magnificence of your being. You must understand that you are creators-in-training, and yet you were once a portion of Creator. One could certainly say, without being magnanimous, that you are still a portion of Creator, yet you are training for the individual responsibility of being a creator, to give your Creator a coffee break. This book will allow you to understand the vaster qualities and help you remember the nature of the desires that drive any creator, the responsibilities to which a creator must answer, the reaction a creator must have to consequences and the ultimate reward of any creator. 435 P. $19.95 ISBN 1-891824-01-5

❺ EXPLORER RACE: PARTICLE PERSONALITIES

All around you in every moment you are surrounded by the most magical and mystical beings. They are too small for you to see as single individuals, but in groups you know them as the physical matter of your daily life. Particles who might be considered either atoms or portions of atoms consciously view the vast spectrum of reality yet also have a sense of personal memory like your own linear memory. These particles remember where they have been and what they have done in their infinitely long lives. Some of the particles we hear from are Gold, Mountain Lion, Liquid Light, Uranium, the Great Pyramid's Capstone, This Orb's Boundary, Ice and Ninth-Dimensional Fire. 237 P. $14.95 ISBN 0-929385-97-7

❻ EXPLORER RACE and BEYOND

With a better idea of how creation works, we go back to the Creator's advisers and receive deeper and more profound explanations of the roots of the Explorer Race. The liquid Domain and the Double Diamond portal share lessons given to the roots on their way to meet the Creator of this universe, and finally the roots speak of their origins and their incomprehensibly long journey here. 360 P. $14.95 ISBN 1-891824-06-6

ZOOSH AND HIS FRIENDS THROUGH ROBERT SHAPIRO

⑦ THE EXPLORER RACE SERIES
EXPLORER RACE: The COUNCIL of CREATORS

The thirteen core members of the Council of Creators discuss their adventures in coming to awareness of themselves and their journeys on the way to the Council on this level. They discuss the advice and oversight they offer to all creators, including the Creator of this local universe. These beings are wise, witty and joyous, and their stories of Love's Creation create an expansion of our concepts as we realize that we live in an expanded, multiple-level reality.
237 PP. $14.95 ISBN 13: 978-1-891824-13-5

⑧ EXPLORER RACE and ISIS

This is an amazing book! It has priestess training, Shamanic training, Isis's adventures with Explorer Race beings—before Earth and on Earth—and an incredibly expanded explanation of the dynamics of the Explorer Race. Isis is the prototypal loving, nurturing, guiding feminine being, the focus of feminine energy. She has the ability to expand limited thinking without making people with limited beliefs feel uncomfortable. She is a fantastic storyteller, and all of her stories are teaching stories. If you care about who you are, why you are here, where you are going and what life is all about—pick up this book. You won't lay it down until you are through, and then you will want more.
317 PP. $14.95 ISBN 13: 978-1-891824-11-1

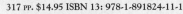

⑨ EXPLORER RACE and JESUS

The core personality of that being known on the Earth as Jesus, along with his students and friends, describes with clarity and love his life and teaching two thousand years ago. He states that his teaching is for all people of all races in all countries. Jesus announces here for the first time that he and two others, Buddha and Mohammed, will return to Earth from their place of being in the near future, and a fourth being, a child already born now on Earth, will become a teacher and prepare humanity for their return. So heartwarming and interesting, you won't want to put it down.
354 PP. $16.95 ISBN 13: 978-1-891824-14-2

⑩ EXPLORER RACE: Earth History and Lost Civilization

Speaks of Many Truths and Zoosh, through Robert Shapiro, explain that planet Earth, the only water planet in this solar system, is on loan from Sirius as a home and school for humanity, the Explorer Race. Earth's recorded history goes back only a few thousand years, its archaeological history a few thousand more. Now this book opens up as if a light was on in the darkness, and we see the incredible panorama of brave souls coming from other planets to settle on different parts of Earth. We watch the origins of tribal groups and the rise and fall of civilizations, and we can begin to understand the source of the wondrous diversity of plants, animals and humans that we enjoy here on beautiful Mother Earth.
310 PP $14.95 ISBN 13: 978-1-891824-20-3

⑪ EXPLORER RACE: ET VISITORS SPEAK

Even as you are searching the sky for extraterrestrials and their spaceships, ETs are here on planet Earth—they are stranded, visiting, exploring, studying the culture, healing the Earth of trauma brought on by irresponsible mining or researching the history of Christianity over the past two thousand years. Some are in human guise, and some are in spirit form. Some look like what we call animals as they come from the species' home planet and interact with their fellow beings—those beings that we have labeled cats or cows or elephants. Some are brilliant cosmic mathematicians with a sense of humor; they are presently living here as penguins. Some are fledgling diplomats training for future postings on Earth when we have ET embassies here. In this book, these fascinating beings share their thoughts, origins and purposes for being here. 350 PP. $14.95 ISBN 13: 978-1-891824-28-9

⑫ EXPLORER RACE: Techniques for GENERATING SAFETY

Wouldn't you like to generate safety so you could go wherever you need to go and do whatever you need to do in a benevolent, safe and loving way for yourself? Learn safety as a radiated environment that will allow you to gently take the step into the new timeline, into a benevolent future and away from a negative past. 208 PP. $9.95 ISBN 13: 978-1-891824-26-5

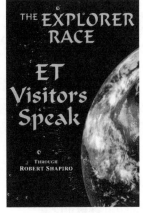

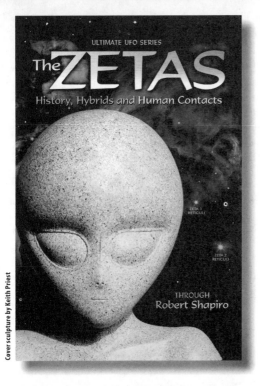

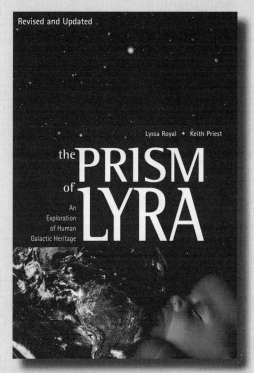

BEYOND THE LIGHT BARRIER

by Elizabeth Klarer

This autobiography of a South African woman is the story of the interstellar love affair between the author and Akon, an astrophysicist from the planet Meton in Alpha Centauri. Elizabeth Klarer traveled to Meton with Akon, lived there for four months with his family, and gave birth to his son. Featuring fascinating descriptions of the flora, fauna, and advanced technology of Akon's people, this classic is being reissued in a long-overdue new edition.

$15.95
Softcover, 244PP.
ISBN: 978-1-891824-77-7

LIFE WITH A COSMOS CLEARANCE

Daniel M. Salter

On May 9, 2001, the Disclosure Project hosted a major event at the National Press Club in Washington, D.C. Those of us who were military witnesses of UFO history showed official government documentation with our detailed testimony. The people who had been employed in agencies within the military and knew the truth about UFOs had been sworn to secrecy. Now I am finally relieved to speak the truth. Aliens have been waiting on the government, and if the government does not come forward with the truth, then the aliens will take a more public role in disclosure.

as told to Nancy Red Star

$19.95
Softcover, 198 PP.
ISBN: 978-1-891824-37-1

THE FASCINATING BOOKS OF TOM DONGO

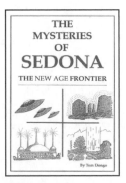

$6.95
Softcover, 85 PP
978-0-9622748-0-0

$7.95
Softcover, 130 PP
978-0-9622748-1-7

$9.95
Softcover, 146 PP
978-0-9622748-2-4

$9.95
Softcover, 122 PP
978-0-9622748-3-1

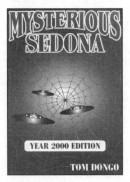

$9.95
Softcover, 118 PP
978-0-9622748-6-2

$14.95
Softcover, 203 PP
978-0-9622748-4-8

Tom Dongo is a long-time resident of Sedona. During this time, he has camped on and hiked over thousands of miles of the Sedona/Flagstaff/Prescott mountains, mesas, deserts, and canyons. He is a recognized world authority on UFOs and paranormal occurrences. He is also a writer of mainstream magazine articles and has written seven books on UFOs and the paranormal. His work and personal interviews have appeared many times on national and international television.

$4.95
Softcover, 30 PP
978-0-9622748-5-5

MAURICE CHATELAIN

Author Maurice Chatelain, former NASA space expert, has compiled compelling evidence to show that a highly advanced civilization existed on the Earth approximately 65,000 years ago. Further, his work indicates that the knowledge of the advanced civilization had been "seeded" by extraterrestrial visitors who have aided mankind with advanced information in mathematics, electricity and astronomy.

OUR COSMIC ANCESTORS

Our Cosmic Ancestors is a dynamic work, unraveling the messages of these "universal astronauts" and decoding the symbols and visual mathematics they have left for us in the Egyptian Pyramids, Stonehenge, the Mayan calender, the Maltese Cross and the Sumerian zodiac.

SOFTCOVER 213P.

$14⁹⁵   ISBN 0-929686-00-4

Chapter Titles:

- The Apollo Spacecraft
- The Constant of Nineveh
- The Mayan Calendar
- The Secret of the Pyramid
- The Maltese Cross
- The Rhodes Calculator
- The Kings of the Sea
- The Signs of the Zodiac
- The Polar Mysteries

- The Universal Calendar
- The Four Moons
- The Mystery of Atlantis
- Extraterrestrial Civilizations
- Mysterious Visitors
- Conclusion

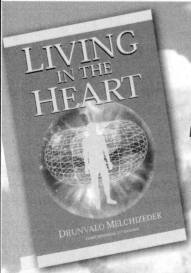

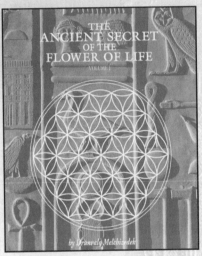

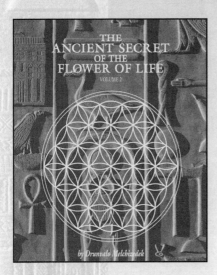

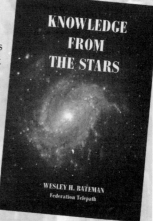